Gumbo for the Soul

A volume in
Contemporary Perspectives on Multicultural Gifted Education
Donna Y. Ford and Malik S. Henfield, *Series Editors*

Gumbo for the Soul

Liberating Memoirs and Stories to Inspire Females of Color

edited by

Donna Y. Ford
Vanderbilt University

Joy Lawson Davis
Virginia Union University

Michelle Trotman Scott
University of West Georgia

Yolanda Sealey-Ruiz
Teachers College, Columbia University

INFORMATION AGE PUBLISHING, INC.
Charlotte, NC • www.infoagepub.com

Library of Congress Cataloging-in-Publication Data

A CIP record for this book is available from the Library of Congress
http://www.loc.gov

ISBN: 978-1-68123-697-1 (Paperback)
       978-1-68123-698-8 (Hardcover)
       978-1-68123-699-5 (ebook)

Printed in the United States of America

CONTENTS

CHAPTER 1

INTRODUCTION

Rejection. Loss. Confusion. Pain. Our past and our future are intertwined. Each distinct memory becomes one life. What once hurt, eventually heals, and the lesson (or lessons) to be learned becomes one with our soul and our spirit. Our experiences provide strength instead of destruction. Our great-grandmothers, grandmothers, mothers—all women of power who came before us—were great descendants of the coastal lands of West Africa. They arrived in strange lands with their Gumbo—their memories, rhythms, ingenuity, creativity, strength, and compassion. Their lived stories and conversation were recipes mixed with unique combinations of ingredients, dropped into the cast iron pot—stirred, dropped in, seasoned, dropped in, stirred again, and again, and again, until done. This Gumbo is savory like the soul, carefully prepared, recipes rich with what our foremothers brought with them from their homeland. They brought the best of what they had to offer.

Gumbo or Gombo is a Bantu word meaning "okra." Okra is a rich vegetable that serves as the base (or gravy) for a delicately prepared stew. (Today's Gumbo cooks use a "roux" as the base—see the recipe on page 3. Gumbo's West African origins have been modified over the past two centuries by people of varied ancestry: Native American, German, Spanish, and French (Moss, 2014). It is essential to understand the manner in which Gumbo is prepared: each ingredient must be placed into the stew at its specified time so that it can cook in and savor its own flavor. When completed, Gumbo is usually served over grits or rice.

Gumbo has become a cornerstone of life in African-descended communities across the south and southwest spanning from South Carolina to Louisiana and Texas. Gumbo is a treasure . . . a reminder of the greatness that lived in the village in a time of strength and abundance . . . a reminder of the resilience and richness of our people over generations.

This book—a collection of memoirs written by Women of Color is shared to inspire and motivate readers. The authors of these precious, soulful stories are from across the globe and represent various backgrounds and professions. What these women have in common, though, is their drive to tell their story. Stories of pain, discovery, strength, and stories of beginnings. Many of the experiences, as difficult as they may have been, made the women who they are today. Telling these stories to a new generation will empower and encourage them in their experiences no matter how troubling or challenging (Harris, 2015). These stories, like our foremothers offering their Gumbo, present the best these women have to offer. These authors want the world to know that deep inside of each of us is a rich, vibrant, purposeful beginning. As our lives develop and we are "stirred and stirred again," like Gumbo, our experiences begin to shape who we are and who we become. When the stirring is complete, a comforting meal—one that says no matter what has gone into the dish, it's going to be amazingly magnificent!!

The authors hope these stories will inspire and motivate girls and Women of Color to trust their experiences—whether good or bad—to help them become. Our becoming means that after all that life has thrown our way, we are strong, purposeful, and powerful people who are a great treasure to a world that sometimes rejects and ignores our existence. Embedded in this book are stories of abuse and triumph, sadness and victory, disappointment and resilience, discovery and victory.

We are very proud to be the keepers of these rich recipes. They represent the first in what we hope will become a collection or series of inspirational memoirs that will be shared to help others live out their destiny and become the women they were born to be.

REFERENCES

Harris, J. (2015). Dear Black girls: Letters from the souls of Black women. *The Root.* Retrieved from www.theroot.com/articles/culture/2015/10/dear_black_girls _from _the_souls_of_black_women.html

Milton, R. (n.d.). Chicken and Sausage Gumbo recipe. Unpublished. Vinton, LA.

Moss, R, (2014). The real story of Gumbo, okra, and file. Retrieved from http:// www.seriouseats.com/2014/09/history-new-orleans-gumbo-okra-file-powder. html

A Recipe
Sausage & Chicken Gumbo

12 oz. or 2 cups of Roux
1 Fryer (cut up)
3 cups of chopped onions
$^1/_3$ cup of parsley

1 Gallon of water
1 lb. of Sausage
$^2/_3$ cup of green onions
1 medium bell pepper chopped

Season the fryer w/salt, red cayenne pepper, black pepper, and garlic powder. In a large pot, add ½ gallon of water. Bring to a boil. Add roux. Stir continuously until dissolved. Add ½ gallon of water and boil for 15 minutes. Add fryer, onions, and bell peppers. Boil over medium heat with the lid off for 30 minutes. Add sausage and boil another 15 minutes. Add green onions and parsley and simmer for 10 minutes. Serve over rice.

Roux Recipe

4 cups of flour
1 cup of cooking oil

Using a cast iron pot or heavy gauge pot, mix flour and oil over medium heat and stirring continuously until roux mixture becomes light brown to dark brown.

Note: Do not overcook or burn. Roux is bitter when too dark. Remove from heat and let cool. Leftover roux can be stored in a jar and used later.

Gumbo Key Challenges		
Name	**Title**	**Key Challenges**
Sheree Nicole Alexander	*At Risk. . . . And At Promise Too!*	Poverty, devastation of drug epidemic, urban challenges
Natoshia Whaley Anderson	*Pushing Past Trauma*	Abuse, self-esteem, poverty
Melanie Askew	*At Your Best, You Are Love*	Divorce, domestic violence, parental illness and death/loss, self-esteem, bullying, overcoming, forgiveness
Margaret Barrow	*Sweetest Candy—Education and the Love of Teachers!*	Foster family, poverty, perseverance
Margarita Bianco	*The Seven-Mile Divide: From Intellectually Gifted to Remedial*	School challenges, low expectations, poor school advising, bullying, negative peer pressure, Latino/a family
Rhonesha L. Blache	*Against the Grain*	Alienation/isolation, over-achievement, peer pressure, single mother
Dionne Blue	*I Am a Composite of All My Experiences*	Poverty, child of a teen mom, single-parent family, school changes and transitions
Mercedes Cannon	*From Homeless to Hopeful: Overcoming Tragedy to Persevere*	Foster family, blended family, sexual abuse, teen pregnancy, loss of child, marital challenges and divorce, school challenges
Marissa Campbell	*Racism and Giftedness: A Double Whammy*	Racism, segregated schooling
Disha Lynch Charles	*Forging Ahead in the Midst of Challenges*	Bullying, parental illness, immigrant family, academic self-concept
Johnita Collins	*I Needed My Mother and My Daughter Needs Me (Biggest Fan! First Defender! Best Advocate!)*	Low teacher expectations, poor academic advising, high achieving but unidentified gifted, parental loss, single-parent family, low income
Kimberly Phillips Dabney	*Making Beauty from Ashes: On Learning to Forgive and Love*	Violence, parental death, single-parent family, parental incarceration, extended family, forgiveness
Joy Lawson Davis	*Surviving, Thriving and Rising Above*	Lack of academic challenge, rural school, teen pregnancy, faith, family

Gumbo Key Challenges (continued)		
Name	**Title**	**Key Challenges**
Crystal A. deGregory	*Forgiveness: The Unexpected Gift of Fatherlessness*	Single-parent family, academic challenges, self-esteem challenges, immigrant challenges
Isi Ero-Tolliver	*Finding My Academic Self: Snapshot of a Bigger Picture*	Single-parent family, low-income household, international challenges, poor mentorship, work-life balance
Donna Y. Ford	*Beyond Zip Codes and Genetic Codes: Black and Poor and Gifted, Too!*	Poverty, single-parent family, racism, peer pressure, teen pregnancy
LaTonya Frazier	*Despite the Score: Removing Barriers from Access to Gifted Education*	Low income, single-parent family, extended family, test bias, academic under-challenge
Jessica A. Fripp	*Free to Fly*	Racial pride, isolation/ostracism, racism
Vernessa T. Gipson and Brianna T. Morgan	*"Can't" is a Four Letter Word and Life Rolls Along*	Health issues, dual exceptionality, special education, low expectations, academic isolation, employment challenges
Kristy Girardeau	*I Read to Live*	Low teacher expectations, parental incarceration, parental low education, finances, parental divorce, teen pregnancy
Derria L. Ford Glover	*The Day I Found Pain*	Parental loss, peer pressures, (over)weight
Jamye Hardy	*The Difference Between Giving Up and Moving On*	Imposter syndrome, goal setting
Breshawn N. Harris	*Never Put Rocks on an Eagle's Back*	Extended family, single-parent family, poverty, deficit thinking
Tiffany Hollis	*Bendable, Yet Unbreakable*	Single-parent home, poverty, behavioral issues, underachievement, deficit thinking, first generation college, domestic violence
Amina Humphrey	*Being Called a Nigger: Reflections as a Student and in Teacher Preparation*	Racism, peer pressures, affective issues

Gumbo Key Challenges (continued)

Name	Title	Key Challenges
Zeynep Isik-Ercan	*Like a Leaf in the Wind: Growing up Gifted in Turkey Without Privileges and Capital*	Poverty, low teacher expectations, behavioral challenges, lack of academic challenge, procrastination, time management, language as ELL student
LaShonda M. Jackson-Dean	*To Thine Own Self Be True: Stand Tall*	Peer pressure, self-esteem, school challenges, perseverance
Patricia Jahaly	*Fighting the Good Fight as an Afro-Rican Leader*	Racial identity, biracial, racial isolation, academic identity, poverty/financial challenges, single parent
Donna M. Johnson	*People Come into Our Lives for a Season*	Sexual assault, career choice challenges, loss of friend/friendship challenges
Jennifer M. Johnson	*From "Smarty Pants" to Scholar: A Personal Journey of Self-Acceptance*	Peer pressures, acting White, social isolation, poverty
Charemi A. Jones	*From Heartache to Head Up*	Single-parent family, poverty, abuse, violence, perseverance
SaDohl Goldsmith Jones	*Passion and Purpose through Pain and Dysfunction*	Family transitions, verbal abuse, physical abuse, sexual abuse, neglect, self-worth, overcoming, underachievement, misdiagnosis
Tammy D. Lane	*My Life Began to Bloom at Forty*	Parental loss, aging process (e.g., late bloomer)
Tonya Leslie	*The Perils of Being Too Young to be Grown*	Peer pressure, behavior issues, under-achievement, anger
April J. Lisbon	*Push Back and Stay in the Game: Life Goes on After Mistakes*	Peer pressure, rejection, self-esteem, identity, perseverance
Arleezah Marrah	*Learning to Love Myself After Sexual Abuse*	Sexual abuse, self-concept, overcoming and resilience, Christianity, forgiveness
Renae D. Mayes	*I'm not an "Oreo." I'm Focused!*	Racial identity, acting White, racial discrimination, isolation, negative peer pressure, first generation college student
Heather Cherie Moore	*The Dark Side of Giftedness: A Hidden Curriculum of Rejection*	Bullying, isolation, acting White, racial identity, self-esteem and self-concept, low expectations, academic challenges/rejection

Gumbo Key Challenges (continued)		
Name	**Title**	**Key Challenges**
Shondrika Moss-Bouldin	*The Greatest Gift of Love*	Divorce, family cohesion, father-daughter relationship, self-esteem
Mildred Moveda	*Sancocho: How Mami's Stories Fed My Curiosity and Continue to Sustain Me*	Biracial, peer pressure, poverty, language issues, parental education and literacy, cultural barriers
Barbara Mullen	*Fear is Not an Option*	Decision making, fear of failure, Imposter syndrome, self-efficacy, academic goals, career challenges
Janice Nix-Victorian	*The Garrison Finish: Learning to Live on Purpose, Not Just on Time*	Scholar-athlete, rural living, illness/disability, extended family, value of faith
Quinita Ogletree	*I Am Not Alone: Overcoming Abuse and Rejection*	Sexual abuse, suicide ideation, self-esteem and self-concept, anger management
Charissa M. Owens	*Adversity is Knocking... Let Success Answer It*	Underachievement, low/negative academic self-concept, single parent, loss of parent
Alexis Riley	*A Family and a Dream: A Journey from South Central to Life Beyond*	Identity, school challenges, self-esteem first generation college student
Cynthia Rivers	*Beyond Overcoming: Living Out God's Plan*	Single parent family, school challenges, poverty
Kelly A. Rodgers	*The Other "Big C"*	Divorce, homelessness, parental drug abuse and addiction, school challenges
Yolanda Sealey-Ruiz	*Getting to Here from There: My Journey from the South Bronx to the Academy*	Poverty, immigrant family, college academic under-preparation
Chinequa Shelander	*Why Not You? My Story of Inspiration and Determination*	Divorce, extended family, anger, over-achieving
Victoria Showunmi	*A Journey into racial identity: A Black Woman and White Socialisation*	Foster family, identity, self-esteem, perseverance
Aisha K. Staggers	*No Safe Space*	Health issues, physical abuse/sexual assault, police brutality, racism, single parenting
Michelle Trotman Scott	*Being Above Average: Hearing, Accepting, and Believing*	Parent death, single parent, resilience, underachievement
Desireé Vega	*School Changed My Life*	Divorce, violence (fights, excessive spankings)

Gumbo Key Challenges (continued)		
Name	**Title**	**Key Challenges**
Nicole McZeal Walters	*I Am Because of Her*	Parent alcohol addiction and abuse, parental loss, poverty, overcoming
Tuwana Wingfield	*Move Over World ... Here I Am*	Peer pressure, isolation, academic challenges, poor mentoring
Jemimah L. Young	*From Special Ed to Higher Ed: A Black Girl's Journey in Discovering Her Giftedness*	Biracial, English as a Second Language, special education misdiagnosis, behavioral challenges, juvenile delinquency, underachievement

*Like eating Gumbo, telling our stories
is good for the soul.*

—Donna Y. Ford

CHAPTER 2

AT RISK. . . . AND AT PROMISE TOO!

Sheree Nicole Alexander

> **Key Challenges:** poverty, devastation of drug epidemic, urban challenges

"*At Risk*" was something I saw scrawled across a folder on top of my middle school guidance counselor's desk. *Low SES* was yet another box checked on the form that was inside of that folder. I would later learn that the words scribbled on the folder meant that I was most likely headed for trouble, had problems, or needed to see the guidance counselor all of the time. I would also learn that the checked box meant that I was poor, even though I never received free *or* reduced lunch. My mother worked every day and I felt really normal (whatever that is).

It seemed like Ms. Wooden, our African American school counselor, called me out of class daily (but it was probably more like weekly) to come down to her office. I didn't mind going down to her office because she had a kind smile, smelled good, had a fly haircut—and she always spoke very softly and had a way of making something that was really bad seem as if it

Gumbo for the Soul, pages 11–15

wasn't so bad after all. Her office was neat and she winked at me when she saw me in the hallway, every time, not just when the principal was around. She was also respectful and kind to my mother, who would just stop by the school to bring my lunch or gym clothes when I forgot them at home. Ms. Wooden would also tell me things about her daughter Dani and even told me that she wanted me to meet Dani because I would like her. Hmm . . . now that I think about it, Ms. Wooden felt real regular and never made me and the other students feel like we were "at risk." Instead, she saw promise in us. Truth is, she was concerned about me and so was my single mother, who must have been terrified by my increasingly aggressive behavior.

Ms. Wooden always told me how smart I was. My mom always reminded me that Ms. Wooden thought I was smart. Even in eighth grade, I wondered why what everyone else at that middle school thought mattered so much to my mother. It was there at that middle school my mother sought help—refuge—from something she didn't understand, was not used to, and couldn't put her hand on, but it was something that was affecting her every day. At that time, there wasn't a name for it, but there was something happening all around all of us. All of a sudden, senses were heightened and we looking around . . . but for what? Was it something that was hushed, hidden, and tucked away but was escaping and running down our neighborhood streets like slow bubbling hot oil, scorching and changing things in our community, day by day?

Neighbors just seemed to be missing, moving or "disappearing". Some even "disappeared" in the middle of the night. When the "night disappearances" happened, my mother and my grandmother (who lived directly across the street) would quickly turn off the lights and peek through the front windows in the upstairs bedrooms. I would hear them whispering on the telephone about the whirling red and blue lights of the police cars that idled on our small one-way street. Sometimes, a blanket was draped over our neighbors, but other times, that was not the case. When I would ask what happened, the answer was always, "they had a heart attack". I clearly remember rubbing my chest, wondering if I would be next because the heart attacks seemed to happen all of the time.

Some of our neighbors, who did not move away, disappeared right in front of our eyes. Round and full faces with plump lips that whistled on the way to work or sang the oldies during the block parties, morphed into ghosts with gray ashen, itchy skin. For some, the doors on their homes opened and closed all night. For others, doors were eventually boarded up and the homes gutted from the inside out. Then there were those who would sit on the steps together to listen to music, or, just to escape the scalding summer heat of a row home—but then all of the sudden, stop coming outside all together. Delicious smelling dinners that signaled us to come inside for dinner, no longer wafted through screen doors. Nor was the streetlight the signal to get on the steps and play with someone that lived on my block. The open screen doors were replaced with decorative steel bars that stood in front of heavy, silenced, suffocated, and locked steel doors. I wondered if we were locking something out or locking ourselves in. I missed the breeze that flew through the small houses on my childhood block. All that steel made everything inside of our tiny homes stand still and become silent, literally.

Meanwhile outside, loud expensive colorful cars circled and circled our one-way streets. Sometimes, one of those cars stopped and blasted the latest rap song for everyone to hear. Before long, we were all dancing. Soon, the crowd diminished and separated into two groups. Some of the guys stopped moving and stood still in small groups on the street corners and waved as the shiny cars continued to circle. Some of the girls sat in the passenger seats of the cars and adorned cheap, gigantic gold-hooped earrings with their name spelled across the opening so big, that you could read it from far away. The other guys and girls appeared disheveled, as they scooted up to those standing on the corner, with their hands scooped, full of change.

One day, sometime later, my father sauntered down the street. I ran to meet him, expecting the crisp $20 that he would always give me as he flashed his dimpled smile. But on this day, he just asked, "Where's your mom?" and continued down the street. He didn't live with me and to cover it up, I actually told anyone who asked, that he was in the service; but, he was long gone, before I was even born. I used that story to explain away why he was not here, there, or anywhere between his every now and then appearance. He came that day and when I woke up the next day, he was still there. The same thing happened the next day.

On the fourth day, my mother went to work and I came home to him sitting on the couch with his legs propped up on the arm, something of which I could not and would not dare do because my mother always explained how important it was to take care of everything you had. Mom and I had a routine and it did not include his new demands. On that fourth day, he demanded that I cook some food while he went to the store. I thawed, seasoned and cooked the hamburgers that I took out of the Murry's box in the freezer and placed them between two slices of white bread. I placed the burgers on the table and sat a tall glass of red Kool-Aid, filled with ice, next to the plate.

The next morning, when I came downstairs to go to school, my mom was sitting at the table in front of those same hamburgers. The bread was now hard and stale, and she was smoking a cigarette. Hair still in rollers, she slid her glasses up and asked if I moved her bill money. When I answered 'no', she kissed me and told me not to miss the bus because she would not be able to take me if I did. When I got half way up the street, I noticed that her car was not in its usual parking spot, so I ran back in and asked her where it was; she replied: "Getting fixed. Now hurry up before you are late". That was all she said as she slowly took a drag from that cigarette.

When I came home from school, everything in the house was displaced. Furniture was turned over, the dining room table was pushed way in the corner and the lampshades were dented and bent—and that is just how I felt. I went to the kitchen and asked my mom what happened. But, she just smiled as if our house did not appear to have had been hit by a tornado. I noticed the red, blue and yellow wires poking through a hole in the wall where our rotary phone had once been. Mom saw me looking at the hole and said, "You think you can run over to Grandmom's and help her out while I clean this up?" The only sound that escaped from my throat was a weak, "OK." I then ran upstairs to grab some of the money, 90 dollars to be exact, that I had saved to buy a bomber jacket, but it was not there. By the time I ran down to the bottom of the stairs, mom was at the bottom and said, "It's gone, but don't worry, we'll get your jacket. Grandmom is waiting." When I ran across the street, I looked back and saw the red and blue lights that now flashed in front of my door. That's when I knew . . . no one was leaving my house or neighborhood because of a heart attack, nor had any of my neighbors gone away or disappeared. As a matter of fact, they didn't leave . . . it was crack that came.

This was one of my earliest memories of devastation that crack caused in my immediate community and immediate family. There were numerous instances of violence and crime that plagued the city where I grew up. I not only had to adapt, but I had to grow up very fast in order to survive and not succumb to daily threats that existed in my neighborhood. I also had to work very hard to avoid either side of the war on the drugs that became my new neighbors. I vowed to avoid becoming a user and buyer, but it was less easy to avoid the lure and temptation that the easy money, improved life style, and ability to buy big, gaudy things that depreciated before I got them home.

Throughout high school and college, some of the people with whom I came into contact, had very low expectations for me and counted me out. Some of those people, I did not know and others, I knew very well—and was even related to. However, I shared this memory for every other little brown girl who may feel trapped inside of her past, defined by her parents, neighborhood, socio-economic status, or any other identifier. You are not your circumstances. Some may identify me as the daughter of a crack addict. I identify myself as Dr. Sheree Nicole Alexander. You decide who you will and can become, for it is not the environment that defines you but how you use the whole experience to strengthen you over time.

Sheree N. Alexander, EdD, has served as a P–12 public school administrator in Pennsylvania and New Jersey, and as an adjunct faculty member at Rowan University. With 22 years in the field of education, she has served as a middle school Literacy teacher, Instructional Support Officer, Assistant Principal and Principal in both urban and suburban school districts. She holds a BS in Elementary Education from Millersville University of Pennsylvania, MEd in Educational Administration from Cheyney University and EdD in Educational Leadership from Rowan University. Dr. Alexander's research interests include the intersection of race, class and gender and the impact it has upon the schooling experiences of African American females, culturally responsive teaching, urban education and P–12 school leadership.

CHAPTER 3

PUSHING PAST TRAUMA

Natoshia Whaley Anderson

Key Challenges: abuse, self-esteem, poverty

I know that God doesn't put more on us than we can bear. I say this because my life has been an interesting journey—it has had so many twists and turns—much like that of a roller coaster. I am a gifted girl and proud of it! I hope my story gives the reader the courage to persevere, persist, and succeed.

In 1979, my mother remarried and moved from the city of Atlanta to a suburban neighborhood on the outskirts (20 miles) of Atlanta. Coming from an all-Black school to an all-White school was a culture shock of the worst kind. My siblings and I arrived at the elementary school academically behind, and the school's administration suggested we be placed into special education classes. We worked really hard to catch up with schoolwork, and of course, my siblings and I proved those administrators and our teachers wrong. The next year, we tested into the gifted program. I went from reading *below* grade level to reading four to five grades *above* grade level before I entered high school. My favorite subject in school was math. At home, I was very curious about how things worked, so I would break my toys just to see how they worked.

HOW IT ALL BEGAN

In 1981, my aunt Fern met and fell in love with a man named Paul. He would become my uncle by marriage the following year. My aunt moved out of our house and into a new house with her new husband. We liked Paul. He was fun. He would take us to the store and buy us candy and toys. He always made time for us when we would visit. He knew our aunt played an important part in our lives. Our aunt was like a second mom to us and we loved her dearly. Soon, we began to spend almost every weekend with Aunt Fern and Uncle Paul. One of them would pick us up from home on Friday and bring us back home on Sunday. We would have popcorn, watch a movie, and/or play games Friday night. Saturday we would go to the amusement park or visit their friends with kids our age. On Sunday we went to church and then headed home. This was our ritual from 1983 to 1986.

While we were at Auntie's house there was always a trip to the candy store and time spent with just Uncle Paul. He would tell us stories about his upbringing, his siblings, and his wild adventurous youth in Cincinnati, Ohio. We were totally fascinated. He had us all hooked with the stories. After a while, my brother stopped coming with my sister and me every weekend because he was starting to play various sports. When we started to go to Auntie's house by ourselves, that's when weird stuff starting happening to me, and I later found out that it was happening to my sister as well. When my brother stopped coming, my sister and I decided to not share a room because we each wanted our own space. We would find magazines sprawled over our bed in each of our rooms. The pictures in Playboy and Penthouse magazines were very graphic. I moved them off the bed and put them on the nightstand where I thought they belonged. Uncle Paul would also leave books in the bathroom. These books always had interesting titles and covers so that made me curious. At the time, I didn't see anything wrong in flipping through these books and magazines. Sometimes, my sister and I would talk about the books and magazines.

What I didn't know was that this was all a set up. Uncle Paul was a pedophile. He started to come visit both my sister and me during the night hours. He would wake one or both of us up, and take us to the back family room. He made me feel that because I looked at the books and magazines, I was a naughty girl and that I deserved the fondling, groping, and after a while, penetration. This went on for about a year. My sister and I starting protesting about going to my aunt's house. My mother was concerned. She would ask if anything was wrong. We couldn't or didn't tell. I often have thought that my mother had some inkling of what was going on but didn't know for certain. I would pray that Uncle Paul was out of town or had something to do that would have him coming home really late. When someone betrays your trust on this level and at such a young age, it can cause you to mistrust everyone. Trust of others doesn't come easy and it has also made it difficult for me to trust myself. My inability to trust myself has led to me making a lot of mistakes in my life. Now, when I make a mistake, I have learned to look for the lesson in it. Situations and mistakes are here to teach us valuable lessons that we can apply in our lives. It's our job to get the lesson.

I knew that what was happening to me was not right, but I didn't know what to do about it. While my mother talked to us about sex in general, "good touching" and "bad touching" were never mentioned. I saw an afterschool special on TV about sexual molestation. I had never heard the term before. It was then that I realized that this is what was happening to my sister and me and that it was not normal. My gut instinct told me that I had to say something.

One night, at my Aunt's house, he came in my room and started rubbing his hands against me. This was his signal that "it" was going to happen. I told him that this was wrong and that I was going to tell my aunt what he was doing. He laughed at me and told me that I didn't have the guts. He was almost right. He looked so confident that I almost believed him. But I gathered my courage and went to my Aunt's room. I woke her up and told her that Uncle had been touching my sister and me.

She was in shock, but she believed me. She asked a lot of questions. How? Where? How long? She confronted him and demanded that he leave. They fought and argued that night and I remember falling asleep (my sister and I slept in the same bed that night) to the noise. The next morning, Uncle Paul was gone. This was the demise of my Aunt's marriage.

SURVIVING THE (HARD) LESSONS LEARNED

I stop here to give advice based on things that have happened to me in my life.

I want every gifted girl to know that you must: (a) Celebrate your victories and believe in them. Know that it isn't luck—it's you; (b) Learn from mistakes, but don't let the mistakes define you. Get the lesson and move on; (c) Learn to trust your instincts; (d) Do not give your trust to everyone. Let them earn it. This does not mean don't trust anyone, but use #3 to guide you in who to trust or not trust; and (e) Education is your friend. Use it wisely and judiciously in your life.

The after-effects of sexual molestation are long lasting. I suffered from low self-esteem, or have a lack of confidence in my own abilities; I don't trust others easily; From time to time, I still suffer from guilt as I felt that I couldn't save my sister from the abuse; I have intimacy issues which has made my marriage and other relationships more difficult than necessary. *The Imposter Syndrome* has been the hardest to overcome. Impostor syndrome can be defined as a collection of feelings of inadequacy that persist even in face of information that indicates that the opposite is true. It is experienced internally as chronic self-doubt, and feelings of intellectual fraudulence. I have and continue to work through this with the help of a good therapist.

All of the things that I have been able to do in my life thus far are a testament to my faith and a lot of personal hard work, and that is cause for celebration. For every milestone in my life, I celebrate it big. We are often really quick to put ourselves down when things go wrong; we need to do the opposite and celebrate when things are going well. I make it a habit to celebrate after every event or success (no matter the size) that I have. I graduated from high school in the top 10% of my class. I attended college and earned a degree in Mechanical Engineering Technology. I spent many years as an engineer designing train cars, and HVAC systems for all types of buildings. I've had to learn to trust and work with others. I have also learned to trust myself and those same instincts that saved me when I was younger.

I have always used education as a way to grow myself. When I was younger, I remember doing a project on sexual molestation. My teachers didn't know what to make of this and neither did my parents. I needed to do that project and I learned so much from it. It was like free therapy, before I knew what therapy was. When I'm feeling insecure about something or if there is something that I just don't know, I am inclined to research and educate myself about it. I've always used education as a way to soothe myself. I have gone on to earn an MBA and a doctorate (EdD) in Educational Leadership. My particular passion is encouraging and supporting girls in pursuing a future in a STEM or STEM-related career. Molestation might have stolen my youth, but it did not steal my future. I won't let it! You don't have to let the molestation define who you become. Have hope about your future and know that you ultimately are the one who defines it. Being gifted is indeed a gift. Be sure you use your gift to uplift and sustain yourself and others.

Natoshia Anderson, EdD is the Dean of the School of Education, New Media and Strategic Partnerships at Georgia Piedmont Technical College. She has a BS Degree in Mechanical Engineering and an MBA with a specialization in Marketing from Southern Polytechnic State University and a doctorate in Educational Leadership from the University of Phoenix. Her research interests include the intersection of race and gender in STEM with an emphasis on minority women (African American), the experience of AA (gifted) girls and young women in school and college especially those pursuing a STEM degree, and experiences of Women of Color in higher education as academics and administrators.

CHAPTER 4

AT YOUR BEST, YOU ARE LOVE

Melanie Askew

Key Challenges: divorce, domestic violence, parental illness and death/loss, self-esteem, bullying, overcoming, forgiveness

By the age of three, I had learned to read fluently and was beginning to comprehend most of what I read. I would pursue the attention of family and friends in hopes that they would serve as a potential audience to my reading prowess often holding them hostage in order to read my favorite books to them. Unbeknownst to me, reading would be a skill that served as an escape from the reality of a world that required that I cope with some very unsettling matters. Reading books became my way of coping with the hills and valleys that surfaced while growing up in a household overshadowed by domestic violence. As matters became increasingly worse overtime, Arthur and Corduroy, characters from one of my favorite childhood books, would serve to distract me from the reality of turmoil and turbulence.

In the middle of any given night, my reality consisted of waking up to a loud bang from my parent's room. Typically, moments later my mom would come into my room and lay next to me with hope that my father wouldn't display his rage in front of a daughter that he seemed to adore. Years later, I would find out that my father had actually thrown a phone at her that particular night but there were other nights in which various other items or whatever he could get his hands on, had been thrown. His constant bouts of rage became the norm and could be attributed to him mixing a combination of alcohol and prescription drugs. Years earlier, he had been diagnosed with lupus and prescribed Prednisone to fight the disease and Xanax, a strong tranquilizer to remedy his depression. But the problem was that he was an alcoholic and not only did he take his medication with beer; he literally drank all day. This dangerous combination resulted in his having numerous mood swings and impromptu meltdowns...one moment he could be the nicest man on the planet, but in an instant he would turn into your worst nightmare.

After undergoing physical, emotional, and mental abuse for years, my mother filed for a divorce. One day, several years later I stood in the foyer of the home in which I grew up, with a black hefty trash bag in my hands, waiting for my mom to pick me up. My father, who was standing at the top of the stairs, leaning over the rail, put me out of his house. He was the first man that I had ever loved, but that didn't stop him from putting, his eight-year old daughter out of his house. I would not see my father for another six years. I'm not sure if I reminded him too much of my mom or if it was my ability to comprehend more than I should have at my age, but one day, after much alcohol, he decided that it was time for me to exit. When I walked out of the door, I looked up at him and told him I'd never come back.

When I was 14, my sister received a phone call from my brother who was home after a tour in the military, who told her that we should come visit our father. Similar to me, my sister hadn't seen him in several years as her relationship with him was also estranged. But, after much contemplation and discussion, we decided to visit. Ironically, my father lived only five minutes from where I lived with my mom, but I had not seen him for six years. When I arrived to his home, I recognized several family members that I had not seen in years, but my eyes were searching for my father. With intense nervousness, I saw a very skinny figure of a man, who wore a black baseball hat and limped with a cane. It was my father. Although it had been six years since I had last seen him, he seemed to have aged at least 20 years. The Lupus that he fought for so long had taken a drastic toll on his body. It was as if he was slowly deteriorating. It was in that moment that I knew why my brother had reached out. It took everything for me not to wallow in tears. My entire body began to tremble, my stomach was in knots, and I had to dig deep for strength to even get out of the car.

My father turned around and said, "What's up, Bud? It's been awhile. You grew up on me." He spoke to me as if nothing ever happened. I said, "Yep. Since you put me out." He responded, "Ahh, I don't remember that.

Must have been fooling around. How's your mom doing?" I said, "She's doing well." He responded with a vulgar remark, but I told him, "I came to see how you were, not to hear you talk bad about my mom. Keep on and I'll leave for another six years." He laughed and mumbled, "Must get that mouth from me." I continued to greet the rest of my family members. It wasn't a moment of reconciliation but it was a start. I was hurt, angry, and confused as to why he did not love me enough to reach out over the last six years.

During this time, I was experiencing bullying at school. During my visit with my father, I managed to tell him about the bullying that I was experiencing at school. I also shared that my mother and I had been looking at private schools as an alternative. He was very empathetic and told me that I could use his address in order to attend school within his district. As time progressed, my being estranged from my father began to get better, but at the same time, the bullying became worse. Girls threw things at me on the bus and would make lewd comments. They had no idea as to what I was dealing with and how their comments and threats of "jumping me" were killing me spiritually and emotionally. My self-esteem waned and I questioned everything from my appearance to my abilities. Each day I had to ride the "torture bus" as I began to call it, to my father's house. During this time, I learned more about my father and why he was the way he was. It took years before I really understood why he struggled to demonstrate love to his children.

Half way into my eighth grade year, an announcement over the P.A. system chimed into my classroom telling me to come to the office immediately. When I arrived to the office, I was told that there was an emergency, and my mom was on her way. When my mother arrived, she told me that things had taken a turn for the worse; my father had suffered a stroke due, in part, to his lupus. At age 15, after a year and a half after I had reconciled with my father, I would lean over to him, in his unconscious state and say my last words to him, "At your best, you were love." The lyrics were significant. Prior to the Lupus diagnosis, he had sung professionally for years and the lyrics were from a song that I had practiced singing with him. My father would never understand the lasting impact he would have on my relationships and the trajectory of my life. For at a time, he was a fun, loving, and caring guy but reality made him keenly aware that he was never to realize his dreams. He had the voice of a songbird but was unable to pursue his dream of singing, his parents weren't supportive nor where they loving. He experienced the ills of the Vietnam War, then when diagnosed with Lupus, he succumbed to alcohol and lived with the many bad decisions that he made in his life based on his own insecurities.

My father's death actually afforded me the ability to attend a private high school where I was no longer bullied. I excelled during high school as an honor roll student, president of the senior class, and a cheerleader. Up until high school, I had never been athletic. However, after watching me perform a gospel pantomime at a school event, the track coach approached me and asked about the possibility of me joining the track team. Ironically, he proposed that I specifically run the hurdles.

As I reflect back, the hurdles proved to be a perfect match for me because my life had been one set of hurdles after another. Reading helped me to overcome the hurdle of domestic violence because it allowed me to escape the commotion; the separation and divorce of my parents was another hurdle I had to clear, while the bullying served as another hurdle that allowed me to forgive and come back into his life at a time when he was fragile.

Overcoming hurdles can lead us to winning the race but it takes strength and endurance. To this day, I do not make excuses for my dad. But I do understand who he was, and I take the strength that I have gained from my experience to inspire others. I have learned how my experience with him could have the potential to impact my relationships with others and have proactively learned to trust and love. Thankfully, I had a chance to see him in a different light. Aaliyah's song, says it best, "At Your Best, You Are Love," which is the way that I see him now.

Melanie Askew, MEd, is the Founder and Head of School of Élan Academy Charter School in New Orleans. Ms. Askew received a Bachelor's of Science in Human and Organizational Development and a Master of Education in Organizational Leadership from Vanderbilt University's Peabody College. With the drive to provide a quality education for all children regardless of ethnicity, locale, and socio-economic status, she worked as a founding teacher, instructional coach, curriculum content specialist, adjunct professor, and education consultant. Ms. Askew was selected as a 2015 Fellow with the Building Excellent Schools Fellowship. Now, and through her work in the Building Excellent Schools Fellowship and with a committed founding team, she is humbled at and driven towards the opportunity to open an excellent K–8 school that provides a quality option rooted in the voices of the community of New Orleans.

CHAPTER 5

SWEETEST CANDY— EDUCATION AND THE LOVE OF TEACHERS!

Margaret Barrow

Key Challenges: foster family, poverty, perseverance

"Life for me ain't been no crystal stair," wrote Langston Hughes in the poem "Mother to Son." As an African American and Native American woman, I have struggled to survive—to become someone with racial pride, who was successful, and who made a difference. From the age of two, I was raised in a foster home by Ms. Pinto, who was African American and Portuguese. Four of my siblings were also sent to the same foster home (a brother and three sisters).

I was very close to my biological half-brother, Carl who was a few years older than me. One of my fondest memories about learning was when he introduced me to his fourth grade teacher, Mr. Levitt and his wife Mrs. Levitt, who was also a fourth grade teacher at our elementary school. The school was located a few streets from where we lived in the suburbs of Randolph,

Massachusetts. Before Carl introduced me, I had seen my brother with his teacher after school on a few occasions while I was on the basketball court shooting hoops with my friends. Carl loved school, but I didn't because the boys in my class picked on me and the teacher never did anything when I complained to her about them pulling my hair and calling me names. Her uncaring attitude made me distrust all teachers. So, when my brother told me that the Levitts were different, I didn't believe him. However, I promised Carl I would give the Levitts a chance. I found out after spending some time with them that they were pretty nice people. After Carl begged for weeks, our foster mother allowed the two of us to spend a few hours a month with them at their home in Braintree. Our sisters were encouraged to come along, but they didn't want to, and so they never came with us. They called us "teachers' pets." My youngest sister was too young to join us. Personally, I was happy to take a break from our noisy, crowded home filled with bickering and fighting children.

At the Levitt's home, it was quiet, and my favorite room quickly became the kitchen. They had what Carl and I referred to as "the golden drawer"— full of sweets that made our mouths water just thinking about them. Each visit, we were allowed as many treats as we wanted. I could hardly contain myself thinking about the moment when I would slip a sugary Mary Jane into my salivating mouth. There were also mounds of butterscotch candy that found their way into my deep empty pockets. While we sat in the living room eating sweets, Mr. and Mrs. Levitt talked to us about school, learning, books, places to visit, and films they watched. We were fascinated with their lives. They went places and did exciting things.

In our foster home, there were 12 kids and not a lot of money to do all the fun things the Levitts enjoyed. With our foster mother's permission, they were allowed to take us around Boston to visit museums, art galleries, and bookstores. While I enjoyed these outings very much, I didn't think much of them at first. Don't get me wrong, I was fascinated by the African art, the films about exotic places I'd never heard of, and the history of Black people blew me away. I was overwhelmed as a child. There were no people of color in positions of authority in my life, except for my foster mother. I had a difficult time understanding what I was seeing and what I was living. At a young age, I began to question why there weren't many Black people in leadership roles in my life. The Levitts often told us that if we wanted to be someone when we grew up, we only had to apply ourselves. I can still hear Ms. Levitt's voice when she'd say to me: "You're a smart kid. You can do anything you set your mind to do."

I can't claim to have been gifted, but at an early age there were teachers like the Levitts who saw potential in me, something I could not see at the time as my vision was often dulled by the limitations of my home life where violence rested; curled up like a rattle snake preparing to strike at any moment if I made the wrong move, used the wrong tone, or said the wrong words.

In our foster home and neighborhood, young girls were getting pregnant and depending on welfare to support their families. In our own home, three teens were pregnant, one as a result of a rape. When I was nine years old, my twin biological sisters (ages 14) were sent away after they proved to be "too sexually promiscuous" for our foster mother. One left behind a baby that I would have to take care of—and I was only nine years old—too young to be a mother to my niece. I wouldn't see my sisters again until I was in my twenties.

Young Black boys were becoming fathers, selling drugs, arrested and sent to jail for committing crimes. We saw a lot of kids turn to drugs in our suburban neighborhood. Violence was a normal part of our lives. I watched as one of my foster brothers had his fingers cracked by a one-inch thick wooden stick held by my foster mother. Another was forced to place his fingers in the door jam while my foster mother slammed the door on them. At a young age, one of my foster brothers molested me. Years later, the same foster brother beat me in the face black and blue—nothing was ever done to him. I had nowhere to go and nowhere to run.

When I was 11, we all moved to a remote part of Arizona. Life was different and we had no electricity or running water. There were no neighbors for miles around. Our home was a single trailer parked in the middle of the desert. Books became my best friends. I started to write in a journal. In high school, I began to work hard, realizing that after four years, I would be out in the world on my own. It was in my English class that I became aware of my potential. I was placed in an honors English course where I excelled. Without my knowledge, my teacher Ms. White took one of my essays and entered it into a regional writing contest. I didn't know about it until one day while reading the newspaper in a journalism club meeting, a classmate pointed out that my name was in the local newspaper and that I had won a first place prize for my "True Meaning of Democracy" essay. It was the first time I felt proud of myself. It was also at that moment I began to believe in myself.

After graduating from high school, I went to a broadcasting school in Arizona and then traveled to Massachusetts, fell in love with a musician, got married, and moved around the world for three years. I felt like a wanderer. Three years later, I tired of tagging along, following someone else's dream, and set out on my own. We lived in England then. I left my husband and arrived in New York with a dream. I would go back to school. I got a secretarial job at Standard and Poor's and went to classes in the evening. Not long after, I married again and brought into the world a beautiful little girl in 1992. At the completion of my bachelor's degree in 1996 my second daughter arrived. I charged forward without skipping a beat. I earned my master's degree in 2000. It wasn't easy but I was determined. I was an honor student throughout the six years, and was invited into the Golden Key Honors Society.

After teaching part-time for a few semesters, a number of people interested in my career encouraged me to apply to an Ivy League college. However, as far as I'd come, I was still dealing with self-doubt. Yet, I sent out my application. When I received the acceptance letter from Teacher's College, Columbia University, I was still unsure of myself. I started in fall of 2000. I was awarded a Minority Scholarship, which I desperately needed to complete my doctoral degree in English Education.

Along the way, I met an extraordinary teacher who, like the Levitts, cared for me as a human being and was interested in my success. Dr. Mikki Shaw came into my life when I needed encouragement. Going to college at night and teaching at a community college was wearing me down. But, I continued to move forward. In August 2009, I defended my dissertation and became Dr. Margaret Barrow. I never dreamed that a poor, mix-raced Black girl with the odds stacked against her would become a teacher.

There weren't a whole lot of role models around me while growing up. In my heart and mind, I've always held on to the love and caring these three teachers gave me when I most needed to be shown love. The Levitts' caring attitude and actions developed a love for learning in both my brother and me. Ms. White's insistence that I see the potential inside myself, and Dr. Mikki Shaw's interest in me as a person ignited a roaring fire within me. I started out not really knowing what I wanted to do. The one thing I was convinced of was that I wanted to make a difference in the world. I wanted to prove to my foster mother—who had said when I was a kid that I'd end up a prostitute like my mother—that I could be someone and that I had the brains and determination to do it.

Today, I am an Associate Professor and Deputy Chair in the Department of English at the Borough of Manhattan Community College. Working at a community college where many students enter ill-prepared for the rigors of college course work and are often the first in their families to go to college, is where I belong. In many of my students, I see myself. Marlene and Jeffrey Levitt, Ms. White and Dr. Mikki Shaw taught me that a good teacher cares about her/his students, sees their weaknesses as temporary, supports their efforts, and inspires their potential. My challenge is to spark an interest, a responsibility, in my students to reach beyond their personal doubts and discover a love for learning—to indeed, offer them the sweetest candy—Education.

Margaret Barrow, EdD is an Associate Professor of English and Deputy Chair at Borough of Manhattan Community College, City University of New York. She earned her doctorate at Teachers College, Columbia University, and earned her MA and BA at City College, City University of New York. Margaret Barrow co-created the national bi-annual community college conferences Transitions and Transactions that focuses on teaching literature, creative writing, and journalism in the community college. She also co-designed the BMCC Teaching Academy, which is a two-year faculty development program for new faculty that supports and guides them as they learn to teach in a community college setting. She has written articles on pedagogy and teaching in higher education. Her interests are literature and creative writing pedagogies, contemporary literature, Native-American literature, developmental education, composition theory, discussion practices in the teaching of literature, English Education. As a former foster care child, she gives motivational talks to foster care teens and young adults about education.

CHAPTER 6

THE SEVEN-MILE DIVIDE

From Intellectually Gifted to Remedial

Margarita Bianco

> **Key Challenges:** school challenges, low expectations, poor school advising, bullying, negative peer pressure, Latino/a family

Washington Heights, located in in the northern portion of New York City, is where I call home. A richly diverse community, "the Heights" is bordered by Harlem to the south, the Hudson River to the west, and the Harlem River to the east. Growing up in the Heights during the 1960s provided an unparalleled opportunity to experience the richness of a truly diverse and multicultural community comprised of Chinese, German, Jewish, African American, Puerto Rican and Cuban families. Walking along 173rd street, you would see children of all nationalities playing hopscotch on the sidewalk or sitting with their family elders on the steps of the red brick buildings. The diversity of our neighborhood was reflected in the classrooms of our school, Public School (PS) 173.

Memories of my early elementary school experience include the smell of glue, the cigar box full of crayons and, along with several other girls,

Gumbo for the Soul, pages 31–34

being pulled out of Miss Lilly's third grade class for "IGC" several times a week. I never questioned why I was being taken out of class or the meaning of "IGC." I only knew that this was a time when only a select few of us were taken to a small room down the hall where we would play games or be interviewed by strangers. Decades later, I learned that the IGC class was a special program was for "intellectually gifted children" and the curious strangers were college students helping to identify a small group of students for admission to a program for gifted girls affiliated with Hunter College.

I never did attend the special school for gifted girls; however, I often wonder how that might have changed my life. Like many other Latino/a families, both then and now, my family had no interest in separating me from my neighborhood or taking me out of my neighborhood school. My parents never questioned their decision and neither did I—at least not then.

The Washington Heights neighborhood started to change. Although still rich in diversity, gangs and drugs started to infiltrate the neighborhood. My parents decided it was time to leave. Like many other immigrant families that made their way to New York City, a common dream was to own a piece of land to call your own. Upward mobility meant no more apartment rentals. It meant crossing the Hudson River via the George Washington Bridge, driving seven long miles to unfamiliar territory, and buying a house in the suburbs of New Jersey.

Bergenfield, New Jersey was our new home. Streets were named after trees that I never heard of or saw before, and schools were named after presidents, not the street number of its address. Children did not play hopscotch on the sidewalk but instead played games unfamiliar to me by kicking balls and darting between trees. There were no more bodegas[1] on street corners or children sitting with family elders on the steps of apartment buildings. Nights were particularly eerie with darkness and quiet—I was unaccustomed to this having grown up in the city. I was a stranger in this new land; not just because of my new surroundings, but also because we were among the very few non-White families in this working class town.

Children can be cruel. I was taunted, teased, and called names I'd never heard of before. The brownness of my skin, the fullness of my lips, and the vowels in my name made me the target of harsh ridicule. Adults can be cruel too. Children were not allowed to play with the new Puerto Rican girl in town.

The long seven-mile divide was especially felt in school. School administrators made lasting decisions based on my brown skin and Latina name. Despite being identified as "intellectually gifted" in a school only seven miles away, I was now placed in the lowest level classes for students who needed "remediation." I don't know how this was explained to my parents or on what basis this decision was made. What I do know is that my parents, like many other Latino/a families, didn't and wouldn't challenge the decisions made by the all-knowing, all White, school authorities. After all, unlike my parents, these people were college graduates and had letters after their names.

Children have a remarkable ability to live up to, *or down to*, the expectations held for them in schools. I was no different. If a remedial class is where I belonged, then I needed to act the part—and so I did. For the remainder of my public school years, I was "remedial." There were remedial reading classes in middle school where we pulled color coded cards from a large box sitting on the teacher's desk while she drank coffee and read the New York Daily News. While other students studied advanced biology, I was relegated to a general science class where we learned about the inner workings of a toilet bowl. It is no surprise then why Mr. Bené, my high school counselor, would tell me during my senior year, "You are not college material." I almost believed him; almost . . . but not fully.

Graduation day was bittersweet. As the first in my immediate family to graduate from high school, I remember a sense of pride as I walked off the auditorium stage and handed my high school diploma to my Abuela. My family was proud—and I was confused, nervous, and scared. Since I was *not college material,* I had no college plans. Certainly, if I had applied, I wouldn't have been accepted anyway—so why bother trying? Or at least that was my thinking at the time.

Working part-time for minimum wage left me with nothing. Fortunately, I was able to live with my parents and borrow their car to get to and from my job as a teacher's aide. I was also fortunate to be working among people who were attending college or had already graduated. They had access and knowledge that I needed and wanted. They knew how to navigate the system that I too wanted to participate in, but I didn't know how to or where to begin. Being in their presence was enough to give me the confidence to enroll in college and to think that I might be "college material."

Without question, the first year of my undergraduate program was hard. Learning about the inner workings of toilet bowls did nothing to prepare me for my anatomy and physiology class, and reading those SRA cards had no relevance to college level textbooks. It would have been easier to believe Mr. Bené, but I chose not to. I was right where I belonged. I was college material! I was worthy and deserving of my first college degree and the several others that followed!

The seven mile divide taught me many lessons. I learned the damaging effects of making assumptions about children's intellect based on race or ethnicity. I learned the power behind teachers' and counselors' words as they try to control and underestimate your power and destiny. I learned how ill prepared students are for college when not provided with opportunities for academic curiosity and college readiness skills in their P–12 school experiences. I also learned the power of being self-determined and unapologetically claiming your rightful space in life. Lastly, I learned how to use my story to motivate other gifted, bright and talented Black and Brown girls to claim their own destiny. I learned to believe in myself—despite what others believe about me. As a college professor, I know the power of expectations; I communicate positive expectations to students at all ages so that they know how to cope with teachers like Mr. Bené. I want them to defy low expectations, negative expectations, and stereotypes. Many do, and so can you.

NOTE

1. Spanish word for small grocery store.

Margarita Bianco, PhD, is an associate professor in the School of Education and Human Development at the University of Colorado Denver. Dr. Bianco is also the founder of Pathways2Teaching, a program designed to encourage high school students of color to become teachers [http://www.Pathways2Teaching.com]. Professor Bianco's research interests include the underrepresentation of teachers of color and gifted students from underrepresented populations. Dr. Bianco is the recipient of several awards including the Outstanding Researcher Award from the Council for Learning Disabilities, University of Colorado Denver's Rosa Parks Diversity Award, the 2011 University of Colorado President's Diversity Award, the University of Colorado's 2012 Teaching Excellence Award, and most recently honored with the Council for Learning Disabilities (CLD) Floyd G. Hudson Service Award.

CHAPTER 7

AGAINST THE GRAIN

Rhonesha L. Blache

> **Key Challenges:** alienation/isolation, overachievement, peer pressure, single mother

Unapologetically different from the majority of people, including family members, in my early life, it seems that going against the grain has been a way of life for me. Being different has afforded me many amazing, life-changing opportunities that have helped me continuously grow both personally and professionally. If success is being happy with your journey through life as you focus on and reach your goals, my life has been quite successful thus far, despite ongoing adversity at every cornerstone.

My mother, aunts, uncles, cousins, two older brothers and even my younger sister had attended and graduated from the local high school in our community, but I decided to attend the rival high school, despite the longer commute and lack of popularity. This rival school was on the other side of town in an area perceived to be of a higher socioeconomic status than my low to middle class, predominantly Black and Mexican, gang affiliated, and drug-infested neighborhood. I was not allowed to walk down certain streets and always walked quickly to get home after getting off the

Gumbo for the Soul, pages 35–39
Copyright © 2017 by Information Age Publishing
All rights of reproduction in any form reserved.

school bus. Still, my family and friends tried to encourage me to follow the family tradition by buying me South Mountain spirit T-shirts and constantly expressing their disappointment. Some of my friends who had chosen to attend the local high school reminded me about the rival's past losses to the local school in sports and called it a "nerd" school. Yet, I attended the "nerd" school and was able to be exposed to the most rigorous curriculum available through the International Baccalaureate program. I gained new lifetime friends in my peers and teachers, earned college credits, and developed a taste for all things international, which grew into an international career and travel experiences of which most people only dream.

Many people considered me an 'overachiever'. My undergraduate college years were quite active as I earned my Bachelor of Science in Psychology with honors, more college credits than I needed, and experiences that still shine with relevance on my resume today. I was president of the two largest Black organizations on my college campus and an active member of several others. However, my closest friend and roommate at that time often felt the need to tell me my college education would not be enough to make it in real life and that I was still naïve to the knowledge one needs to be considered "street smart".

When I decided to become a teacher, my mother warned me that teaching does not pay very well and suggested that I get a job working for the local city government like her, with options to be promoted throughout the years and make increasing amounts of money with what she considered great benefits. She believed that I would not make enough money to live a comfortable life, but ultimately, as a top-level secretary for not only the local city government but also the state's Supreme Court, I have made more than she did.

As a 24-year-old, single woman with no children, I bought my first home with my own money and credit. Yet, my family was disappointed that I did not buy a home with a big backyard and more rooms available for them to move in if they needed to. Some of them even felt uncomfortable in my home. They considered me to be bourgeois and disapproved of my choices since it did not accommodate their desires. Yet, I had to remind myself that my home was my private sanctuary, a major investment, and no one else was going to help pay my bills.

When I earned my Master of Arts in Education/Curriculum and Instruction, my Black, elder female supervisor and supposed mentor asked me whom I was trying to impress, as if I had no other valid reason to have completed a Master's degree. I thought she would have been happy for me since it instantly afforded me a significant increase in salary and made me more marketable for international teaching positions overseas. Fortunately, I did not need her approval to further pursue my career aspirations.

At age 26, I decided to move overseas and teach at an international school. My father refused to speak to me for several weeks until it was almost time for me to leave the country. He was upset that I was leaving because of concerns about not being able to get to me if I ever needed help. However, he already lived three time zones away and rarely made an effort to come to my aid when his support could have made a significant difference.

My friends at least appeared to be excited for me and made sure to tell me how much they would miss me and wished I would stay. However, I later learned that some of them resented me for leaving. Many people questioned why I would even consider leaving the United States. Nevertheless, I found it easy to leave, because I was excited about the endless possibilities of what I could learn. The world instantly became my playground, and my daily life felt like endless recess. Since then, I have lived in four different countries and traveled to many others.

Currently, I am pursuing my doctoral degree, and as you may have guessed, there are people close to me who have been a source of discouragement. Again, I am considered to be the overachiever and have even been accused of doing too much and wasting time. I have learned that it is more important to follow your own dreams than to follow the advice of those who have not accomplished what it is you have set out to do. Perhaps, they have yet to set goals to reach their dreams or have failed to dream at all.

Sometimes, it is necessary to break the rules in order to create your own set of standards and establish your own traditions. Paradigms are meant to shift at the point of discovery, when you first become conscious of a need for change. Then, it is important to explore the possibilities of the options that ultimately meet that need. Since we cannot control the actions of others, our focus must remain on our own actions. Mahatma Ghandi said, *"Be the change you wish to see in the world."* In other words, the bottom line for each us is what we each choose to do with our own life. It is when we decide to take responsibility for our own success that we are most likely to influence others to do the same for themselves. Each of us has a purpose in life that no one else can fulfill. Own that responsibility and free yourself mentally and spiritually through the fulfillment of that purpose.

As you strive toward your goals, keep in mind that everything you need is already within you. However, seek out mentors who will support and guide you toward your goals by providing you with an example of what to do in order to maximize your experience along the way. Be aware that your strongest supporters may not be relatives or family members, but they will nurture you in ways that challenge you to develop and grow in the areas you need it most. Find a healthy outlet for the inevitable stress that comes along with pursuing success and chasing your dreams. For example:

> My happiness is a result of the quality of life that I live
> Therefore, I often seek out the healthiest alternative
> I choose to use a form of release that's quite constructive

As it allows me to remain happy and productive.
Thus, I write.
Ink provides me an outlet for my mental overflow
And in the midst of momentary sorrow,
I cope through hope for a better tomorrow
The ink starts to flow, and I let it all go
So, I write.
To reveal my subconscious thoughts and become aware
Of the thoughts that are too heavy for my heart to bare
Rather than scream, shout or swear
And risk damaging a relationship beyond repair
I stop and write.
I inscribe my thoughts on paper to clear the air
I have found that they are best there
There on the blue lines of white pages habitually confined
within the red margins
Or I transform my thoughts into words on the keyboard
before others barge in
I write.
Rather than allow the doubts of naysayers to invade my brain,
Hinder my efficacy and induce pain
I let the words pour out like Seattle's rain
And continue to excel against the grain.
For me, this art form works well
I can describe heaven even when I'm going through hell
I pick up a pad and a pen and begin to tell
My stories from within
I pray that this helps someone who may now be where I have been
No matter how tough the fight, if you never give in, each day you win.
It has proven to work for me and for you it might.
So when things in life don't seem right
Look for peace and clarity as you write.

Rhonesha Blaché has worked in the field of education for 20 years. As a passionate educator, she has purposely diversified her experience by working with students at each level from P to 20, public to private, rural to urban, small to large, traditional to alternative, and local to international including Europe, Africa, the Caribbean, and the US. She earned a Bachelor of Science in Psychology from Arizona State University, a Master of Education in Curriculum and Instruction from the University of Phoenix, and is currently pursuing a Doctorate of Education in Interdisciplinary Studies at Teachers College, Columbia University. As the graduate assistant for the African Diaspora Consortium, she is committed to uplifting and bridging the gap between people of African descent worldwide, thus her research interests include the leadership and identity development of Black women, culturally relevant pedagogy, international and comparative education, experiential learning, and study abroad.

CHAPTER 8

I AM A COMPOSITE OF ALL MY EXPERIENCES

Dionne Blue

Key Challenges: poverty, child of a teen mom, single-parent family, school changes and transitions

Looking at someone from the outside, you never really know what struggles that person has experienced and witnessed. Most of my acquaintances and co-workers look at me and assume that my background and life story are the same as theirs. As an African American woman, my struggle is often subsumed within the common culture and practices of my surroundings. I am often not asked to share myself outside of the cursory 'How was your weekend?' and even then, most don't really want to entertain the details. They ask because they think it is polite or right to do so.

In reality, if most of my co-workers and peers knew my background, they would be surprised. Not because I am the exception to some unwritten rule (although in their minds I may be due to being professionally successful), but because the expectation for a Black girl from Newark, New Jersey, who was born to a teen mom, is not that she will go on to achieve the highest

Gumbo for the Soul, pages 41–44
Copyright © 2017 by Information Age Publishing
All rights of reproduction in any form reserved.

level of education in her field . . . the expectation is that she would certainly be an urban statistic.

My mother grew up being told by adults around her that she would never amount to much, especially after she had a baby so young. They thought she was doomed to be the 'teen welfare mom' that so many people associated with young women of color in large urban areas. Fortunately for her and for me, all of those negative people made her even more determined to make sure that I never had to endure the animosity people sometimes feel against someone who is doing positive things with their lives. Even though it took her twice as long as others, she still finished college despite having me at the age of 16. She did so with sheer will and the support of her family and a circle of close friends.

There are always going to be those who have negative things to say when you are doing well in school, making good choices, have a special talent or underlying potential. But my mom and I didn't listen to them. Instead, we lived by the quote *"Let your haters be your motivators."* My mom had that drive, and she instilled that same determination and drive in me at a very young age.

My mom attended college during most of my elementary school years. She had to work to pay for school, so she was what was called a 'stop-out:' She withdrew from college several times, usually for a semester, but once for an entire school year, so she could work and raise the money to go back. She had no reliable transportation and no reliable childcare. We rode the city bus everyday everywhere, and she relied on whoever was available to babysit me. Sometimes that meant I would stay with my grandma or great aunt for a few weeks at a time, sometimes her old roommate, other times the lady who lived downstairs from us, who had a dangerous, alcoholic and abusive husband. Because of that volatility, I too had to withdraw from school, and then re-enroll in whatever neighborhood school I was near, depending on who I was staying with. I never knew how long I would have to be in any specific school, and I never really fit in to most places because I was always the 'new kid'—here one week, gone the next, and back again in a month. I never had the luxury of making friends, or knowing what lessons had been taught in the new schools. I just had to get in wherever I fit in, and figure it out as I went. I was considered a student with high mobility, which meant I changed schools for reasons other than being promoted to the next grade. Kids like me were automatically considered high-risk; between Kindergarten and second grade, I was never in any school long enough to get a continuous semester of schooling. Once I reached third grade, my mother joined the army, which meant I was still moving a lot, just for a different reason. In 13 years of school (including Kindergarten), I attended nine schools as a regular student, and at least two others as a temporary student, on and off.

Once I reached second grade, I was a latch-key kid: I walked home from school, either alone or with other kids; let myself into our apartment, and stayed alone or with my cousin who was the same age as I was, until she got home. Every day I had the same the routine—come straight home from school, lock the door, change clothes, fix a peanut butter and jelly sandwich, do homework, watch TV. That's just how it was; I never questioned it, and it never seemed odd to me, because all of the kids in my neighborhood did similar things.

In the schools I attended in Newark and East Orange, "gifted" was an unofficial title; it just meant that you could skip a grade if your family pushed for it, or that you could just do some portions of your day with the "big kids"—those in the grade ahead you. I started reading by age four, and by the time I reached Kindergarten, I may as well have been the teacher's aide, because there were few concepts she taught us that my mother hadn't already drilled in to me in the two years prior. I could even tell time on a traditional analog clock before I was six.

Although I was considered gifted most of my elementary years, I never took it seriously. I knew I was good at some things, but not so great at other things, but I never felt like I was overly challenged to excel. In all reality, I thought I was just lucky, because if my mom hadn't started me off on a good track, and herself been a good example of working hard and staying focused, I may not have made it all, let alone been considered exceptional in any way.

It wasn't until I went to college at an all-women's Historically Black College and University (HBCU), that I realized that Black girls from any background can grow up to be strong, focused, poised leaders. On the outside, we were all African American young women, but underneath that, all of our struggles had been different. I had friends and peers who grew up with a lot of money, and others who grew up with hardly any money at all. Some were already mothers, while others of us had never even had a boyfriend before. Life had been difficult for some and easier for others, and even though we were from different places across the country and had different life experiences, we were all highly intelligent young ladies with a purpose. All we needed was the tenacity to persevere. As Henry Ford once said: "Whether you think you can or think you can't—you are right." My mother knew she could, and she convinced me that I could. Could do what, you ask? Whatever I wanted! I know that there is always someone out there better, thinner, smarter, prettier, or more popular than I am, but the "me" that I am can still be the best that I can be no matter the circumstance. Even if no one else ever knows what my struggles have been, because all they see is what is on the outside, I know that I am who I am today because of the experiences I have had that have shaped me into the woman I am today, and I am proud to be that person.

Dionne A. Blue, PhD is the Chief Diversity Officer for the Evansville Vanderburgh School Corporation. She received a Bachelor's Degree from Spelman

College where she majored in English and minored in Spanish. She has a Master's Degree in Literacy Education from Washington State University and a PhD in Integrated Teaching and Learning from The Ohio State University where her research focused on racial identity development and the impact of social contexts on education. Dr. Blue has written a number of publications, and is a member of several organizations for professionals in the fields of educational research, multicultural education and diversity.

CHAPTER 9

SANCOCHO

How Mamí's Stories Fed My Curiosity and Continue to Sustain Me

Mildred Boveda

Key Challenges: biracial, peer pressure, poverty, language issues, parental education and literacy, cultural barriers

---

Throughout my elementary, middle, and high school years in Miami Dade County Public Schools, teachers often underestimated me. By the time we were sophomores in high school, it became an inside joke between my two best friends and I. "How long will it take for the teacher to figure out that Mildred was one of the top students?" Perhaps it was my brown skin, the big hoop earrings I wore, or my talkative outgoing nature. For whatever reason, it was not until the results of the first assessments were out—typically a week or two into the semester—that a teacher would take notice of me. In contrast, today I find that when I am at professional educational conferences people are too quick to pay attention to what I say or do. Perhaps it is because of my brown skin, the big hoop earrings that I wear, or my talkative

Gumbo for the Soul, pages 45–48
Copyright © 2017 by Information Age Publishing
All rights of reproduction in any form reserved.

outgoing nature. For whatever reason, complete strangers have no qualms with approaching me with flattering statements and with the expressed interest of staying in touch.

As a high school student, I did not allow teachers' low expectations to discourage me and today I am not puffed up by the White gaze and sense of wonder that I frequently encounter. There came a point in my upbringing when I gained an understanding that I am more than my academic gifts and talents and more than others' desires to acknowledge my abilities. As an educator who interrogates the effects of intersecting identities, I now know that this early realization was critical for me (a light-skinned-Black girl/dark-skinned-Latina born to Dominican immigrant parents) to survive in the 'hood and to thrive in the equally savage context of American schooling. In this chapter, I explore how I developed two critical attributes that I greatly value even though they were never assessed in traditional academic settings: an understanding that everyone is a potential source of knowledge and a purpose-driven curiosity. Through the telling of narratives from my family and school experiences, I explore how I developed these critical aspects of who I am and the role that self-awareness and an inquisitive nature played in navigating challenging and unchartered contexts.

Growing up, my parents never read me bedtime stories. The only two books in our house were the Bible and the phone book. My first exposure to children's literature came only after I entered public schools. Although I did not learn about the Ugly Duckling or about the adventures of Raggedy Ann and Andy until an elementary school teacher read me those stories, my early childhood memories are nevertheless filled with numerous narratives about my parents and siblings' lives in the Dominican Republic. My mother, for example, was too poor to attend school during a time and place where compulsory education did not exist and only the affluent were able to pursue a basic education. Both of my parents worked from a very young age in order to support themselves and their families; my mother was able to afford her first pair of shoes at the age of 16. The repeated telling of stories that vividly described life before I was born in the United States heavily influenced my attitude toward school and my respect for the educational opportunities available to me. My parents were never able to check my homework or talk directly with most of my teachers, but they established a tacit understanding that it was my responsibility to do my best in school and to take advantage of all of the resources they never had at their disposal.

When I was born, my parents were in their 40's and my siblings, who are 15 and 16 years my seniors, were already preparing to leave the nest. My cousins closest to my age did not move to Miami until I was in the third grade. Spending most of my pre-school years surrounded by adults and immersed by the oral tradition, I became the type of student who was excited to be around other children at school; I constantly talked to all of my classmates.

Teachers would often reprimand me for being too chatty, and would heap praises on the students who were able to stay calm and remain quiet. There was a clear message conveyed that the best students were the ones who were able to remain quiet. At home, on the other hand, my family indulged all of my questions and my mother was the primary source of answers.

For a woman with no formal education, Mamí was amazingly apt at giving responses to my insatiable inquiries. Not only would she tell me her own stories, but through her impeccable memory she would recount stories about her father who died when she was 11, her mother who raised eight children in the rural parts of the Dominican Republic, and countless stories about notorious government leaders such as Rafael Trujillo. Sometimes my aunts worried that she was too forthcoming, but I thank God that Mamí never withheld the truth from me. I heard tales about resilient and resourceful men and women who were ethical and worked hard to support themselves and their people. As I got older, the details about the challenges the matriarchs of my family faced became more specific, and at times, horrific. I learned that life, though precious, can be unfair. Regardless of what obstacles they confronted my family pressed on; because they pressed on, I am here. I only have seen three pictures of my mother before she moved to the United States. Nevertheless, the stories I heard in school rarely represented characters who looked or sounded anything like me, but the narratives about my family always did.

Having explicit understanding about my family's trajectory—the challenges they faced and the obstacles they overcame—gave me a perspective about our living situation in Miami. I often say that the potential for violence was as much a part of my public school experience as was having to carry a book bag to school. It was not until my 20s that I realized I had become desensitized to the brutality of my urban school context. Although we lived in some of the toughest parts of the city, I understood that where we were was a sign of immense progress from where my family had originally come from. Consequently, I could not succumb to the destructive futility of self-pity or to the lower expectations that others had of me. By comprehending and honoring my family's struggles, I avoided the gangs, drugs, and other common snares typical in my urban community.

Although my family lacked the middle class' economic, cultural, and social capitals typically rewarded in schools, I can identify several ways in which my family's agency and example of resourcefulness kept me focused. For example, during elementary school, science fair projects were especially challenging. Unlike other children whose parents were able to help them with their science boards, I had to complete the projects completely on my own. I never won a ribbon and my board was usually one of the least attractive of those presented in the exhibit hall. But because I took the scientific method very seriously and engaged in the experiments to the best of my ability, by the fifth grade I was able to participate and win first place for our school's Science Bowl. Had I focused on the ribbons instead of the lessons learned from completing the projects, perhaps I would have been discouraged and turned off to science. My emphasis was on taking advantage of the opportunity to learn, an opportunity that some in my family never had, and as a result I developed a true passion toward research and inquiry that I still have to this day.

Mamí's stories were critical in helping me understand my place in the world. My parents did not have any academic credentials, did not speak English, and could not understand how to navigate the local school system. I frequently served as the translator in my parents' infrequent interactions with school staff. Yet, with all of the qualifications that they seemingly lacked, they always emphasized the opportunities that schools provided. In retrospect, I entered school as an English language learner, defied many people's low expectations, and graduated with an acceptance to several Ivy League institutions because I was driven by my family's high expectations. Although I am the most educated person in my family, I continue to aspire to be half as brilliant as the elders whose stories initially sparked my curiosity. It is the stories of their journeys that continue to inspire me as I navigate new and complex academic spaces in pursuit of the expansion of access to high quality education for all. I hope you find inspiration in my journey. Stay focused. Stay committed. Do all you can to not give up and feel defeated . . . and choose wisely in spite of pressures and social temptations and ills.

Mildred Boveda is a Doctoral Candidate in Exceptional Student Education in the College of Education at Florida International University. Her research interests are in collaboration in teacher education, preparing teachers to teach a growingly diverse student population, and the application of intersectionality theory to teacher education practice, research, and policy.

*My first bowl of Gumbo was like nothing
I had ever tasted before. I slowly consumed it.
Each ingredient was there at its peak, tasty and full
of its uniqueness . . . somewhere in the middle of the
bowl . . . there it was—that power, that magnificent
richness. It took me to a familiar place, but a new place
all at once. Like our stories, the best Gumbo
is uniquely rich, familiar and new and filled
with soul-enriching power!*

—Joy Lawson Davis

CHAPTER 10

FROM HOMELESS TO HOPEFUL

Overcoming Tragedy to Persevere

Mercedes Cannon

> **Key Challenges:** foster family, blended family, sexual abuse, teen pregnancy, school challenges

In this world you will have trouble but take heart! I have overcome the world.
John 16:33 (NASB)

In the world of my childhood years, I did not know love. Instead, I knew troubles too great for a child to bear. My mother died unexpectedly when I was four years old. My identity as my mother's daughter changed irrevocably at the moment of her death, and the agony of her absence lingered in my life for many years. I did not speak for the first year after her death and was consequently labeled as having a speech and language disorder by a staff person at the elementary school I attended.

Gumbo for the Soul, pages 51–55

Upon my mother's death, my father was unable to care for me. So, immediately after my mother's passing, I was placed in foster care with three other families who were all related to each other. Everyone there called the woman who was my foster parent 'Grandmother'. She was a strict disciplinarian. I called her daughter, Aunt, and her son-in-law, Uncle. Grandmother's family didn't interact with me or the other foster children, but Aunt and Uncle's daughter was my age, so we often played. Grandmother also had two sons who lived with us, one of whom had an adult son of his own who was slightly younger than me.

Grandmother eventually began abusing me verbally and physically. Then, sexual abuse by someone else in the house soon followed. One summer, at the age of 12, I ran away from home after an episode of sexual abuse. I returned only after I learned that my father had come to Grandmother's home hoping to visit with me. I begged him to take me with him back to Indiana where he was living with his wife, and he obliged. I was finally able to escape the abuse I'd endured at Grandmother's house, or so I thought.

Shortly after my thirteenth birthday, my father molested me for the first time. I spent several years in his house before I finally found the courage to leave, which I did at 16, choosing homelessness over the trauma I was experiencing. I survived by rotating among friends' homes, including that of my high school boyfriend.

At 17, I managed to complete high school early, the summer before what would have been my senior year. I had no idea what I wanted to do with my life. I only knew that I wanted to love and be loved, to be married, have children, and live happily ever after. But instead, I soon became pregnant while dating a physically abusive teenager. I was totally unprepared to raise a child, yet knew that I wanted my baby in spite of the undesirable aspects of my situation. I also knew that I had to get away from my boyfriend. I left his home during my first trimester and as I had done after I left my father's house I stayed with different girlfriends and their families.

During my sixth month of pregnancy, I was hospitalized and underwent an emergency caesarean-section. A beautiful boy emerged from the womb beneath the large incision on my abdomen. I had become a mother. The thrill of that realization temporarily dulled the excruciating pain radiating from my stapled belly scar. Looking down on my newborn for the first time, I thought to myself, "Here is someone who will love me just as I am." At the time, I did not realize the selfishness of this; nor did I realize then that I was still a child myself. But although I was desperate for love, I saw a helpless premature son who also needed unconditional love.

I was struck by the brightness of the incubator during my first visit with my baby. The nurses shared that the incubator's light kept his temperature regulated and protected him since he was not immunized against human or environmental dangers. Also, he could not breathe on his own and had been born with water on his brain, a condition known as hydrocephalus. My son survived three operations within three months, but eventually he died. I buried him in a small box donated by the state of Indiana and I was devastated. I was left to grieve alone, without the support of my son's father or my own family.

The death of my child haunted me long after his precious soul left earth. I blamed myself for his death, judging myself for being unable to withstand the pressure I was living under while pregnant—pressure that left me psychologically and physically unable to carry him full-term. I was so depressed after he died that the doctors urged me take anti-depressants. I refused, feeling that if God existed, he would help me heal. I needed to bear the pain I felt, I thought, not run away from it through a pill. I wanted God to guide me in using my suffering as a means to grow and transform my life.

After my son's death, I remained homeless, shifting between girlfriends' houses for a half-year until I met a young woman through one of my friends. She invited me to stay with her and her husband and children until I could find low-income housing. With her help, I had my own apartment within weeks. In addition, I was accepted to a four-year university in Indiana's largest city but I only attended classes for one semester before walking off campus one afternoon. As a young adult, I did not understand how higher education could help me take care of myself. What was being taught in those college classrooms seemed irrelevant to my struggle to pay my bills, so I walked away and began to search for work . . . and the love and affection I was still desperately needed.

At age 23, I got married and had my second son. My marriage however ended after three years due to my husband's infidelity. At the end of our relationship, I found myself alone, fighting for custody, but after a grueling four-year court battle, I won. Throughout this time, I supported my son and myself through odd jobs that included working at a fast food restaurant and driving a school bus. Eventually, I earned my cosmetology license and opened a salon. At the age of 30, I got married again and with this marriage, I gained a daughter who my husband had via a previous relationship. Although I was happy, I could still tell that there was still something missing and at the age 32, I realized that I needed to release the reigns and surrender my faith to Jesus Christ. Today, the Holy Spirit is what I call my daily God consciousness that empowers the life I live.

I returned to higher education later in life, and earned a master's degree in Counselor Education at age 50 and am currently working on my PhD in an urban education field where my focus of study is on the educational experiences of Black women and people who have been diagnosed as learning disabled. I examine how certain experiences shape people's identities, including their faith.

Faith has been at the center of my life and work since I placed myself in the care of Jesus Christ over 20 years ago. Before I began living in faith, I did not know what I was supposed to do with my life. However, I now see that my life has been divinely crafted for me, but before I could see, I had to seek that change I wanted to see, and I chose God as my mentor. He changed my mind, heart and soul . . . and led me to others who could assist in my needs. I had to learn that there are people who care. In the midst of suffering, God did something very intimate and personal in my life. He set my heart aflame with Himself and deposited love beyond measure into my soul to the point where I now have what it takes to help others.

You too have everything it takes too—you have your mind, your will, and your emotions, which are shared attributes of God. Faith believes there is something more and good for you than what you are currently experiencing. It takes faith to believe God cares about people who feel lost and lonely! We have the tendency to look at what we see with our eyes, which results in fear and causes us to remain stagnated in oppressive situations.

Teenage years can feel like a roller coaster ride; they are filled with highs and lows. You start to ask major questions about your identity and how you fit in with others; you may feel unsure about what you want to do with your life. Many times, society, family, and your personal dreams and goals can pull teenagers in different directions. In school, you may become very aware of your teachers' expectations of you, while at home; you may face the wishes and demands of parents. During these times, you may not be able to explore your *own* wishes and dreams; but your time will come when you are on your own.

Whether you attend college or move straight into the work force in order to take care of yourself, at the end of the day, you must balance your personal desires with the demands of others as you decide what you want to do with your life. During this time, it's important to decide upon your goals and what it will take to achieve the goals. This may require you to venture outside of yourself with the help of a mentor or guide (hopefully), who is living in a way that you admire and would like to create for yourself. This will require you to get out of your own way and open yourself up to others who show that they are willing to be in the trenches with you and willing to help you as you establish your identity and grow into yourself and your relationships with others. The process is not easy, but it's important for you not to allow fear and difficulties trick you into thinking that you do not have what it takes, or trick you into believing that you should quit for another reason. Just as I had to do a few years ago, you have to believe first . . . then you have to do it! Our outlook on life often affects the ways in which we live—take heart, God has overcome the world and is always there to help you do the same.

Mercedes Cannon is a doctoral candidate of an Urban Education Studies Program in a Midwestern Urban University. She is interested in programs that advance Black women with disability labels (e.g., High-incidence categories) progression to degree attainment in post-secondary education.

CHAPTER 11

RACISM AND GIFTEDNESS

A Double Whammy

Marissa L. Campbell

Key Challenges: racism, segregated schooling

I first became aware of racism when I entered the first grade. My parents moved our family of nine from the "projects" to a single-family home in East Nashville. It was the early '60s and urban (inner-city) neighborhoods were being abandoned during waves of "White suburban flight." To my family's benefit, upwardly mobile Blacks were moving into residential communities, hoping to improve their (our) lives and circumstances. Not only would we be living in a more stable and secure environment, but we would also be attending better schools and be walking distance from the church of our parents' choice.

The year was 1966, and I was seven years old. As only one of "just seven"—as my mother was known for saying—I had been re-zoned to attend 1st grade at Jere Baxter Elementary School, along with an older brother and sister. Jere Baxter Elementary and other neighborhood schools had

Gumbo for the Soul, pages 57–63

only recently integrated, and since I was so young, I knew little about what to expect. Until then, I had attended an all-Black (with a Capital "B"), pre-school class and an all-Black kindergarten class. I had lived in an all-Black neighborhood, played at the all-Black Hadley Park, and frequented the businesses along Jefferson Street, including the all-Black Ritz Theatre, which—before re-gentrification—was regarded as the Black Folks' Main Street of Nashville. During that time, not only were businesses on Jefferson Street owned by diverse people thriving; but quite a few Blacks—even my Dad—owned and operated businesses in the area, which allowed them to carve out their piece of the economic pie.

Despite my family's segregated existence, life for us seemed to be good. There had always been home cooked meals; most needs and many wants had been met; and to the envy of some and admiration of others, we were exposed to a broad array of cultural experiences. Over the years, my mother became the "designated driver by default," and she hauled kids back and forth to practice and to game locations for football and cheerleading demands. Likewise, my father was revered by the neighborhood boys, who were in need of a surrogate Dad, since many of their fathers were military men serving duty at home and abroad. Others had fathers at home who worked during inconvenient hours, so they didn't have much time available to interact with their kids. Dad was also known for having two or more jobs, which was a necessity to support his bulging family.

At the time of our move, I didn't really understand what the concept of integration meant. I knew that great changes were taking place; and suspected from what I had heard, that those changes would indeed benefit us. I knew about those who were featured in the trilogy of photos on the walls of nearly every Black home—Jesus Christ, John F. Kennedy, and Dr. Martin Luther King, Jr. These and others were highly esteemed champions of justice and they inspired me to pursue my dreams.

I had heard chatter about Nashville resistance, sit-ins, and marches. I was in awe of "the movement" and would decide as a sixth grader that I would attend Howard University and follow in the footsteps of the Great Thurgood Marshall. I would later grow to appreciate the fact that *Brown versus the Board of Education in 1954* was the conduit for my opportunity to enjoy educational opportunities and advancement. I was also inspired to practice law by the late Great Justice Marshall who demonstrated to me that commitment to a good cause, knowledge, wisdom, and zealous advocacy can and may yield progressive results when there is a dire need for change. With a general understanding of the Civil Rights Movement, I sensed that something big was going on and I wanted to be a part of it.

Prior to entering first grade, in 1966, I had not, to my recollection, experienced any incidents of racism or discrimination. Nor was I conscious of any other negative experiences that might later find their way back, to wreak havoc in my life. However, at seven years old, my innocence was shattered once I was transferred to an integrated school. It was then that I began to realize that my race made a difference. It first became apparent when I noticed that the attitude of some of the White students, with whom I had bonded and had formed friendships at school, would turn cold while in the presence of their parents. This reality also became vivid on birthdays when parents were invited to share lunch with their son or daughter at school. It didn't take long for me to notice that the friends with whom I had held hands; and had worked and played with in pairs, would never invite me to sit with them. Indeed, when their parents were around, they would not even speak to me, and, at times, would be quite mean.

After school and weekends were also off limits. Once, a brave and true White friend invited me and another Black girl to her weekend slumber party. I was the only one of the two who accepted the invitation and had a great time at the party because everyone treated me the same as all of the other guests. I later learned, however, that several girls had not been permitted to attend the party—for no reason other than the fact that I had been there. The news hit me like a ton of bricks—and that was my first discriminatory experience. I remember tearfully inquiring, "What is wrong with me?" and my mother replying, "Nothing, except that you are Black."

That would be the first of many times that I was conscious that my being Black would affect who might choose to be in my company. Likewise, that was the first time of many that I would be reminded of the fact that being Black alone, could be dictate whether I would enjoy opportunities and/or benefits that my White counterparts took for granted and regularly exploited.

Despite the increasingly obvious, I was an exceptional student and focused on doing my best. Indeed, my White sixth grade teacher saw great promise in me and encouraged me to pursue my dreams. Despite the odds, he expressed confidence that I could be whatever I chose to be... even President, if that were my will. Heading a class for gifted students, he engaged us like no other educator, challenged us to expand our minds; and involved us in practical learning experiences, which gave us an edge in preparation of Jr. High School. It was during that time of my life that I decided to become a lawyer; and from that point on, all of my academic efforts were directed towards that end.

By the time I reached Jr. High School, I had decided that I would "be all that I could be." I joined the high school marching band. I was a cheerleader and became active in forensics, debate and student government. When I was in the ninth grade, I decided to run for the President of the Student Government of Litton Jr. High School. During that same period of time, I also became the first Black student to be inducted into the newly formed Honor Society; and was honored to be elected as its first President. I am also the first Black student to be elected to lead Litton's Student Government, making me President of both organizations—two firsts. Although I had been fairly elected for both positions; mainstream alumni and parents were outraged. A Black student had never led Litton's students; and racist alumni and parents were determined not to start a precedent. They were already resentful and resistant to the mere prospect of integration, so they furiously protested against my holding either position. In the end, I was able to maintain my elected position as President of Student Government; but would have to relinquish my role as President of the Honor Society. That position was later given to a White male student, instead.

While still in the ninth grade, I applied for and was accepted into the A Better Chance (ABC) Program. As it still does today, the program enabled underprivileged urban youth to earn scholarships to attend boarding schools, thereby giving them an academic advantage and creating a pathway to college.

Living in Wisconsin was like nothing I had ever imagined. There were great opportunities for educational advancement; but the trade-off was that I was living in a town where only one Black Family resided and most of the other (predominately White) families had had little exposure to Blacks. Indeed, we lived in a homogenous University town, where all other Blacks were either there on a college scholarship from the local University; or were on ABC scholarships, like myself. Seven minority girls lived in a huge house with me, while seven boys lived in a house nearby.

During the weekend, we stayed with one of two alternative host families—both of whom were White; and both of whom had opened their homes to a Black student in an environment where there had been little exposure to

Figure 11.1

Blacks; and where racial myths proliferated. More than once, I was asked to prick my finger, so that my friends could note the color of my blood. I often had to explain racial concepts to the small children of one of my host families. For instance, I had to explain that what appeared to be dirt on my hands and arms that would not wash away, was in fact, the color of my skin. There were always those who wanted to touch my hair, which would only remain groomed if we ordered hair products from Milwaukee, since none of the small towns in Wisconsin sold hair products for Black people or any other items used exclusively by Black folks. Several times, I was chased by White guys in cars, which forced me to run through private yards and climb over fences just to safely make it back home. *"Go back to where you game from N---- "* was a familiar chant. It was also a frightful experience, an experience that I had never had before—not even during those times when I was only one of a few "token Blacks" in Nashville.

Those were thought-provoking times. For the first time in my life, I was isolated from family support and learned about racism through the eyes of others. I realized then that we as Blacks folks, were totally exposed to the White culture and adopted much of it as our own. On the contrary, many Whites had actually existed in total isolation from other cultures and knew nothing about them, except for the limited information they had gained through home, church, school and media. For me, being the "token Black" was somewhat of a culture shock and I viewed it in a way in which I had never done before. Nearly everywhere I went, I was a treated like a novelty by almost everyone.

Despite the awesome opportunity afforded to me through the ABC Program, it was a lonely existence, devoid of diverse culture, family engagement, and support. So, rather than completing High School in Wisconsin as planned, I returned to Nashville, where I eventually graduated from Nashville's first Comprehensive High School. I resumed my choice of extracurricular activities and excelled academically and qualified to be inducted into the Honor Society. However, when the day of induction arrived, I had yet to receive my invitation. But I had a praying mother who was also an activist who set an essential example for her children. Mom was known for interrupting whatever she was doing to fight for the rights of her kids. So, she investigated the matter, showed up at the school, and demanded to review my transcript to ascertain the basis for my exclusion. There was none—the records showed that I scored high on the list. Then, the Beta Club Administrator struggled to explain that I "had simply been overlooked," as had several other Black students who had qualified for the honor.

Due to my mother's insistence, I was inducted—to the apparent disappointment of those who obviously sought to deny me and others the honors that we had deservingly earned. Insult was added to injury when graduation date neared. When the time came to distribute tassels to affix to graduation hats, McGavock conveniently ran out of the gold ones, which were intended to distinguish honor students from the typical graduate, who would wear a red, white and blue tassel, instead. They had plenty to go around for mainstream students, but when it came to students of color, they seemed to have exhausted their supply. Once again, Mother had to rise to the challenge. Immediately upon being informed of the shortage, she made her way to the school, offering to assist administrators in discovering more gold tassels. When all was said and done, I was issued my gold tassel, as were all of the other Blacks students. Likewise, we were recognized along with other Beta Club members for being the high academic achievers that we were.

Based on these and other experiences, I realized that, despite the much-celebrated accomplishment of integration, those who possess hatred and resentment toward Black people would do everything in their power to undermine our opportunities to succeed. Whether blatant or subtle, the result would be the same—the deliberate and intentional denial of equal educational opportunities for Blacks, regardless of how competitive we might be. Integration gained us admission through the doors of educational opportunity and advancement; but it also provided no guarantee that Blacks would be allowed or permitted to matriculate the challenge, without interference. Blocks and barriers would be erected all along the way and we would need to knock them down, one after the other, one block at a time.

All of the racism I faced in school was sobering. It was not enough to academically compete and excel during the course of my primary education. Throughout those 12 years, I had to fight for the right to compete, to be acknowledged, to be recognized, and to be rewarded for my accomplishments. Years later, I would find myself fighting for the same rights for my son and his similarly situated classmates. Time and time again, I would engage in battles in the same war for justice; only during a different period in time.

Achieving educational equality, employment opportunities and upward professional mobility had been quite a feat, but the journey was not yet over. There would be numerous reality checks and constant reminders that "integration" was more than just a word, with broad social, economic, political and cultural implications. The concept did then, and still does necessitate a mutual effort on the part of racially diverse people, who share a desire to interact and co-exist. However, it had become clear over time, that with respect to many Whites, there was little desire; but a lot of disdain and resentment of compulsory change. That revelation being duly noted, I was traveling on my road to success with a self-written playbook on integration in hand. Eventually, I became a lawyer; one who would go down in history as a first, just as I was in Jr. High School when I integrated a 100-year-old firm. Not only did I contend with racism, I also confronted sexism. I did both with my self-esteem intact and vivid memories of the challenges I faced over time to keep me strong.

Marissa L. Campbell, Esq., is a native of Nashville, TN. She is a graduate of Howard University and Georgetown University. She earned her Juris Doctorate at Georgetown. Attorney Campbell was the first Black attorney to be hired at a 50 year old firm in Tennessee. Her areas of expertise and practice are family law, estate planning, contracts and intellectual property. She enjoys research, writing and speaking with varied audiences, sharing her expertise and empowering others. She has served as Chair of the Domestic Violence Committee of the Lawyer's Association of Women.

CHAPTER 12

FORGING AHEAD IN THE MIDST OF CHALLENGES

Disha Lynch Charles

> **Key Challenges:** bullying, parental illness, immigrant family, academic self-concept

I was in the third grade when I was given an exam that changed my life. I must have performed well because, the next year, I was in the academically talented and gifted class where I would remain for the next three years. I had heard about the class before—I even knew people who were in the class, but never really imagined that I would one day be in the class. I thought I was a good student, but was I good enough?

Everyone in the class was "smart." Why would I stand out? What would make me as special as I had been in other classes? As time progressed, I became lost in the class and felt as if everyone expected me to know how to do everything. Even when I was uncertain, I would never admit this was the case. I was expected to just do and while I did, it was certainly not close to what I *should* have been doing. As a result, my skills were not developing as strongly as they should. Could it have been that I really did not belong in

Gumbo for the Soul, pages 65–69
Copyright © 2017 by Information Age Publishing
All rights of reproduction in any form reserved.

the class? Were they mistaken about me? Self-doubt set in and I became the little fish in a big pond, as the saying goes.

It took the help of a teacher who believed in me and my abilities, even when I didn't believe in myself, to make me realize that I did belong and that even those who are "gifted" need help at times. Despite the hard time I gave her in the beginning, she worked with me, not only to enhance my math skills (I struggled most with math), but also to motivate me to push myself. This teacher never let me give up; she encouraged me to achieve my goals.

I entered junior high school feeling confident and ready to tackle my classes. Little did I know that academics would be the least of my troubles. The work came naturally to me and I was excelling, but being labeled smart brought on a slew of different challenges. Some girls didn't like me because I was "too smart." Others wanted to be my friend only so they could get the answers to homework assignments. I thought I was popular because of my involvement in various clubs and activities at school but, for some, I was just a way for them to get an A on an assignment. I recall a particular quiz that was given in my ninth grade English class. I knew something was strange because she handed each person in the class his or her quiz paper and then went into an inner office that was located near the rear of the room. I remember thinking to myself, "why would she leave the room?" Several of my classmates started asking for answers, but I pretended that I was afraid to give them because I didn't want to get into trouble. But actually, I was annoyed because the quiz was based on a book that we were assigned; therefore, everyone should have been able to answer the questions independently. One student actually got up and stood over me and copied my answers and then called them out to the class. The next day we not only received our quiz scores but also a tongue lashing from our teacher who was very disappointed. I was the only student who scored 100%. Although there was only two or three additional A's, the majority of the class failed. She had given us different quizzes because she suspected that students were not doing their own work; clearly, she was right.

As a result of this and other incidents where she suspected students of using my work, my English teacher and I developed a tumultuous relationship. Things got so bad that we ended up speaking with the guidance counselor on several occasions. I thought to myself, "why does this woman care so much about what I do?" It wasn't until I was named the Valedictorian of the Arthur A. Richards Junior High School Class of 1993 and she offered to help me write my valedictory address that I understood her concern. As we sat in her study at her home working on my speech, I realized that much like my ACT teacher, she too saw something in me that I still had not seen in myself.

I continued on to high school and as expected, excelled in my academics and continued my school and community involvement. The bullying because of being smart continued and so did the people who wanted to copy homework or work with me on an assignment because they figured I'd do the work and they'd get the A. One high school experience that sticks out in my mind was when my Spanish teacher asked me in front of the class, "Have you ever taken an IQ test"? He followed that question with, "You're really smart." The next day people who never spoke to me in class were suddenly saying "hi" and I suppose if the majority of them could sit next to me, they would have done so.

As I reflect on my pre-college years, not only am I reminded of the social challenges I faced because of my academic ability, but also the many losses I encountered. I recall lives of some of my peers destroyed by drug and alcohol abuse and lives forever changed because of teen pregnancy (some of whom were also gifted). I definitely recall my mother and aunt battling breast cancer and the toll this took on me emotionally. All of these events seemed to occur all at once or in a chain reaction. But instead of allowing them to break me, I chose to let them strengthen my mind and spirit.

My aunt Octavia was one of my greatest inspirations. She was one of the kindest, and most loving women I knew. When she was first diagnosed with breast cancer, I was not worried. She was always strong and I just knew that she'd be okay. I realized that a greater power had a different plan for her life. But, despite the chemotherapy, radiation, mastectomies, she grew more ill. The family gathered at the hospital one evening for a visit and I recall hearing my mother's outburst of cry. The doctor told her there was nothing else they could do for my aunt but keep her comfortable. I began to wonder, who was going to help me with my history projects? Who was going to play board games with me? Who was going to save me when I got in trouble with my mother? It was at this point that I understood the finality of death, and the day before her birthday, I gained an angel as my aunt Octavia passed away.

About two years later on my sixteenth birthday, I learned that my mother had breast cancer. I couldn't help but flashback to my aunt's last days. I was not prepared to lose my mother, but I knew that I had no control over the outcome. My older sister was away at college and my mother flew to the mainland for surgery while I remained at home, on the island of St. Croix.

At 16, I became the adult at home as my two older brothers found themselves entangled in the elements of the world. Unfortunately, they were oftentimes under the influence of "something" that made it difficult to even reason with them and I presumed that everyone was trying to cope. I drowned myself in my academics because I knew my mother would expect for me to continue to do well in school. My mother was also a teacher and she wanted more for her children than she had for herself. I didn't want her worrying about me because I needed her to focus on getting well so that she could hurry up and return home. I was emotionally exhausted and spiritually defeated, but I had to hold it together.

My mother returned home the end of my junior year, but that was when even more nightmares began. Unfortunately, my mother could not receive her chemotherapy on the island, so she had to travel to nearby Puerto Rico to receive treatment. Air travel was not covered by her insurance, so she had to travel alone as resources were limited.

Have you ever had a stomach bug that made you vomit so much that you were so weak you couldn't do anything but remain still? Well, imagine that times 10. I would cry myself to sleep many nights as I listened to my mother in the bathroom or in her room vomiting. There was nothing that I could do to ease her pain or make her feel better—and that destroyed me. But my mother was a woman who believed in the power of prayer and she taught me how to pray and that's what we did.

After what seemed like forever, she was cancer free! As I walked across the stage at high school graduation to receive my diploma, I saw her jumping and cheering and the tears rolled down my cheeks. I was ecstatic to have her there. I couldn't even imagine the day without my mother. Thankful doesn't even begin to describe how I felt. While some of my classmates cried because they knew it would be the last time many of us would see each other, I cried tears of joy that my mother survived.

Everyone has a story. Some are more colorful than others, but all are meaningful. We never know how sharing our experiences may impact another's life. There may be that one person who identifies with you or your experiences and finds hope in your story. I shared a snippet of mine in hope that someone would be encouraged to continue to forge ahead even when the future looks gloomy and filled with despair. I knew from a very tender age that I wanted to be successful and was intrinsically motivated to do so. You may not be, which is why I am honored and humbled to leave you these words of encouragement by Edgar A. Guest.

Somebody said that it couldn't be done
But he with a chuckle replied
That "maybe it couldn't," but he would be one
Who wouldn't say so till he'd tried.
So he buckled right in with the trace of a grin
On his face. If he worried he hid it.
He started to sing as he tackled the thing
That couldn't be done, and he did it!
Somebody scoffed: "Oh, you'll never do that;
At least no one ever has done it;"
But he took off his coat and he took off his hat
And the first thing we knew he'd begun it.
With a lift of his chin and a bit of a grin,
Without any doubting or quiddit,

He started to sing as he tackled the thing
That couldn't be done, and he did it.
There are thousands to tell you it cannot be done,
There are thousands to prophesy failure,
There are thousands to point out to you one by one,
The dangers that wait to assail you.
But just buckle in with a bit of a grin,
Just take off your coat and go to it;
Just start in to sing as you tackle the thing
That "cannot be done," and you'll do it.

Disha Lynch Charles began her academic quest on the tropical island of St. Croix, Virgin Islands. She holds a Bachelor of Science in biology from Montclair State University and a Master of Public Health degree from Hunters College. In 2010, she earned her doctoral degree. Dr. Charles has worked as a Science teacher at several New York City Public schools and currently works at the Bronx School for Law, Government and Justice. Dr. Charles also enjoys spending time with her husband and family, reading, event planning and traveling.

CHAPTER 13

I NEEDED MY MOTHER AND MY DAUGHTER NEEDS ME

(Biggest Fan! First Defender! Best Advocate!)

Johnita Collins

> **Key Challenges:** low teacher expectations, poor academic advising, high achieving but unidentified gifted, parental loss, single-parent family, low income

I sat in the guidance counselor's office during my last year of middle school, excited about being accepted to Overbrook High School's prestigious Music Magnet Program. I loved and excelled at music. My White guidance counselor leaned back in her chair as I shared how nervous I had been during my audition. She paused before pulling the pin on her grenade, "You don't need to go to that school." She did not mask her disdain for the predominantly Black music magnet school that was my preference, "You're too intelligent to go there." She now launched the grenade, rolling it to the

Gumbo for the Soul, pages 71–75
Copyright © 2017 by Information Age Publishing
All rights of reproduction in any form reserved.

place I had, until then, stood firmly. "You need to attend Bartram Motivation Center and major in French!" French was not my thing. And I had no idea what school she was talking about. "What's that?" She boasted, "A college preparatory school for smart girls like you."

Bartram Motivation was a predominantly White school that accepted "intelligent" Black children, filtered in through the guidance counselor's recommendations and the few Black families who integrated that neighborhood. Bartram Motivation was an academic only, college preparatory school that offered nothing to support my cultural needs or creative side. And both were central to who I was as an intellectually gifted child. That highly credentialed counselor, whose mission was to guide students toward their best future, clearly did not fully see me for who I truly was. I was not identified as gifted nor was anyone in my school or neighborhood that I knew of. This was one of countless times that misguided people along my path did not recognize me as a gifted Black girl, and tried to contain rather than sustain me.

I remember being pulled out of reading and given more difficult material than my classmates. Always at the top of my class, I was often chosen to lead. I was called smart, sometimes too smart for my own good. But I was never identified as gifted. Until that point, being ill-advised, I had not second guessed my high school choices. I began to feel uncertain about whether my musical and academic pursuits could coexist. Later that night, I helped my sister cook dinner. While sitting at the kitchen table, I shared that I had made it into the music magnet program. "Is that what you want to do?" was her response. Perhaps she didn't see my passion for the arts and music, and did not see it as a potential career. In moments like this, I missed my mother. I needed my mother, her support, especially then at 14 years old; I needed the guidance of the one person that knew me better than I did. She died on September 1, 1986, just before I entered the seventh grade.

Sixth grade was difficult, I spent the first half in Milwaukee with my Dad but even then my fight was being shaped. I knew my mother didn't want me to see her sick and dying but I wanted my mother, whom I cared deeply about. I had only known my Dad through the telephone, a few letters and weekend hangouts when he visited Philly. But, while living with him, we had great jam sessions and intellectually stimulating conversations. He allowed me to begin to find my voice. However, for six months of my life, I cried almost every day and asked to go home until an airplane ticket was sent, and I was back in Philly. I believe I realized that if I ask, and keep asking, eventually I would get exactly what I was asking for—tenacity developed. It was somewhat hard to believe my mother had been gone for less than two years and I was graduating without her by my side.

Growing up the youngest of my mother's six female children had its challenges, but wasn't bad for me, relatively speaking. We were very close knit and I had no idea that we were poor and on welfare. I knew that those white paper bills with brown, blue and green numbers on them that we pulled from a perforated booklet were different than the regular green dollar bills, fives and tens I would usually see. That was about the extent of poverty for me.

My mother worked hard to sever her relationship with the government's welfare rolls. She attended the Philadelphia Opportunities Industrialization Center (OIC). OIC assisted people who were unemployed, underemployed, homeless, or otherwise economically disadvantaged. The goal was to achieve self-sufficiency and empowerment, through things like education, training, job placement, housing and economic development. That's where my mom and dad met and fell in love. Their love for the arts, music and education could not sustain their relationship, which would be short-lived. My parents separated when I was a toddler.

My dad moved to Milwaukee and landed a job with the city as an arborist. My mother became a driver for SEPTA, Philadelphia's public transportation system. She was a trailblazer of sorts in the 80s as one of few women in that position. She navigated Philly's roadways for SEPTA until she died from cancer. My father retired early because of health challenges, he went back to school and earned his bachelor's degree at age 52 and a master's degree at 54. Now, in his late 60s, my father is pursuing a PhD. His educational pursuits made clear that it is never too late to step fully into your destiny.

I have little doubt that my father *and* mother were unidentified gifted Black people. My siblings and I were unidentified gifted too. When we were young, my mom was a single mother who ran a tight ship, making us leave the TV off, instead making us read and play challenging games like Boggle, Scrabble, chess, crossword puzzles, monopoly, backgammon, homemade *Family Feud,* and *The Gong Show.* Laughter often permeated the atmosphere of our home. It is why I still find laughter in the midst of life's fires.

It was this time spent together that she used to nurture critical thinking, responsibility, independence, leadership and negotiation skills. We were six independent thinkers who had to come together for a common good. It did not matter the age, you better have a strategy and a fight because we played to win. By the time I was 10, I could run many aspects of my home, without assistance. Really! I could create the grocery list, cut coupons, earmark sale items, handle food shopping, pay the bills and clean house. We were well organized and everyone could handle the household business as needed, and As and Bs were the norm on Ethel's girls' report cards.

Evidence of my mother's focus on critical thinking surfaced in an interesting way while I was in the seventh grade. I became my math teacher's public pet and secret assistant. Instead of doing pre-algebra homework, she began assigning me algebra. Soon, she began to send the class test home with me to grade. Yes, I graded my classmates' math tests. Sometimes I created tests and a few times, I taught the class. While in an odd way, this signaled the teacher's recognition of me as a gifted student. But it also underscored a void in teachers' ability to identify gifted learners like me and support our learning needs. Yes, I learned to score, develop exams and challenge my peers but I certainly missed out on being challenged at a level I was prepared to handle but I figured out a way to some degree. And, not just in her class! This experience taught me that just because someone is willing to accept less than my best, I should not.

My eighth grade year went well. My teacher put aside concerns that I might be too much of a challenge and she challenged me academically. She stretched me in every subject. The music director challenged me as the viola section leader, lead vocalist in the citywide Philadelphia Cluster String Ensemble. That meant I played classical and jazz viola and sung jazz and R&B music during every performance; often being pulled out from class to practice and pulled from school to travel the Tri-State area as a musical representative of our school. I was achieving and excited about school and life, again. The year went well. And I was ecstatic when my father flew in from Milwaukee to see me graduate. After surviving my mother's cancer related illness in the sixth grade and her death in the seventh grade, the eighth grade underscored my resilience as a young Black girl.

At graduation I received honors awards for science, math, English, and music. A special leadership plaque accompanied with flowers for my hard work as an orchestra member, vocalist and violist provided the icing on my cake. While I lived during a babies-having-babies era, with many friends who did not graduate alongside me, I poured all I could muster into my academics and music. And it paid off. What a lesson. I would need to tap into that lesson in the fall when I got to the academic high school I was sent to instead of the music magnet school I wanted to attend. I wound up at the academic school because my guidance counselor sent my transcripts to the school *she* preferred rather than the school I wanted.

Although my parents and teachers may not have been able to identify my giftedness, their support and affirmation of my strengths helped me to keep believing in my capabilities and empowered me to endure challenges that could have led to me losing sight of my potential—or worse, my passion. I was learning to recognize and absorb the goodness people poured into me and to filter out paternalistic marginalization that has no place in my life.

I also learned to recognize teachers who cared, beyond the books about me and my overall success. I learned to absorb their mentoring and mothering, and to see my potential more clearly through the reflection of me in their eyes. They made clear how important it is for Black gifted children to have people lighting and championing their path. It's why I mentor girls and young women to this day. They need us to see them fully. Of course, the one who needs my insight the most is my daughter.

I recognized my daughter's giftedness very early on and have been advocating on her behalf ever since. I had her formally tested, something I did not have done as a child. And that test officially identified her as highly gifted. But, to be the best gifted person she can be, she needs a balance of support. So, I nurture her emotional, social, cultural and academic needs. I see my daughter holistically. Make sure her thirst for music, theater and arts are satisfied, and that she learns how to navigate friendships. I believe if she feels great about who she is first and is comfortable in her own brown skin, as she is, then she will continue to use her giftedness in a naturally resourceful way. This allows her creativity and intelligence to grow to unimaginable heights in ways that leave her happy and healthy. This is how my daughter needs me. She needs me to love her. And she needs me to understand and see her in a way only her mother can.

As, they say, hindsight is 20/20. Today, I see clearly and draw on my life experiences as an *unidentified* gifted student to ensure that my *identified* gifted daughter obtains and enjoys emotional, social, cultural, academic and artistic success. Consequently, I am her biggest fan and number one defender. I advocate for my gifted Black child as well as children and young adults like her, who need and deserve it too.

Johnita Collins is a business owner, artist, pastor and passionate parent. As a spiritual life mentor, her empowering workshops reinforce resilience, renewal of the mind, leadership and the importance of developing emotional intelligence. Johnita Collins' work speaks to people's pain, with healing truths about surviving trauma. She is a living reminder of the power of God in each of us.

CHAPTER 14

MAKING BEAUTY FROM ASHES

On Learning to Forgive and Love

Kimberly Phillips Dabney

> **Key Challenges:** violence, parental death, single-parent family, parental incarceration, extended family, forgiveness

I never saw her face, perhaps only in my dreams. At that time, no one actually said she was gone, I just knew. There was never much mention of her name in our household. It was perhaps a dark secret that no one wanted my sister or me to realize. Perhaps to say her name would stir up her memory, some blocked or suppressed emotions. She did exist, didn't she? Yes, she did. Around the Sunday dinner table, I saw my grandmother, my grandfather, my sister and, of course, there I sat.

Each meal was attended by all. All heads were bowed, the blessing was said, and the meal was consumed by my "family." The most non-traditional sense of the word, grandma, grandpa, and granddaughters—where's the mom and dad? I can still remember saying the words "by thy hands we all

Gumbo for the Soul, pages 77–81
Copyright © 2017 by Information Age Publishing
All rights of reproduction in any form reserved.

are fed, give us Lord our daily bread, Amen." A tradition. After dinner, my sister and I helped our beloved Gran clean up dishes. My Gran was an amazing cook. She taught me well.

It's Sunday afternoon, the Sabbath; we are home from church and we were going to rest. Sunday worship wasn't an option—it was a requirement and one that we looked forward to. The choir sang and the preacher brought forth the word; I got to see some friends and learn about an awesome Savior who had died just for me. On those Sundays that the youth choir sang, I was always present and accounted for. "Soon and Very Soon" was the song I led. Life was good. Or was it? Something was missing though. I felt love, I felt loved, my grandparents, while growing in age were great "parents," but something was missing.

We retire to the living room where there's plastic on the sofa (we must preserve the good furniture). The television was on. It likely served as the tool that would take us to our afternoon nap . . . but this Sunday, something was different. Gran said she has a letter to share with us. "A letter" I exclaimed, "From who?" "Your father," she says. Silence . . . more silence . . . a glance passes from my sister to me. My head drops. I wait with baited breath. She disappears down the hall to her bedroom and comes back with an envelope. She insists on reading it to us, like a bedtime story . . . but oh so different. She unfolded the long, yellow legal paper and all four eyes are on her. We patiently wait to hear what our father has to say. He spoke of missing us and loving us. Of how he hoped we were well and that we should be obeying Mr. and Mrs. Jones. He spoke of making good grades in school, and how we were the most important people in the world to him.

And then, he wrote about being a chef for over 300 people and that, daily, he pealed tons of pounds of potatoes and scrambled tons of eggs for these 300 plus people. That's a mighty big restaurant, I thought to myself. I never said a word; I just listened as my grandmother read those long yellow sheets of handwriting to us, one by one. Each page turning into another... He surely didn't understand brevity. There were several pages (at least four) of long yellow paper filled with words. It never failed; before she could get to the very end of the letter, I could feel the tears running down my face. I would sometimes turn my back and hide so that neither my sister nor my gran knew. But they did. They always knew. Why did I cry? Did his words hurt me? Why couldn't he come by our house and say all those things? Did he really love us? Why was he cooking for all those people? Where was he?

One similar Sunday, the dots were finally connected. I became aware of something that I likely knew, but no one had actually said. Sitting on that plastic covered couch reading the "colorful" ads in the Sunday paper, there was a Murphy's Mart ad with savings on this and that. Here it was in front of me, a BB gun. I said "granddaddy, look at this BB gun, I want that," to which he says, "If your father would have kept a gun out of his hands, your mother would be alive today." Silence . . . more silence . . . even more silence. The truth of the matter is, I knew all of this somewhere deep down in my heart, but it became my reality the moment my grandfather actually spoke those words. I recall briefly the awkward glance between he and my Gran and then, as if he said nothing at all, my head went down, I kept reading the ads and life went on as usual.

I had so many questions as time progressed, but I never knew whom to ask. My grandparents, while loving, nurturing, and supportive, were old school and sitting down and talking about "things" is not how I recall that unfolding. My father, while miles away, could be reached by phone, but my fear is that he wouldn't be truthful. So there we were with no valid explanation of my mother's untimely death. No one said, "If you have questions, I can answer them." In all honesty, I can't blame them. Perhaps they didn't know themselves. Perhaps they just wanted us to have a chance at normalcy. They too were grieving, they too suffered loss and lack of closure. My grandma lost her daughter and there was nothing that she could do about it.

Over the years, I met my mom's high school friends and they gloated and sang their undying love for her. "She was this, she was that, she was so beautiful, you have her laugh and smile, she was feisty, your sister looks like her, but you act like her." I loved and still love meeting people who loved my mother, who were a part of her dash, who knew her silly ways, bubbly laugh and wild side. My uncle used to tell me often, "You are wild like your momma." He speaks of her to this day and his eyes well up with tears and his throat closes with raw emotion.

I sit here today at the age of 40, with vivid memories of that day when those dots were connected for me, when someone said "his actions took her life." I couldn't have been more than seven years young when I acknowledged it in my mind; when I knew she was gone and not coming back. When the only name I would ever say in a maternal acknowledgement was grandma. I am sure at seven, I didn't profess to have the answers and nor decide that I was going to make the best of this hand that life had dealt me, but apparently a verbal confession was required. Thinking back, outside of my mother not being there, life was never all that difficult for me, in my opinion. The essentials were covered—a roof, food, some toys, clothes, and love. I don't think I expected much more from the aging parents of my beloved mother.

In their individual ways, family members loved, protected and made us feel safe, all while clutching somewhere in their minds that their 27-year-old daughter had been shot and killed, and they had to do all that they could to make sure these girls are cared for. My sister and I both have lived longer than she did. That is our reality; one that we ponder often. "The Village" (my mom's siblings) were the stern hand of discipline for us, while our Grandparents took a semi-back seat to the disciplining. My sister would disagree, wholeheartedly. Her entire view of these events will read differently, as she was three-years old and remembers our mom. She remembers her life, but I was only one, and I can only live through others.

As time went on, I finally met the guy who wrote all those long letters. What an awkward meeting. We would speak on the phone, but there he was in my home, standing in front of me. His freedom had been secured. What would I do? I hugged him, of course . . . a bit leery and nervous. He's my dad. My father. The man my mom married. In the back of my mind, I knew he was guilty of taking the life of his wife; but there he was, standing in the home of her parents, with open arms ready to spend the day with us or however long my Grandparents would allow. That act right there said something about the two of them to me that I still think about and would never forget—that they at least trusted him enough to let him take their two grandchildren off for a while. I couldn't begin to say what we did, where we went or how long we stayed; all I know is that when he brought us back home, I was the happiest child on earth. There was safety and security in my grandparent's house; it was home.

My interactions with my father after that point were what I'd like to call "necessary." I talked to him more than I saw him. He called, we called; but there were no Hallmark moments with us. My grandfather and Auntie used to say often that the Bible says to forgive, that the Bible says to honor, that the Bible says to love. Because of this example, I found myself picking up the phone to call him. I would write him letters sometimes in my teenage and college years. I thought about him and I always prayed for him, no matter how I felt about him. This was the man my mom married. He was my father. How could I not try to forgive him and love him? Doesn't the Bible say that if we forgive, God will forgive us? Didn't my Auntie say, "You ungrateful little brat, you forgive and you love to free yourself." Don't harbor ill will. Let the Lord handle that. Now don't get me wrong, all of my mom's siblings did not feel that way, but there was at least one who was more concerned about my soul than anything else.

As days grew into weeks, grew into months, grew into years, I never forgot that message of love and forgiveness. I also never let those unanswered questions that I had in my heart and mind for whomever would answer them, consume me and cause me to act ungodly towards my dad. He was invited to my high school graduation. He came. He was invited to my college graduation, again, he came. He was invited to my wedding. He wasn't asked to walk me down the aisle, but I wanted to invite him. Today, I often look forward to picking up the phone, seeing how he is, asking what life is bringing him. We bear an uncanny resemblance. Our sense of humor is alike. We enjoy the same foods and activities, but I can't recall sharing a roof with him in my entire life. I see so much of him in me, but I also cringe at some of the behaviors we share.

My sister and I have taken our education and our careers to a place that statistics say two young girls with our HER-story shouldn't have reached. We have BAs and MBAs and AVPs and certifications to boot. The Lord has blessed us. I am an investment banker and my sister is an engineer. What is most beautiful about it is that we've invited him to accompany us along each leg of this journey. For me, I still hear the words of my grandfather and my aunt about forgiveness. I still recall the many sermons that various pastors have preached about loving beyond our pain, forgiving beyond the circumstances. I truly believe that my ability to let go of that which would have consumed me and to clench to that which is holy, those fruits of the spirit, saved my life.

I forgave, I didn't forget, but I forgave. In the end, hate and hurt wouldn't bring her back, but the way I live on earth will surely secure me seeing her beautiful face again one day. There's nothing I would do to compromise that reunion. I truly believe that God is using me to spread his message of love. Most people couldn't do what my sister and I do. For most, the door would have been closed the moment she took her last breath. For the rest, it would be their life's passion to make him as miserable as possible. I can't imagine using all that energy for something so unnecessary, something so useless and draining. I forgive, I am loved, and I am able to love.

Kimberly Phillips Dabney, MBA is a Payables Consultant for Wells Fargo Bank, N.A. Serving the financial services industry for over 18 years, she has strived to share the practices of both fiscal and fiduciary responsibilities with all she encounters. Kimberly holds a BA from Norfolk State University and an MBA from Averett University. Kimberly has been married to Christopher for 16 years.

CHAPTER 15

SURVIVING, THRIVING, AND RISING ABOVE

Joy Lawson Davis

> **Key Challenges:** lack of academic challenge, rural school, teen pregnancy, faith, family

I grew up in Newark, New Jersey in the 1950s and '60s, the youngest of six children. My mother and father were laborers. Earlier as youngsters in Virginia, they lived in nearby communities, fell in love and found themselves getting married at the tender age of 16, before they graduated high school. But even without a high school education, they were two of the most brilliant people I have ever known. My mom worked as a domestic. She cleaned the homes of Jewish families that lived on the outskirts of Newark and my father worked at foundries and other metal fabrication plants. They worked hard to provide for our family. My parents had six children, all born by the time they were 25.

In the early 1950s, my parents moved to Newark, New Jersey. Like so many other African Americans who lived in the South during this time period, they were looking for better jobs, better economic opportunities, and better

Gumbo for the Soul, pages 83–90

schools for their children. This period was known as the great migration. All but one of my mother's siblings (and there were seven others) moved to Newark. My father's brothers had earlier come north to live in Brooklyn and Philadelphia (one brother died early while he was in the military and another chose to remain in Virginia). There were six children in my family, four girls and two boys. I was the youngest of the brood. With the challenges of raising six children on limited income, we never missed a meal, we always had a nice apartment that was clean and organized, and we always had warm clothing, which was important in the brutal harsh winters in New Jersey. Having family close by in Newark and Brooklyn, made it easy to visit and establish strong bonds with extended family throughout our stay in New Jersey. Each summer, we took a trip to Virginia to visit my grandmother, aunt and other family members. It was during these times that my father took his '53 green Chrysler out of the garage he rented around the corner from our tenement apartment building. This car was our indication that despite our day to day challenges we could still travel with our family for vacations each year and see a part of the country that most of our friends knew nothing about. Going to Virginia every summer gave us a sense of family and heritage that I value to this very day. Occasionally, on weekends, we would also take trips to Brooklyn, Plainfield, Westfield or Philadelphia to visit other family members. I was well taken care of and protected by my five older siblings **and** my parents.

I loved school. I loved to read, write, and draw. My mother took time after work every day to read to and draw pictures with me as I sat on her lap. Those are some of my most cherished childhood memories. My oldest sister, Ellen would take me to the public library in our community when I was very young. There, I was able to borrow books with my very own library card. To me, the library was such a fascinating place and I was there for every extra opportunity presented by school. Attending Robert Treat Elementary School was the most important experience I had as a young child. School for me at that time was a safe haven. We had large classes, but the instruction was challenging, exciting, and many opportunities for enrichment in theatre, music and art were provided. I absolutely loved school!!

In the second grade, my teachers spoke to my mother about 'skipping' me to the third grade. I was always ahead of my classmates and my teachers noticed that I was deeply in love with learning. After meeting with my mother, the school administrators and my second grade teacher decided to send me to the third grade class every afternoon for math. It was a long walk up that hall and the flight of stairs to the third grade, but I went each day...so very excited about the new things I was going to learn...and all through elementary school and into junior high, school was an exciting, enriching experience for me.

At the cusp of the civil rights movement, in 1967, my parents moved back to Virginia. My dad had saved money over the years to build a new home for us. So, I started ninth grade in a small rural school in central Virginia. Talk about a culture shock! Coming from a large, urban area with hundreds of neighbors within a few city blocks, to living on a road with only ten houses within a five-mile radius was tough. We didn't even have a street address, so I could not even tell my friends back in Newark where I lived. Everyone in the school was African American, even the Principal. In Newark, I attended integrated schools, with teachers from many different ethnic groups, including Jewish, Italian, and Eastern European. In Virginia, all of our neighbors were Black. For me, being in a monocultural school was very different. I knew that the students didn't accept us at first because we spoke different and because I was academically advanced. Some thought that we were arrogant and believed ourselves to be better than others. We did not, but it was hard fitting in for quite some time. The school was very small; and there was no art class, no gymnasium, and no opportunities for enrichment outside of the music program. The community was also lacking, as there were no theatres, museums, and libraries. Thank goodness I loved to sing. So, for my creative release, I enrolled in choir and home economics (where I learned to design and make clothing). At school, I also took advantage of every opportunity to become involved with leadership clubs and organizations.

Before long, my name was well known as someone who was gifted, outspoken, and brave. When anyone had a disagreement or problem with authority or the lack of resources, they would come to me to help organize and speak up on behalf of the student body. When I was a junior, I led a student body on a protest during the school day. We marched out of the school during to the School Board meeting and demanded that the school district build a gymnasium. We deserved to have a gymnasium like other schools had, and our march was successful. Later that year, money was placed in the budget and during the following school year, a new gymnasium was erected.

As I've just shared, there were many great experiences in school. However, my being bored in school led to the development of some very bad habits. Viewing myself as being 'smart' or at least thinking that I was smarter than others, including the adults, resulted in me being disrespectful to the teachers. Soon, I was spending more time in the counselor's office than in the classroom. Nonetheless, Mr. Williams, our counselor, saw the potential in me and encouraged me to use my gifts in a positive rather than a negative way.

It took a while for Mr. Williams' advice to sink in. So, for a period of time, I spent less time on schoolwork and more time on other things, namely boys. Like many girls my age, especially in the 'country,' my extra-curricular choices were limited to church activities, menial household chores, homework, or boys. So, even though I spent a great deal of my time in church-related activities (my mother and grandmother demanded that), for an intense, energetic, creative girl like me, it was not enough. I longed for the intellectual challenge of school, the way a person longed for a dear friend who left them behind. In time, my thoughts about school shifted to a growing relationship with a new boyfriend. And my attention to school decreased.

I developed bad habits. I began focusing on boys and became less focused on academics. These bad habits eventually led to me becoming pregnant the spring of my junior year in high school. The same girl who led the student march earlier in the year began to experience what would be the worst year of my entire schooling experience. I considered this even worse than the year my parents left New Jersey to move to Virginia.

The year I found out that I was expecting, I was also slated to enter my senior year as a model student. I was the Student Government Association (SGA) president. Leadership opportunities like the SGA were enriching and enabled me to develop and utilize my oratory skills. I was always told by teachers and church leaders that I had a gift for speaking and persuasion. People around me spoke about my charisma and my capacity to put words together in unique and convincing ways. I knew it was a gift and it was something I valued. It was one of many gifts that I possessed and I believed myself to be a very fortunate person. All of my dreams and hopes for the future crashed like a nightmare the day I found out that I was going to be a young mother!

The pressure and stress from all of this was intense and overwhelming. College opportunities were ahead of me, and my family was proud. The pressure was on me to select and complete college. Even though my older brother, who I considered to be more gifted than I, attended college on a basketball scholarship in Colorado and had attended college earlier making the entire community proud. To my father's disappointment, my brother came home after one year on academic probation and chose not to return. My father was very hurt about his decision. So, you can imagine the hope and optimism in my family as I was preparing to complete school and go off to college. They patiently waited for me to select a college. I was their last hope. I was the youngest and I would be the first of my siblings to actually enter and complete a four-year program and earn a college degree.

My mother and I had to think about how to tell my father that I was pregnant. That was a painful time for us because my father had a very hard time with the news. As the youngest daughter, and the last one he had a chance to groom to go to college, he was a deeply disappointed.

I was a Daddy's girl. When he was doing shift work, I used to get up early in the mornings and sit with him as he ate breakfast and drank his coffee. He taught me how to read the newspaper and even shared his coffee with me. He truly tried to protect us. For months after the 'announcement', my father could not look at me nor talk to me. He did not utter one word or even glance my way. I hurt him in a way that I couldn't understand at that time.

My mother and I decided that I would have my baby in New Jersey where I could be taken care of by my sisters and my aunt Cora. It was just easier that way and we felt that I would be more comfortable. My oldest sister was my best friend; she had a nice home and gladly took me in and took care of me during the summer until it was time for me to deliver my child. My next oldest sister lived nearby, so going back to New Jersey was a good place for me to be during this challenging period. We also agreed that my parents would take care of my child so that I could finish high school and go on to college. My boyfriend (who soon became my ex-boyfriend) graduated from high school that year and left to join the military. My father insisted that our family would take care of me and I had no need for financial support from my boyfriend or his family at all. It was my father's way of helping me 'cut the ties' and move on. In my heart, I didn't agree, but I didn't dare disobey my father and hurt him again. So, our family took the entire responsibility of taking care of me and my baby. Years later, I told my daughter about her father and took her to visit him. Over time, she established a relationship with his family and had an 'on and off again' relationship with him. She did her best to make it a good relationship, but for many complicated reasons, it was tenuous at best.

When summer break came, I went to New Jersey and stayed with my sister and her family. My sister was so good to me, she made sure that I was healthy and that I kept my prenatal appointments. I had time to spend with my other sister, Mildred, and her family and also my brother James who also lived in the area, as well as my aunt Cora. Even with all the family around me, I was still lonely because I missed my mother. It was difficult, but because Ellen took such good care of me, the summer went by quickly. Before long, I was ready to deliver. I had my baby and returned to school. Thankfully, God allowed me to restore and renew the special relationship I had with my father. What a blessing! I had the utmost respect and love for my parents, because even though I disappointed them, they continued to love me, encourage me and insisted that I continue my education and go to the college.

I survived that deep, dark time in my life. I survived for a reason. I always knew in my heart that my life was purposeful. That I was born, survived challenges and was enabled to thrive so that I could help others, encourage those who needed help and guidance at becoming their very best. I learned early in life that there were no bad experiences, and that things happened for a reason. I learned it was my responsibility to learn from my mistakes, choices, and challenges. I learned that all experiences were opportunities to learn something new, apply our new knowledge and use it to help us continue to grow and, at some point, be able to share our experiences with others.

Because of my family, I was able to get through a period that could have caused me so much shame that I would have found it difficult to walk with my head up high. But I persevered! On September 15, 1970, my beautiful baby girl Alexis was born. Alexis was 8lbs, 11 oz.—perfect and so beautiful. She had the biggest smile and skin the color of caramel. I made a promise to my bundle of joy that I would take care of her and see her through life. I promised her that what I allowed to happen to me would *not* happen to her. Having a child at 16 was difficult; to be honest, it was extremely hard. I lost a lot of my so-called friends. I went back to school and was very isolated from my classmates. It was difficult to restore relationships with even those who were closest to me prior to my leaving to have Alexis. Eventually, a few girls slowly began talking with me again and made an effort to help me feel comfortable.

I had to commit myself to being an adult earlier than most teens. I had to keep my promise to my parents to get my college degree … and to come back and take care of Alexis. I met and surpassed all of these goals. Alexis was and is still a very special daughter. At 21, after finishing college, I got married and have since had two other children, Adrienne and Brandon. All of my children are wonderful people. Today, they are all married, have children of their own, and are doing well in their lives. Each of them knows that they are blessed and live generously so that they can be a blessing to others.

Alexis taught me more than any other lesson that I had experienced that there are no bad experiences. Years later, when I was diagnosed with end stage renal disease, I had to make a decision, to either be prepared to be on dialysis for the remainder of my life or to begin the process of becoming a transplant recipient. My entire family was in shock, but they circled around me with the supernatural kind of love that gave me peace in the midst of a very challenging moment. Alexis and Adrienne were both tested to become a donor. Other family members and friends also offered to donate. As it turned out, Alexis became my donor and gave me one of her kidneys. My daughter from my 'bad experience', my 'mistake' had saved my life.

As time has gone on, I learned that my life is not my own. My life is a life of a servant. Like the great Muhammad Ali noted: Serving others is the rent we pay for living here on earth. I truly believe this. I live to share my gifts with others and to speak up for them. Personally and professionally, I have had numerous opportunities to help others. As a classroom teacher, a pastor, school principal, administrator, and now working in higher education, I live to share my gifts and help others to develop theirs. I have always committed myself to being a voice for those who cannot speak for themselves. I take this charge very seriously.

Just writing this makes me shiver, it is so amazing how life happens and when you are in the midst of the most challenging circumstances of your life and you think you have to give up and that nothing will ever be the same again—a small voice whispers to you and says "remember Joy, there are no bad experiences . . . this is going to be alright. I saved you before and I'll save you again." Alexis, it appears, was meant to be in my life to literally *save* my life.

I learned a great lesson from that experience. The illness strengthened me in a way that I couldn't really define at the moment. I only knew that I would face challenges in my life and if I could recover and survive the challenge of having a child at such a young age, then I could probably overcome almost anything. From each challenge comes new learning and new opportunities to grow and help others. I encourage everyone reading this story to believe in yourself, listen to that voice when it speaks and encourages you to seek out those who love you and those with whom you can share your most private thoughts. Allow the protection of the Almighty to surround you during your times of utmost need. You'll come through, you'll survive, and you'll thrive. And one day, you'll be able to share your experience to help someone else along the way.

You were born for a reason, a purpose. If you falter along the way, as most of us do, don't let your mistakes dictate your future, use them to help you grow stronger, develop more wisdom and consider how you can use your challenges to help others. For many years, it was difficult sharing this part of my life story. I felt shame and embarrassment. But as I grew older and wiser, I came to understand that it was this part of my life that truly shaped the woman I am today. Surviving this challenge created a strength in me that has been a frame for the rest of my life. It is because of my challenge, not in spite of my challenge, that I came to trust in God with strength that defied all the odds against me and not only did I survive and thrive I rose above to become the woman I am today. As you read my story, I hope that you will allow it to give life to your dreams and know that no matter what challenges you may face, you too have the capacity to survive, thrive and rise above to be the woman you were born to be.

Joy Lawson Davis, EdD holds two degrees in gifted education from The College of William & Mary in Virginia. Dr. Davis has held numerous P–12 positions in school districts and served as the first African American State Specialist for K–12 Gifted programs in Virginia. Davis' first higher education appointment was as Assistant Professor of Education at the University of Louisiana, Lafayette. She is author of the award winning, *Bright, Talented & Black: A Guide for Families of African American Gifted Learners* and *Gifted Children of Color Around the World: Diverse Needs, Exemplary Practices, and Directions for the Future*, and several book chapters and articles. For over 25 years, she has consulted with school districts across the nation and been internationally addressing the needs of gifted children of color. Her expertise is examining underrepresentation in gifted education; culturally responsive pedagogy; and the impact of family engagement on student achievement. Dr. Davis is serving her second term on the Board of Directors of the National Association for Gifted Children and is currently an Associate Professor of Education and chair of the Department of Teacher Education at Virginia Union University, where she also serves on the Executive Committee for the Center for the Study of the Urban Child.

CHAPTER 16

FORGIVENESS

The Unexpected Gift of Fatherlessness

Crystal A. deGregory

> **Key Challenges:** single-parent family, academic challenges, self-esteem challenges, immigrant challenges

When I was four years old, I was sitting on the couch in the living room of the house I shared with my parents. Despite the noise from the television, I remember it being quiet, eerily quiet. My father entered the room with his suit bag. He stopped right in front of me. Crouching down on his knees, he said: "Crystal, I'll always love you. But from this moment on, I'm no longer your father. So if you see me, don't speak to me, because I won't speak to you."

These words that I've never forgotten, are words that loomed over my childhood, and words that have remained with me throughout the course of my life. Sometimes I think they are words that I should forget. The pain of them, even today, is so piercing I wonder if it will remain as long as the memory of having heard those words do.

He wiped away the tears that streamed down my face before telling me not to cry. He reached for his suit bag, and with it in tow, walked through the room's sliding glass doors onto the patio, and out of my life.

I didn't scream. I didn't cry out. I didn't pull at the hem of his pants. I didn't chase him. I don't remember moving towards the door at all. I just sat there, silently crying, paralyzed by my father's (still unbelievable) declaration.

Although I didn't know it then, my father's abandonment, his abrupt and unexpected departure, would be co-signed, sealed and delivered by an estrangement from his immediate and extended family. Oh, they'd honk their car horns if they saw me walking along the roadside, but my attendance at family holiday gatherings was no more, as were birthday party invitations. The silence of his family was deafening and their complicity in his abandonment of me compounded the initial rejection with yet another rejection.

My father was much older than my mother. A former politician, he was primarily widely known as a businessman with a chain of furniture stores that were driven by a combination of his industrious nature and his sheer will. Charming, charismatic and good-looking (he would definitely want it stressed that he was good-looking), he had a larger than life personality.

I was a daddy's girl. To me, he'd hung the moon and the sky. He'd let me cut his birthday cakes, open his Christmas gifts and steer the wheel of his car. So the day he walked out of my life, my innocence died. Truthfully, a piece of me died too.

Fatherlessness carries with it, guilt and shame. As a child, it is virtually impossible to separate the abandonment of one's father from feeling that you are responsible for his absence. You blame yourself. You're convinced that somehow, it's because you weren't enough—good enough to deserve the love of your father. The pain is especially acute when you are gifted, which often includes being very perceptive, having a keen sense of justice, and wanting to solve problems. You even want to solve problems that you have little or no control over and those that belong to adults, the ones who should take care of you and be there for you. When you're a child, life is supposed to be sweet. Even your vitamins are gummy bears and your cough syrup is grape-flavored. Rejection and desertion by a loved one is a difficult and bitter pill to swallow, especially when you're a child!

The counterpoint to an absentee father, if you're lucky or fortunate, is a great mother—one who is supportive and tries to fill that void, the hole in your soul when your father is gone. My mother really did everything in her power to make me feel loved and to prepare me for the rest of life's challenges that lay ahead in wait as a gifted Black female. All the while, she discouraged my bitterness, never letting me speak ill of my father despite the fact that he really deserved that and so much more.

When you have a "supermom" single mother, fatherless children often bear the additional weight of feeling like a burden to their mother. It's almost as though missing your father is an affront to her effort and her love. I see this played out every year on social media on Father's Day. In the absence of one's father, it's customary for a child to say that their present parent was both mother and father. Not so, I say, not so. There are uniquely different things, I feel, that mothers and fathers give a child. None is better, none is worse, but for me it was and is different.

There are some things fathers naturally teach and model for their daughters unlike mothers; and the same is true for mothers being able to provide support and guidance in ways that fathers may not do as well. I believe that good fathers who are present in their daughters' lives offer them an unparalleled sense of self-worth. For example, my father was sure of himself, in ways in which few people are. Ever-confidant in himself and in his value, he was honest to a fault; and his word, including hurtful mis-guided ones, was his bond. Not only did he model his belief that he was worthy of happiness, he took responsibility for securing—even if at the expense of the happiness of others.

It took a great deal of effort, mostly on my part, to reunite with my father and his family when I was 12 years old. After eight years of estrangement, he re-entered my life. And it all happened because an acquaintance told him that he was wrong. As a man and a father, he was far from perfect. He messed up. He knew it and I knew it. But he wanted to try again and I let him. His asking for forgiveness was almost as important as my learning how to forgive.

In the time between that day and his death in 2008, we made more than a decade of memories—memories for which I am grateful and will forever cherish. I'll never forget the thrill of watching him swim a 50-meter pool in one breath at more than 70 years old and I still admire fondly, his cheap watches, earth-toned clothes as well as his general disregard for material-ism. Even now, I still shake my head at the fact that my father, a man who sold appliances in his stores, refused to buy a microwave and insisted on re-heating food over a pot of boiling water.

Still, somewhere deep inside me, there is the four-year-old daughter that he passed on city streets and enclosed rooms alike, as though I were a total stranger. Still, I struggle to shirk the unease I feel when vocalizing how I feel because it makes me afraid that someone I love may, in turn, walk out of my life, especially without warning. So, I recommit myself repeatedly and often to a vow I made in the wake of his death—to remember my worth, despite the unworthiness of people who may come and go over the course of my life.

As a gifted child, I threw myself into being the very best at everything I did. I earned good grades, was a star athlete, and was active in every ex-tracurricular activity my mother would allow—including more than a few she struggled to afford. Her decision to keep me in private school after my father withdrew his financial support was an important decision and a decisive sacrifice that provided me with the stability of a school community that affirmed my value.

As an adult, I recommit myself to affirming my worth in many of the same ways I did as a child. I read widely and I write regularly. I am active in the community and I pursue atypical hobbies like mowing my lawn and perusing office supply stores, which makes me unbelievably happy despite how lackluster they seem. Above all, I'm ever mindful that our stories, even painful ones like those associated with fatherlessness, matter. Because it's up to us to decide the ways in which they do, fatherlessness will always be my unexpected gift of forgiveness.

Crystal A. deGregory, PhD is a professional historian and passionate HBCU advocate. A graduate of Fisk, Vanderbilt, and Tennessee State universities, she is the founder and executive editor of HBCUstory, convener of the HBCUstory Symposium, and serves as editor-in-chief of *The Journal of HBCU Research + Culture*. Her widely published research explores various historical and contemporary subjects including Black education in nineteenth and twentieth centuries, with special attention to Black colleges, as well as the relationship of them to the modern Civil Rights Movement. In addition to serving as a co-host of Black Docs Radio, she is a sought-after public speaker and Emmy Award-winning documentary contributor.

CHAPTER 17

FINDING MY ACADEMIC SELF

Snapshot of a Bigger Picture

Isi Ero-Tolliver

Key Challenges: single-parent family, low-income household, international challenges, poor mentorship, work–life balance

---

Getting to this stage I am at now has taken what one of my African American female scientist mentors would call a "divine intervention." I grew up one of five children in a low-income, single-parent household. I was born and raised in Jackson, Mississippi (the state that held the number one spot for teenage pregnancy, illiteracy, and obesity for a while). Both my parents were college educated and so the conversation was never, "Are you going to college?" actually there was no conversation at all. It was assumed that we were all going (and we all did). As a matter of fact, my most fond memory of my dad was a picture of him in his graduation cap and gown, which he sent to us, while my siblings, my mom and I were in Nigeria, visiting for six years, lol. That is another story.

Gumbo for the Soul, pages 95–100

While in Nigeria, we were part of a middle class household and hardly ever wanted for anything because my grandfather saw to that. As a student, we learned a lot about academics and respect. Attending the best schools, I learned that academics were a privilege and not a joke. Most children knew how to stay in their place and if ever disrespectful, they would be checked on site. This was the norm. So years later, when my grandfather gathered enough money to send us back to the United States, my eyes were opened in school to a different culture of different color kids, talking back to their parents and getting away with it, all while attending classes as a joke. It never once occurred to me that this was okay because I could instinctively hear my mom say, "I will slap you so hard, that fireflies will come out of your ears."

Fast forward to the low-income projects (that the government would only support you if you were a single mom, aka, no-dads-allowed) in which we lived with our mom for years. After getting beat up in my first fight ever by the girl who did the windmill to my face (I won the second one), watching my sister skating and losing her tooth from being pushed by a "friend," and hearing of my brother being beat up by a group of boys because he was trying to sound White by being "articulate while Black," I realized that "Dorothy was no longer in Kansas." Things had changed drastically. I wouldn't necessarily state for the worse, because I believe that the resilience, which I recognized mom always had, was born for me in that neighborhood. At that point is when I began to grapple with why some kids were being so mean to us, when all we were trying to do was fit in. I had a mature thought, which was that people were hurting for different reasons and that at the exact moment I was experiencing happiness, did not necessarily have to be the same moment that others would be experiencing theirs. In other words, others are not happy because or when you are happy, so be patient with them.

While at our different levels of happiness, I was attending school with kids from my neighborhood. I noticed that most of us were smart and we were sitting in class with different circumstances. Some found their popularity in being the class clown, being the mean girls, being the flirty boys, being the hidden smart boy or girl (so you don't get beat up), and the etc. I did notice that during certain classes, most of them were afraid of math and science. They would say things like, "Math is hard!" but they would be counting their money and playing card games that included math with ease. In my mind, I would wonder why they didn't think they liked math. Was it the fear of the word, "Math"? Was it the teacher? I couldn't figure it out. So I started learning to teach. I wanted to learn my math and science so I could teach it to my friends in a less intimidating way. That is when I believe my love for teaching began. I learned to teach others.

After high school, I attended Jackson State University for undergrad for reasons that included the fact that both my parents were alums and because I got to stay at home with my mom. She was my rock, next to God. She was my role model of pressing through when love and life seemed to be failing you. She was my role model of raising kids in the midst of turmoil to be the best they could be. She was my role model of taking odd jobs and getting your degrees no matter what! So I knew if she could do it at Jackson State University (JSU), a Historically Black College or University (HBCU), then so could I. At JSU, I excelled and I saw others like me excelling. It was truly an atmosphere that made you feel like "Yes, you can and Yes, we can!" I felt like a big fish in a little pond. Although we did not have a lot of resources, during my Bachelors and Master's program in science, JSU found avenues to still offer you what you needed, sometimes in the form of external summer research internships or foreign exchange programs for exposure. Long story, short, they gave me that "can do" attitude.

With my degrees and love for my HBCU, in tote, I ventured out for my doctorate. I applied to six different schools (all PWI—Predominantly White Institutions). I was accepted into all but one. Of them, I chose to attend Vanderbilt University for academic and personal reasons. Vanderbilt summed up to be one of the most unsolicited roller coasters that I have ever ridden in my life. Keep in mind that I had done many different internships at PWIs, such as Purdue and Berkeley, but those were for a few months. This was for years. For years, I had to endure the perception of being only as good as your last hit record. One of always being aware of the perception of you, like the one hanging on the wall of my first Vanderbilt PIs' (White female) office that stated "being half as good and working twice as hard" that she hung up for women. As I went through ordeals with her, I wondered what her equation was for being a woman that is also Black in academia.

During my face-to-face interview at Vanderbilt, a professor looked at my resume and stated, "Either no one else is doing something at JSU or you are just an overachiever." That was the first form of microaggression I received during my studies, but I didn't realize it at the time. My first few years at Vanderbilt were in the department of biological sciences (in which I was one of two Black girls out of about 50 graduate students at the time). I came in direct admit with a departmental scholarship (meaning that I had the extra load of being a Teaching Assistant during my first few years) but attended a lot of the Interdisciplinary Graduate Program (IGP) activities because they had more structure for their students than I was receiving at the time. Although I was sometimes discouraged from attending their activities by one "nice" young lady in particular, I continued to attend because like JSU taught me, "go where the resources are." Academics were never a problem for me before, and they were not a problem for me while I was there. What seemed to be the problem was with the bench research. I realized that most of my summer research internships had always set me up for success. I was given the "okey dokey" because I rarely had to troubleshoot or think about what would be next in the project. I was given a cookie cutter protocol where everything always worked! So when up against the challenge in my second year, I didn't know what to do. That was the first time I experienced failure on an epic scale.

I reached out to my mentor and told her that I was having difficulty with the next steps and that the results I was getting were not the same as the results my Asian post-doc was getting. I seemed to need more mentoring than she had bargained for. She, nor I, seemed prepared (me, to ask for more help and her, to give it). It slowly started to show that my mentor did not believe in me as I thought she had. When I wanted to take an advanced virology course, she told me, "You may not want to do that because that course is really hard and it might not be a good idea." I told her ok and I took the class anyway. I did so well in the class (A–) that the professor wrote me a personal letter and I shared it with my, PI (AKA "Doubting Thomas"). When things started to fall apart right before my qualifying exam with the research, her true thoughts started to show when she stated, "I am surprised you did as well as you did. You did come from Jackson State and Vanderbilt is of a different caliber." When I wanted to postpone my qualifying exam because I didn't feel ready, she stated, "Do not go to the committee and tell them you need more time, or I will have to share what I really think about you." She went weeks without talking to me. She would walk past my bench and speak to the other students but skip my lab bench. At that point, I started to realize that there was no room for "true mentorship" in her book for me. She was that superficial kind that didn't include more than one session of extra time or personalized direction.

Relatedly, I remember one faculty member telling me "you don't have to finish here at Vanderbilt, you can go to TSU" (Tennessee State University). My response to him was that "I have already been to an HBCU and now I am embarking on a PWI experience to diversify my CV." At first I thought it was just me, but I later saw what happened to the other female students and post-docs at my old lab after I left (all left there on bad terms). I realized it was in my best interest to have finished my degree in a different lab, where I went on to publish articles and graduate with flying colors. My new PI/mentor (older White, male) took a personalized approach to my mentorship. He believed in me and stretched me past my invisible limits—limits imposed by other professors. He encouraged me to go after competitiveness, advanced opportunities, and multitasking (dual-discipline pursuit to my PhD). He saw a part of himself in me. He was from rural Arkansas and knew about missed opportunities and exposures and was creating programs to remedy the situations. He stated, "I am not the smartest person around, but I surround myself with people that work hard and we get things done!" I disagree—he is one of the smartest and productive people I know. He and I did not always see eye to eye, but he respected me as a colleague and it showed. He would say things like, "I don't know how you do it!' because he saw that I had four kids and didn't let anything stop me from achieving my goals and meeting the standards set for me academically. He would take time to talk to my kids when they came to the lab and would ask about their dreams, aspirations, and career goals. He pushed me hard and was always about the scientific data and rarely had time for excuses. He saw greatness in me and if he said, "Let's go to the moon!" I wouldn't wonder "how are we going to get there?" I would ask, "How high?" That was the sign of great mentorship. Both PIs were people of great stature inside and outside their field and at the university. One of the most powerful things that my PI used his power to do, in my eyes, was the push to help me finish. He was so invested in me that I remember that during and after graduation, he walked around with my family and I, took pictures with us, ate with us, and did the most remarkable thing! He got both my parents to come together and take a family picture with me through his diplomacy. That's another story.

In all, I don't know if I would have appreciated my second PI, if I had not encountered my first PI. It's so hard to complete your degree under a different mentor in the same establishment that you almost walked away from earlier. He used his power to work against powers and principalities to stand for me and believe in me. He was mentor and advocate. Under his mentorship, I received a pre-doctoral scholarship from NIH that allowed me to focus solely on research. This was the closest that I got to equity in education at Vanderbilt. It felt like freedom with my own money that bought me time and brought me closer to the same platform as my peers, who didn't have the load of being a teaching assistant, dealing with four children, trying to hold their marriage together, while they spent endless hours and nights in the lab, all while trying to make it look effortless. With the help of my loving husband at home watching the kids during most evenings, it was still a chore coming home after a long day and helping my children with their homework and sometimes cooking dinner. Balancing that work-life was hard and delicate. I honestly don't know if it ever got balanced because something always came to tip the scale, but I finished my degree.

If I had stayed in my old mentor's lab, I know I would not have finished with my doctorate from Vanderbilt. My own family knew I could, but didn't know if I would. Due to my resilience; proper mentorship and direction from many mentors inside and outside of Vanderbilt; and the love of and from my family, love and support from my husband (which was tested on several occasions), I was able to complete an Interdisciplinary PhD in the area of Biological Sciences and Science Education (the first one ever granted by Vanderbilt). Looking back, I am glad I went to an HBCU first because it cultivated the intelligence, resilience and tenacity in me that carried me through my graduate studies. I am the true product of good mentorship and the African Proverb of "it takes a village."

When some people tried to give me lemons, it was divinely turned into lemonade (wink!!). I am at Hampton University (HBCU) giving back what was given to me . . . in an environment where the students may one day choose to pursue degrees in an alternate environment. I stand here as a symbol for them that they too can thrive in any environment they choose, by sharing my story of overcoming in the face of adversity and not leaving till you get what you came for. I look forward to them also paying it forward by being living testimonies and great contributors to society. I am truly an example of how far mentors can take you when they believe in you. When you have the right mentality and people behind you, your possibilities are endless. And like Maya Angelou said, "And Still I RISE!"

Isi Ero-Tolliver, PhD, is an Assistant Professor of Biological Sciences at Hampton University. She graduated with an Interdisciplinary PhD in Biological Sciences and Science Education from Vanderbilt University. Her research interests include investigating the development of science identities amongst Blacks and Latinos and the role of mentorship in the process.

To eat an onion alone is not appealing, but when it simmers with other Gumbo ingredients, it creates a flavor that one longs to savor . . . like our stories blended together, simmering and becoming more appealing . . . the longer they seep . . . into your soul.

—Michelle Trotman Scott

CHAPTER 18

BEYOND ZIP CODES AND GENETIC CODES

Black and Poor and Gifted, Too!

Donna Y. Ford

> **Key Challenges:** poverty, single-parent family, racism, peer pressure, teen pregnancy

I am (now) proud and blessed to say that I grew up in and survived poverty. I learned a great deal about struggling to meet basic needs. This was not always the case. Instead, I have been ashamed of being on welfare, of living in substandard housing and attending poor quality schools. Lifelong experiences and numerous opportunities to reflect on my childhood have given me a new perspective on my journey as a child, teen, and young adult. I have learned so much about struggling and striving as a gifted Black female seeking to desperately find a way out of poverty for my mother, and sisters, myself, and years later, my son.

Growing up in a low-income family and community helped and helps me to appreciate the finer things in life, to devalue material things, and to

Gumbo for the Soul, pages 103–110
Copyright © 2017 by Information Age Publishing

be mentally resilient. My mother, who raised three girls in Cleveland and East Cleveland, Ohio, taught us to move beyond our current circumstances and the limitations imposed on us by others because we were Black girls. She armed us to deal with—to confront head on and without apology—racism, sexism, and classism, and in this order. Race was always at the forefront of mom's parenting and educating. My mother, who served in the Air Force to defend our nation, also knew how to defend her children and others in our community. She and my father, whom I barely knew, separated when my sister and I were toddlers, he and my mom divorced a few years later. I recall meeting him when I was 10 and then 17. I was neither happy nor sad nor angry. I don't recall any emotions other than curiosity. Who was this person? What did he stand for? Why are we meeting him now? Why did we need to meet him now? Thus, mom was our only caregiver, role model, and advocate in school . . . and then later in life. She taught us Black girls that we could move from the margins to the mainstream—in spite of discrimination and social injustices—and we faced many based on race, gender, and income.

In this chapter, I focus on a few memories from my life as a gifted Black female and mother of a gifted son. I was not raised around males but had to find a way to raise a Black male—the most marginalized students in general, special, and gifted education. The struggles were great and numerous. Yet, my sisters and I exceeded odds and are deemed successful in many ways. Our story does not have to be the exception to the rule. Our story *must not* be the exception to the rule.

I was identified as gifted early in school. My obsession with reading played a major role. Mom read to us daily and had us watching educational television shows like Sesame Street. She demanded that we read in the morning and/or at night. She demanded that we read even if there were no homework assignments. Kids in the neighborhood hated coming to our house because mom made them read too. She'd ask about their grades and then lecture them (in a motherly and caring way) about doing better. She was the community educational advocate who schooled us all on how education, as Horace Mann said, is the greatest equalizer. She reminded us that knowledge is power, powerful, and empowering. Some got the message. Some did not. Those who did were more successful than others. My sisters and I 'got it.' We had no choice.

My love for books paid off. I recall being summoned to the office to be evaluated for gifted education and skipping a grade, although I had no idea then what was happening. My favorite book was, *Are You My Mother?* by P. D. Eastman. I had it memorized and was quite the actress while 'reading'. I 'read' it to school personnel and was formally identified as gifted. I laugh and scoff at this now. What a way to get identified! That was the mid-1960s. I spent a half-year in first and then was advanced to the second grade. And

I did well. I recall teachers trying to have me skip another grade in upper elementary school, but mom was not supportive because my older sister and I would have been in the same grade (she is two years older). I was not upset with her for this; that would put me in classes with big kids. No way, especially given my short stature. The educational, social, and psychological needs of my sisters mattered as well. We are a small family and cohesion was and is valued. So while I was not challenged in upper elementary school, there was peace in our home because mom tailored education to our needs and personalities. This is a balancing act.

The next time I recall being told I was gifted was in the seventh grade. A White counselor pulled me out of class to say that I had a very high I.Q. and achievement test scores. Decades later, I cannot get her expression out of my mind—it was a look of pity...like 'you poor child.' She said that I was being inducted into Mensa. At the time I did not know what this meant. I was afraid, thinking it was for people who had mental issues! Soon after that, I recall being sent to the office where I was asked to take a test to become a student in the A Better Chance program. Since 1963, A Better Chance has been opening the door to educational opportunities for thousands of young people of color in this nation. Their mission is to substantially increase the number of well-educated young people of color who are capable of assuming positions of leadership in American society. I recall teachers and staff saying that I had to go to a private school—and they were 'saving' me from public schools. Then, I was confused. Now, I understand as someone who has devoted over 20 years to desegregating gifted education and saving high-achieving and gifted children in the worst performing schools.

Within a few months of being in the program, my mother and I were summoned to the principal's office, at which time we were informed that I had been awarded a scholarship. I was given a number of private high school options from which to attend. Too many of my classmates were less fortunate. Those who did not take the test seriously, who suffered from test anxiety, who succumbed to negative peer pressure, who believed negative stereotypes about Blacks in general and Black females in particular, and who had other priorities did not score at the designated level to receive a scholarship.

After some discussion with my mother, I chose to attend a local private high school that was close to my family and friends. I had never been away from my mother and sisters, so staying close to home and commuting each day was best for me. I thought this was the best choice for my family and me—close to home meant that I'd be in a safe haven. Ironically, this is where my story begins, for my life changed forever. Everything plummeted—my grades, self-esteem, academic self-concept, racial identity, and my dignity. My most pleasant memories about school was the food. I gained over 50 pounds that year.

I attended this private school for females in a Cleveland suburb. In grades 9 to 12, there were only four Black females, including myself. I was the only one on scholarship and poor. I quickly learned that one could face discrimination based on not just race, but also socio-economic status. I could not identify with my wealthy White classmates. They spoke a language foreign to my ears—vacations, housekeepers/nannies, inheritances, personal jets, swimming pools, yachts, Jacuzzis, Porsches, Jaguars, and Mercedes. I, literally, carried a dictionary with me to translate. I understood the language of my Black classmates, but they, too, had little in common with me. While not rich or wealthy, they were well off, but they were lost racially and culturally. I was on scholarship. Further, they were, on the surface or superficially, part of the 'community', having attended the school for a number of years. I was truly the proverbial fish out water—I connected with neither the more privileged White girls nor the Black ones. I was low income; they were not.

Back home, there were other trials and tribulations. My 'friends,' whom I'd known for years, resented my being at that 'uppity White' school. I was now deemed a 'sell out', a trader, who was 'acting White' and disowning my community and sacrificing my racial pride. Survival guilt weighed heavy on me as a teenager. I contemplated the myriad of sacrifices I was making to become successful as a gifted Black student who was also female, low income, and ambitious—and wanting so desperately to be accepted, affirmed, and to fit in . . . somewhere.

I remember vaguely, my teachers, for I have a tendency to push to the subconscious unpleasant memories and thoughts. My English teacher had the most significant and negative impact upon me. She violated my trust and respect in her as an educator, professional, and responsible adult. One of our class assignments was to read *The Scarlet Letter* by Nathanial Hawthorne. For the first time in my life, I learned the potency of bibliotherapy, of the catharsis one can get from identifying with a character. Being in this school, I now realized that I, too, had a scarlet letter—the color of my skin. Some 60 years later, and six decades after legalized and legislated desegregation via *Brown vs. The Board of Education of Topeka, Kansas* (1954), I still get frequent reminders (sometimes daily) that because I am Black, little is expected of me, and I should expect little. However, unlike Hester, Hawthorne's heroine, I committed neither a sin nor broke the law; I was born into my circumstances—this was not a choice. My zip code and genetic code are not my destiny.

I wrote about my 'scarlet letter' for a class assignment at this private school. I analogized that my scarlet letter was being Black—it was a curse, along with being poor. Since this was a school for girls, gender was not on my mind. My White female teacher was so 'surprised that I could write so well' and was so 'insightful' that she requested that I share it with the class—a group of 15 or so rich White females with whom I had so little in common; females who lived in mansions, drove the most expensive cars, had personal drivers, personal planes, and yachts. I refused to share my essay. My teacher's request eventually became an order and ultimatum. The A+ eventually became an F for 'lack of cooperation and comradeship.' My teacher simply did not understand—and maybe did not care to understand. The reading and writing assignment had been a welcomed relief, a mental and physical catharsis and implosion. I was able to vent, rant, rave, and scream in text; I felt relief but not vindicated. Reading my paper would have been like sharing a piece of my soul; like reading a page in my diary. Although I was a teenager who stood against an adult who cloaked as an educator and professional, I did not read my paper to classmates.

The school administrators are also fuzzy images in my mind. They often searched my person, my possessions, and my locker when money, jewelry, or other items were stolen or misplaced. They violated me in almost every respect—psychologically, physically, academically, and more.

It was the 1970s. It was not long, perhaps a month after school started, that I began to withdraw, to show classic signs of educational disengagement or burnout. I spent the day daydreaming and procrastinating. I turned in incomplete assignments, came to class late or not at all some days. Eventually, I committed the ultimate act of educational disengagement and apathy; I dropped out of 'schooling'—not physically, but socially, psychologically, and emotionally. This disenchantment and disconnect revealed itself in my lowered motivation and grades, which plummeted from As to Cs. To my recollection, I had never made a C in my life. My mother was worried and distraught. I blamed the low grades on everything else but the truth I had been concealing from her. I never told her about the academic, social, and emotional hell and torture that I had to endure for 280 days. My mother (my number one fan) believed that the private school meant or guaranteed a promising future—the first step on the upward and social mobility ladder that my mother wanted my sisters and me to climb. I could not and would not disappoint my mother by telling her about my daily trials and tribulations at school.

After a year, I dropped out of that school and transferred to my neighborhood school—almost all low income and overwhelmingly Black. I needed to be affirmed socially, culturally, intellectually, and academically. Had my mother insisted that I return to the private school, I would have dropped out completely. I felt like a soldier must feel after battle—both battle fatigue and survival guilt were common to me. I was suicidal. My self-esteem, academic self-concept, and racial identity had been shattered. I needed to be among students and teachers who shared my struggles, who looked like me, who talked like me, who understood (or wanted and tried to understand) me. These students and teachers did not have to look like me, they just had to care.

My less-than-rigorous neighborhood school had its share of problems. I remember that I was being taught material in the eleventh and twelfth grades that I had learned in the tenth grade at the private school. Even now, as I reflect on my experiences, it is clear that I received what some educators and researchers consider an inferior education at my neighborhood school. Yet, the teachers (all White) were wonderful—caring, humanistic, energetic, and skilled. Over time and slowly, my love for learning and motivation began to return.

As do many adolescents, I also experienced a dilemma, a conflict between my need for achievement and my need for affiliation—the latter won out. Although teachers were caring, I felt unchallenged in school and was fearful of doing well; many of my Black classmates accused me of 'acting White' and the females threatened me physically. It had been too easy to make the honor roll, to be at the top of the Bell Curve, to win writing scholarships, and become President of the National Honor Society. I begged my teachers to not share my grades and accomplishments. They agreed. This is one reason I persisted in school. I was so afraid of the females that I wanted to drop out. Being attractive and intelligent was a dangerous combination, one that could get you bullied and harassed daily. The males wanted little to do with smart girls, and the girls wanted little to do with girls who were pretty and/or smart.

To fit in, I downplayed my looks—hid my long hair, wore no makeup, and played 'dumb' when asked questions. A few males showed interest. I ended up dating one—and became a teen mother. In June 1979, at the age of 18, I graduated and my son was born six months later in December.

I graduated from high school with several academic scholarships. I decided to attend, on a full academic scholarship, a local, private university where I was majoring in mathematics/engineering. Before the semester ended, I dropped out—not because I was pregnant, but because of the overwhelming racism and sexism I experienced. Two professors had convinced me of three things. First, I did not belong in math because I was a female. Second, and more importantly, I did not belong in math and science because I was Black. Third, I would never earn a degree from that university—they would see to it. Again, I found myself underachieving and the flight from academics was the only option I could see.

I stayed out of college for one year, got caught in the vicious cycle of being a single mother, and trying to envision life without a college degree, life without a career in engineering or math. My mother, barely 40 years old, eventually gave me the most important ultimatum of my life—get back in school or else! I was blessed! She agreed to take care of my son, her grandson, while I attended classes.

In 1980, I enrolled in a different university, Cleveland State University. After changing my major four or five times (maybe more), I graduated within four years with a degree in both communications and Spanish. I barely had a 3.0 grade point average, and Cs were familiar and even comforting to me—at least I had not failed.

In 1986, I applied for and was accepted into a Master's degree program. I was still supporting my son and learning how to advocate for him and other gifted Black students. As a graduate student, I worked hard and excelled academically, but I felt incomplete, still searching for selfhood and what I wanted to be when I *grew up*. I was unfulfilled academically and did not think a Master's degree was enough to make an impact for gifted people like my son and me, so I sought a doctorate. Even though my grades were excellent as a graduate student, I had barely scored at the mean of 1000 on the Graduate Record Examination (GRE). I felt lucky to have been admitted, but also believed that the college would benefit in some way from my presence and experiences. They were lucky to have me too.

It was not until I entered the doctoral program (in Urban Education) that I began to feel comfortable and confident on personal, social, racial, academic, and professional levels. I felt empowered and powerful. I majored in urban education as an educational psychologist and was challenged to explore education in the context of urban life where race and income collide; the focus on social justice was refreshing. I could identify with the issues discussed in class—issues of underachievement, achievement gaps, tracking, low teacher and deficit expectations, irrelevant curriculum, achievement-affiliation conflicts such as peer pressures, poverty, racism, sexism, and other ills that permeate society and plague schools. I learned to consider, appreciate, and respect the importance of multicultural education or culturally responsive education, teacher diversity, gifted education and Advanced Placement classes, comprehensive educational and counseling services, family involvement, and motivation for success in school and, ultimately, life.

I have achieved beyond my childhood goals and dreams as a professor and accomplished writer. This poor gifted Black female defied her zip code and let naysayers know that genes are not one's destiny. More priceless than fame and fortune is having saved my only son, a gifted Black male, from an educational system that too often denies their gifts and kills their dreams. My story and that of my son have positive endings, albeit not the kind that movies are made of; but the told and untold stories of so many others are not so positive. This can and must change. This is why I have shared a slice of a life—to give hope to others who know racism, who know poverty, and who know sexism. And understand that when we know, we can act—we can advocate.

Donna Y. Ford, PhD, is a professor in the Department of Special Education and the Department of Teaching and Learning at Vanderbilt University. All of her degrees are from Cleveland State University (BA in communications and Spanish; MEd in counseling, and PhD in Educational Psychology with a focus on urban education and gifted education). She conducts research and writes extensively on: (a) the achievement gap; (b) recruiting and retaining culturally different students in gifted education; (c) multicultural curriculum and instruction; (d) culturally competent teacher training and development; (e) African American identity; and (f) African American family involvement. Professor Ford consults with school districts, and educational and legal organizations on these areas. Dr. Ford has authored some 200 articles and chapters, and more than eight books.

CHAPTER 19

DESPITE THE SCORE

Removing Barriers From Access to Gifted Education

LaTonya Frazier

> **Key Challenges:** low income, single-parent family, extended family, test bias, academic under-challenge

Early life experiences transform us into the adults we later become. These experiences continually shape you. My childhood experiences definitely are the basis for my passion and drive as a school administrator. I am proud to be a part of the district that educated me and now employs me as one of their home-grown talents.

I can say many great things about my experiences growing up and working in my current district. I had a diverse experience being educated with children from many backgrounds and socioeconomic levels. This gift of exposure was due in part to my county's late mandated busing rule in 1975, which was five years before I entered kindergarten. I am still grateful many days that things had somewhat calmed down before I was bused across the county to be integrated into segregated neighborhoods for two years.

Gumbo for the Soul, pages 111–114
Copyright © 2017 by Information Age Publishing
All rights of reproduction in any form reserved.

As an elementary student, I soared in school. I had some of the best teachers and a few that were not up to par. I can say my grandparents and mother may not have known everything about the educational system when raising me, but the one thing they did know and advocate for was me being treated fairly. Therefore, I did not remain in an uncaring professional's room too long, as the school did not want Rosie Abernathy (my grandmother) to make the hike to the building to explain why my removal was a necessity for the duration of my school year.

During my primary years, I recall being a quick reader and natural leader. In the 80s, basal readers, leveled books with short stories, were the choice of curriculum for teachers to teach reading in elementary schools. My first grade teacher was phenomenal. She was just everything you think of when you say teacher—motivating, tender voice, and an advocate for her children who mainly came from the predominately Black neighborhood where the school was located. My teacher, (Ms. Love), did not look like me and probably did not have a similar background. But, what she had was a love for all children and it showed every day when she entered the classroom.

Reading was one of my favorite subjects. Not to show my age, but teachers used to circle reading levels on report cards. I can recall setting personal goals to raise my reading level each semester. On one particular day, Ms. Love must have administered a formative assessment to monitor my growth. The term formative assessment was coined during my tenure as a teacher, but dynamic teachers used this common sense practice in education well before we called it a new phenomenon. My teacher was one of those educators who challenged and put students in the appropriate groups based on their academic needs. I recall during my assessment for learning, I kept reading passages at her request and she kept adding more. She would ask comprehension questions and I would answer them correctly. Ms. Love was so impressed that she immediately got up and told the teacher next door, who came over and also marveled at my reading level. My teacher was animated and excited for my learning. I remember feeling so proud of how I learned so quickly. I believe this is how I ended up in front of the dreadful intelligence screener.

Excited about the intelligence screener, I went in to take the test. Even as a young child, I knew there was a difference between my class and the gifted class across the hall. One reason I knew there was a difference was due in part to the lack of students in the room who looked like me. There were never more than a handful of African Americans in the class and most had assimilated to White culture in my eyes. None of these students joined me at the walker door during dismissal. There was a sense of elitism as these students pranced down the hall. But I wanted to be a part of the group.

I don't know most people's familiarity with aptitude tests. But I have found many of them to be similar in nature and most have been classified as somewhat culturally biased. In other words, making it difficult for someone with my background to do well on this type of assessment, even though I outscored many of my peers in class. The reason I have discovered that many minorities and students from low socioeconomic levels struggle is because most of the material is not taught in school and there is a lack of understanding of the vocabulary on the test. In other words, these type of tests generally do not cater to students who grow up in non-nuclear families with a full time swing shift working divorced mom with a high school diploma, and grandparents with strong work ethic but no opportunities to earn their diplomas. It also does nothing to capture students who are gifted in leadership, as I was.

After bearing through three hours of torture trying to remember what happens if I punch holes here and open it up there, endless strings of mathematical equations that hadn't been introduced, and vocabulary that seemed like a foreign language, I completed the test but knew the results were not good. I do not recall ever discussing the results with my parents, but do remember the following year I was bussed out of that school and did not enter my former school's gifted program. As an adult, I now know that if I would have passed the screener, I could have remained at my home school that I loved but instead I struggled through several years of mediocre teaching. Finally, my family had an educator friend help them through the hardship transfer paperwork to bring me back home to the school where I belonged.

Finally, back at my home school, I endured another half year of low level instruction and made decent grades, not as great as before because I wasn't in a nurturing teacher's room and I wasn't challenged. As I stated before, my family knew to advocate for my fair treatment, so my grandmother made that hike to the school and like magic my movement to a teacher's room who loved all children regardless of their background occurred.

My fourth/fifth grade teacher knew I was smart, and to this day, when she sees me, you see a sparkle in her eye that still lets me know I can do anything. She had a "despite the score" attitude. Although, I had taken the gifted assessment a few times and did not get the results expected, she made learning challenging and fun. Despite the score, in the non-gifted room, I won the school spelling bee and was a runner up for the Young Author's literary award. I had this teacher for 1½ years. As a fifth grade student, she made sure she had me placed in a program that would challenge me as a middle school student, despite the score. I was given an opportunity to be in honors courses. In my county, these courses were designed for people who were high achievers but could not overcome the barrier of the biased gifted screener. My teacher had high expectations and as students we were expected to meet her requests.

This transition to honors classes is one of the reasons I am where I am today. Being in this room, we were exposed to higher level rigor and the expectation that after graduation, we were going to college. If I had to estimate, I would say 90% of my class entered college after graduation. My honors class was well balanced, with people from a variety of cultures and economic backgrounds. I could relate in these classes as there were students who looked like me and walked home with me to the neighborhood.

Decades later, as I have been charged to lead and transform our district's gifted program. I often reflect on my own experiences of trying to break into the elite room. I also chuckle that I am the sole coordinator of a program that never embraced me in its doors only because of my scores. Although much has changed with our service plans, there is room for improvement. We use multiple measures to determine placement. The test score is one of those measures, but not the only factor. We have given permission to school officials to support families on the cusp with appealing their decisions and to develop policies to allow students to take part of the curriculum if they have the other characteristics of giftedness, but not the score. We are continually trying to raise awareness with professional development and we are even implementing a Javits grant to look for nontraditional ways to nurture young talent, modeled after Young Scholars in Fairfax, VA. Life is funny as it has a way of bringing us back full circle to advocate for what we believe in. My passion and background will not allow me to rest on what we can do for all children despite their scores. Putting people in the right seats in classrooms is crucial and can be the difference between a child going to college or going astray, especially with the changing dynamics of family and neighborhood life.

I hope you enjoyed a slither of my "gifted" experience and consider this when you are encountering students that you know need a little extra push. Caring educators really do make a difference. Please advocate, advocate, and advocate—despite the test score!

LaTonya Frazier, MEd has served as an elementary primary classroom teacher, elementary math lab teacher, instructional coach, and adjunct faculty member for the University of Louisville's gifted and talented department. With 17 years in the field of education, she currently serves as the Advance Program Coordinator (Gifted and Talented) for Jefferson County Public Schools. She holds a BS in Elementary Education from Spalding University of Kentucky, and MEd in Education from Indiana Wesleyan University, and a Rank One in Gifted and Talented Instruction as well as a certificate for Educational Leadership from Indiana University Southeast. Ms. Frazier's passion includes diversifying the Gifted and Talented populations by integrating culturally responsive teaching and collaborating to determine ways to remove barriers from gifted programming in public education.

CHAPTER 20

FREE TO FLY

Jessica A. Fripp

Key Challenges: racial pride, isolation/ostracism, racism

For to be free is not merely to cast off one's chains, but to live in a way that respects
and enhances the freedom of others
—Nelson Mandela

I live in skin that has constantly fought to survive, fought to breathe, and fought to live. This skin [my identity] is not dichotomous; I'm not just Black and woman; I'm not simply educated or artistic. To quote Meek Mill, "There's levels to this." My identity is rooted in my experience, self-expression, artistry, language, years of systemic oppression and I could go on. The African diaspora has been both fetishized and ridiculed, both envied and restricted in attempts to take away access to the freedom to be ourselves. There is no "oneness" or "sameness" for People of Color. Our movement towards freedom, to remove the chains placed upon us by dominant structures, continues. History repeats itself, as black and brown skin endure the fight.

If you have not figured it out by now, I embody both the mystery and the aesthetic of being a Black woman. I grew up in a small town, rich with

Gullah history in what is lovingly called the Lowcountry of South Carolina. I am the youngest of four strong, independent women who helped to mold the identity I proudly walk in. I was afforded privileges not unusual to Black families in this community, but not widely publicized because it does not fit the narrative portrayed of our communities. My mother was a nurse who worked with the Navy, and my father, a veteran, went on to work in management for over 30 years.

Having the structure and finances of a dual-parent home allowed me to participate in 4-H clubs, private schools, travelling sports teams, field trips, first cars and sweet sixteen celebrations with ease. Although my parents created a comfortable lifestyle, they did not encase me in a bubble that disconnected me from the pressures, criticisms and maltreatment of society. They knew early on what creating this lifestyle would mean: exposure to dominant groups who constantly questioned my presence in these spaces. Like any family, my parents wanted to give me the best they could, the age old desire to "Get better than what we had." However, no privilege comes without a cost or sacrifice for those whom the system was never designed to benefit. As my parents paid out of pocket for me to matriculate at a small, Christian school, the risk toward unhealthy mental and emotional wellness increased. I worked twice as hard, not to be viewed as half as good, but to be seen as an equal, a counterpart. I wanted my way of speaking, my tenacity to learn, and my ability to be both an athlete and a scholar, to be respected. I wanted to speak Gullah in class and not be told I sounded "unintelligent"; instead, this system muted my ability to be myself. *There was no freedom of expression and this was my first shackle.*

Let's be clear: I never desired Whiteness or to pass. I desired my humanity, to embody my culture, to adorn my head with braids without question, to move away from the European example of beauty that flooded the television, magazines and music videos. I wanted to see "me" when I left the house and entered the classroom; yet this could not happen. Instead, all that was left was a shell of my existence. I developed resilience on the outside while I was mostly confused and equally enraged on the inside. Hostile emotions were driven by the inability to be noticed, appreciated and accepted for the layers of my identity. The plight of Black and Brown skin. With this new militancy, I befriended other students of color, an intimate body of people with common ground, much to the disdain of my headmaster. Occupying a space not meant for me and creating an identity within that space was liberating!

Administration treated us like it was a Nat Turner rebellion, mind you; even though this was simply a sanctuary of likeminded individuals who made each other's experiences bearable. However, *there was no freedom to assemble;* add another shackle to my chain. For one reason or another (something I will never fully know but can assume), the few Black students I came to know went on to leave (or be dismissed from) the private school, bringing back the feelings of ostracism. Empowered to finish strong (although surrounded by many who hoped for my demise for no other reason than because I am Black), I graduated from that high school, earning the coveted Valedictorian status. I went on to attend Predominantly White Institutions within the state, where I cultivated meaningful friendships and wasted little time identifying other Women of Color to glean from.

I was not met with challenges in undergraduate and graduate school that were unusual to me, given my experiences in high school. Navigating White spaces became a common practice, so most adversities motivated me to succeed and acquire knowledge to maintain my position within those environments. I was no longer comfortable with being told "no." I was learning to persevere in spite of hardships because I created a network of supporters who knew I was capable of achieving even when the environment I inhabited denied me. I wanted to take advantage of my experience and share what I was learning with others.

The problem I encountered was lacking a formula to help others and limited access to people who would benefit from my story the most. Graduating with degrees in Psychology and Community Counseling, respectively, I took on a career in the healthcare setting. I encountered populations of individuals who lacked opportunities based upon economic status, the stigma of their diagnoses, and education. I worked in the clinical mental health sector, where my knowledge and ability to relate to protected classes were well-received. Although I did not experience poverty and a lack of resources to be successful, I understood the sentiment of being denied. I came to understand how difficult it was to maintain positive mental health when living within an oppressive society. Therefore, I worked to gain trust with my clients, and not position myself as a "savior"; I recognized the last thing my families needed was some person representing the system, but rather someone who would empower them towards the success they desired to attain.

With this outlook, promotions at work flooded my life, but I was unfulfilled. I benefited from and succeeded at the hands of people who lacked the hope, access and opportunity to create a gratifying life. I was not helping to dismantle the **system** of oppression in mental health for Black and Brown families; I was simply sustaining a way of life that was already not fitting for the populations I served. I needed to become part of the institutional structure, not just a warden of the system. Rather than maintaining the level of advocacy I was given, I charted a new course that allowed me to research and distribute information on a larger scale; I made the decision to work on a terminal degree in Counseling with an emphasis on culturally relevant pedagogy and dismantling systems of oppression that suppress the livelihood of People of Color.

Theoretically, my art for writing in graduate school was honed by faculty who cared and desired me to be ready for academia. However, as I look back, my drive to be outstanding was getting weary. I was growing tired of proving myself in educational settings. For every award that I received, it was met with some controversial statement from my cohort members. One of my faculty was affectionately (insert sarcasm) assigned the identity of "Jungle Fever" because he looked out for me and placed me in positions to write well, receive funding, and be awarded for my hard work. I refused to believe people would be jealous of me, but I found my own patience and mental health growing thin due to a constant battle to prove I deserved to be where I was placed. Perhaps, this was the largest chain preventing me from living peacefully and I desperately wanted to learn to care less about the opinions of those around me.

Despite others attributing my success to my appearance and making false accusations about the relationships I cultivated with my faculty, I was the only member of my cohort to receive a faculty line at a research one in-stitution, doing "the work" I thought would propel stigmatized groups in mental health to receive quality resources and counseling services. When I embarked on this new opportunity, I was informed by a trusted colleague to sanitize some of my research topics in order to make my research agenda "safe." Before I even got settled into my new career, I felt I had *no freedom to petition*, to challenge injustices and speak out against inequality at an indi-vidual, community, and/or national level. Although this was the perception I was given, I'm not quite sure if it is reality. Currently, the faculty in my department appear to be supportive throughout these past nine months. People seem to be interested in what I have to say and encourage me to maximize my research by integrating it into my lectures. So, I am either finding my fit or breaking the mold. Regardless, I am realizing with each day that I can only be me and do what I intend and not allow the bondage of people to keep me guessing about my full potential.

I have learned only a few things on my professional and personal journey towards liberation of people bondage. What I do understand is that I can-not allow people access to my worth who have no intention of preserving it. I no longer allow people to add value to my worth. The same story of "you can't" has played out and I no longer have to believe the messages of my youth. I no longer have to be held captive to the beliefs of others; I am fighting to no longer be bound by dominant power structures that have disenfranchised my history for so long. So, I use my position, my freedom to tell a story about a woman who is removing the chains, one shackle at a time, by choosing not to fit in with those around her or seek acceptance from them. Rather, I am finding my own place once again and paving my own way even when those decisions are poorly received. I'm learning to fly without waiting for permission; I am liberating myself so that I can inspire others. This story does not have a happy ending where you can read it and know what to do to free yourself. It is an honest depiction of a work in progress. None of us have made it, but we are learning lessons to self-actualize. Harriett Tubman realized that so many people could have freedom had they known they were enslaved. My change came when I realized that the words and thoughts from other people do not define me, my purpose or my character. I had to let go of looking for people to affirm me and start believing in myself. I had to stop desiring to be a counterpart and walk in the room knowing I have something valuable to offer; I had to take a seat at the table instead of waiting to be an invited guest. My story is here to remind you that who you are is defined by you, not status, not titles and definitely not people; so, you can either reside within the parameters of opinion or you can choose to soar above it. I challenge you to join me and fly.

Jessica A. Fripp, PhD, is an Assistant Clinical Professor in the Department of Special Education, Rehabilitation and Counseling at Auburn University. Her research interests include attitudes and stigma toward mental health services in the African American community, Critical Race Theory in Counseling and teaching culturally relevant pedagogy. She is currently conducting research on active recruitment strategies to engage African Americans and Latinos in counseling services in order to promote positive mental health and wellness.

CHAPTER 21

"CAN'T" IS A
FOUR-LETTER WORD
AND LIFE ROLLS ALONG

Vernessa T. Gipson
Brianna T. Morgan

Key Challenges: health issues, dual exceptionality, special education, low expectations, academic isolation, employment challenges

---

Brianna Tenette Morgan (affectionately called Bri) entered the world on November 20, 1981 at 1:14 p.m. weighing in at 2 pounds and 2 ounces. She required nasal oxygen, but not a ventilator; and lived in an incubator for 28 days and in the neo-natal intensive care unit for 51 days.

On December 5th at 6am, as I was preparing for my daily visit to the neonatal center, the telephone rang, and when I looked at the caller ID, it displayed Carle Hospital. "Ms. Morgan, we need you come to the hospital immediately." I didn't ask any questions, I hung up and I was at the hospital in 20 minutes. Brianna's (Bri) special neonatal nurse met me at the elevator and before I could say a word, she assured me that Brianna was alive

Gumbo for the Soul, pages 121–129
Copyright © 2017 by Information Age Publishing

and I remember collapsing in tears. In the privacy of an office, Bri's doctor and nurse explained that earlier that morning, her heart had stopped beating. He then told me that they were able to resuscitate her after five minutes, but she had to be incubated to restore her oxygen levels. They assured me that she was stable, but they were unable to tell me if her brain suffered any damage; that could not be determined for a few weeks. But, we knew we would need to give her "catch up" time before we could begin assessing her developmental needs. Although I was relieved—I was still afraid; actually a better description would be terrified. This unexpected and uncertain journey was just beginning…and I knew I had a very special baby placed into my life.

On January 10, 1982, 51 days after her birth, Brianna was discharged to go home, weighing a whopping 4 pounds and 5 ounces. She was so small that she was able to wear baby doll clothes. Since then, my life has never been the same!! I was a mother of a healthy and happy baby who loved music, dancing, and story time.

Because I was a mom with a college degree in Child Development, I was always concerned about her motor and cognitive development. At eight months of age, I was referred to a local agency to obtain a developmental assessment for Bri. The assessment revealed a significant delay of 6–9 months, in many motor areas. As a result, weekly services began for speech and occupation therapy for fine motor coordination and oral muscle training. At 12 months, we began receiving intensive gross motor services for delays. At that time, Brianna did not make age appropriate progress with motor skills such as, turning over, sitting up independently or crawling, but she was excelling with her language, communication and cognitive skills. At 15 months of age, Brianna was talking in phrases, identifying pictures by pointing and had rhythm that was out of this world—she could "dance" in her own special way!!! By the time she was two years old, we were able to get an "official" diagnosis; developmentally delayed/quadriplegic spasticity—but I knew that meant—cerebral palsy!!

Cognitively, Brianna excelled; she knew her colors, shapes, numbers, music and memorizing songs and books were her specialties. She was a funny, talkative and very inquisitive little girl When Bri turned three, we entered into the world of early childhood and special education: a world that included wheelchairs, braces, lift buses, Multidisciplinary Conferences and Individual Education Plans (IEPs) and meetings and ongoing therapies—physical, occupation and speech. Also around this time, I gave birth to my second daughter Candace and Bri became a big sister/or little mother. She was extremely attentive to her sister and "read" to her nightly!!

Bri and Candace had a very special bond growing up; almost inseparable. As Candace, grew older, I found myself experiencing "developmental grief" episodes. As Candace reached certain developmental milestones, I grieved for Brianna even though we made as many adaptations as we could. When Candace learned to ride a bike, we bought Brianna a power motorcycle, and when Candace was invited to sleepovers at her friends' houses, we invited Brianna's friends over for sleepovers in our home. Also, we knew that visits to the homes of friends were often difficult; so our home was frequently and by necessity the gathering place every weekend.

In spite of her physical limitations, we worked hard to ensure that Bri was provided with as many cultural and socialization opportunities as her able bodied peers. Brianna was in Girl Scouts, the church choir and took horseback riding lessons. When she was eight years old, she was a member of the local Girls Inc. Club and served as a reading tutor for younger members. She also was quite the social butterfly among her older peers.

Because Bri ambulated primarily with a walker or her "red" wheelchair, all social trips had to be "vetted" for accessibility. Aside from reading and music, Brianna was also quite the sports fan of both football and basketball at the high school, college and professional levels. She could routinely be found sitting among her male peer groups and family members discussing sports statistics, and player and team strategies. In middle school, this gifted and motivated Black girl was a regular attendee at all home basketball games; she gained free admission and served as the team's sideline coach. She was more popular than the cheerleaders and if she missed a game, the team was concerned and/or quite upset with her. Bri's presence mattered to them and this continued throughout her high school years. She was and still remains a diehard Chicago Bulls fan!

We recognized her strengths, talents, and weaknesses early. She had a beautiful singing voice, so she auditioned and was accepted into the community children's choir, the only Black girl and the only child with a disability. Academically, Brianna was consistent. She sucked in all her math classes, but she excelled in all language arts and social studies classes. However, after multiple psychological assessments, it all began to make sense; the part of her brain that had been damaged following a heart attack she suffered while she was an infant was the same part that governed her motor skills and mathematical reasoning ability. Our family then learned that the brain was a wonderful organ that had other sections that become sharper and stronger when one section was impaired, thus her memory, reading, language and musical skills were enhanced.

During her seventh grade school year, my gifted Black daughter who survived and even thrived was inducted into the Junior Beta Club, a middle school Honor Society. Needless to say, the family was thrilled and excited. But we soon learned that Brianna was proud but not excited. She did not want to attend club meetings or participate in community service projects with the club. She later explained: "I am the only Black student and they never take my suggestions for places to volunteer; people need help, not just animals." We would often find her reading and studying about the lives and times of Huey P. Newton, Malcolm X, Tupac, Assata Shakur, the Black Panther Party and the women in the Civil Rights Movement. It was then that I discovered that I had a bit of a radical thinker on my hands.

Brianna was quite competent at navigating, both mentally and physically, among peers. She was slated to attend the same high school with many of her middle school classmates and she was astute at making others aware of her physical needs. It should also be noted that starting in the fourth grade, Brianna was a full participant in all of her IEP meetings. Much to the chagrin of the teachers and principals, I explained to the IEP team that this was her meeting about *her* disability and that she would be working with the staff every day, so, she needed to hear and be a part of all of the meetings.

During the spring of her eighth grade year, Brianna and her occupational therapist made a visit to her future high school to get "the lay of the land." After her high school tour, Brianna and her therapist met with the high school staff and left a detailed outline of accommodations that needed to occur before she arrived. While enrolled in high school, Brianna completed remedial math (she took geometry three times before she passed), and basic science courses. But, she also completed honors and gifted classes for language arts, social studies, foreign languages and other reading-based classes. Standardized tests reflected her abilities consistently—90th percentile and she performed above average in language arts and social science. But, when it came to math in science, she was in the 50th percentile. Her dual exceptionality was a high school counselor's scheduling nightmare. Also, Brianna represented the first student of her high school had to program for a student in a wheelchair—100% mainstreamed and in need of both honors and remedial classes. Thus, the secondary education nightmare began!

BRIANNA

I was super excited about attending high school. I had my schedule set, had friends in my classes and I knew how to get around the school on my own. But, the first month was a nightmare! My locker was on the third floor on the east end of the school (with all the other freshmen) and my first class was on the first floor on the west end of the building. I was required to retrieve an elevator key—but I had to get from the office, go to my locker, and get back to class on time. Plus, I had a manual wheelchair so that, coupled with the slowest elevator in the world, getting to class on time was impossible!! On my first day of school, I acquired enough tardies to last a lifetime. Plus ... the educators and professionals were nuts!! It seemed as if they had NOT read the accommodations list provided to them. I did not want to be a "whiner," so I tried to cope and began to think; maybe I was the one with the issue . . . I mean . . . I was slow physically, and I talked in the hallway. Maybe I could do better . . . so, I made the decision to not go to my locker in the morning and that resulted in a detention, since students were not allowed to wear coats in class!!

I also remember the time when the lunch carts were left in the elevator, so I was unable to get in, so I was late yet again! I began to wonder; didn't they know freshmen hate being late for classes because everybody stared at you? Plus, I was the only Black child in the honors class and because I was in a wheelchair, the students had to move their desks so that my wheelchair could fit. It was so embarrassing! I then had a better understanding why many kids dropped out of school, and, I thought I would scream if one more teacher asked me if I was in the "right" class. I began to wonder if it was my race or my chair that made them ask me that question My mother taught me at an early age to always filter people's comments through three lenses; gender, race, and ability before I spoke, so I would always respond by saying, "My legs don't work, but my brain is just fine! I'm in the right class." I also resisted from asking the teacher if they were in the right profession. Nonetheless, all of the described embarrassing moments took place during the first week of school!

By the end of my first week, I was done with high school. When I went into one of the bathrooms and preceded to the handicapped stall, I learned that they had put the damned door on backwards—the door swung into the stall instead of outside of the stall thus my wheelchair would not fit! It was at that time that I decided to tell my mother. At the dinner table, (yep, we ate dinner together every night as a family) I answered the question "how was school"? And so it began. As I discussed my week, my father was biting his tongue. My mother, the director of an alternative school for boys with special needs (mostly, behavioral problems), calmly asked me, "So Bri, what do you want to do?" I should have known that my mother would have come to me for the solution; sometimes, I just wanted her to be my "Mom" and fix my problems, but I knew better. I told her that we needed to have a meeting at the school with the administrators, my Special Education case manager and the district director of special education and I shared that I wanted my support system with me—two community advocates (one of whom was a police officer). My mom then asked me why I wanted the advocates there, and my response was that I wanted to have more of "us" (Blacks) at the meeting than "them." So my mother scheduled the meeting for the following Monday.

The meeting was held at 9 a.m. I passed out the agenda that my mother and I prepared ahead of time, and made my opening statement. Through my tears, I verbalized the humiliation I felt during my first week of high school. I remember saying, "If you all don't want me here, then just say so. I don't think I am asking for more than the law says that I am entitled to."

When I finished, there was not a dry eye in the room; well, except for my mom! I then provided them with a list of items that needed to be addressed which included me having my own elevator key, emptied elevators, a new locker location, tardy and detention waivers for reasons that were related to accessibility issues and an accessible bathroom stall the floors on which I had classes. Sounds simple . . . right??

Following the meeting my mother told me, "You understand that what you are doing is not just for yourself, but for all the other students who will come to this school in wheelchairs and who will be attending mainstreamed classes. You are the Rosa Parks of the American Disabilities (ADA)!" That conversation has remained with me to this day and I never felt more successful in my life. Life was far from perfect from that point on—I still missed a few field trips because the teacher forgot to order a bus with a lift or failed to check whether the place where we were going to was accessible.

During high school, I quickly learned I needed to speak up and advocate for myself and shouldn't assume people would remember to take care of my needs. My all-time 'favorite' catastrophe was being left in the school on the third floor during a fire drill. The building was clearing out and when I went to the elevator, it would not open because it had been shut off as per legal fire safety procedures. Prior to this point I was unaware of this protocol, so I just sat there. Then, I remembered my mother allowed me to take a cellphone to school for emergencies. /even though cellphones were not allowed in schools at the time I thanked God for our secret arrangement. I went into a classroom and sat by the window and watched all of the students outside. I called my mother on the phone and I still remember what she said as if it were yesterday. After I told her what was going on, she said the "F" word. She then went on to say, "I am in Springfield, Illinois, sitting in the office of the state director of Special Education. This will be a "fun" call to make!" My mother instructed me to call the District Office and ask to speak with the Director of Special Education. I explained the situation and ironically, the director said the same word that my mother said! It was hilarious! It should be noted that the long-time Director of Special Education worked closely with my mother professionally. She was devastated! To make a long story short, I was safe, but the school was given a $3000 fine by the Fire Marshall. But in my opinion, that was a miniscule degree of accountability.

My struggles in math and science classes often caused me to be depressed at times, but overall I loved school. But having a "normal" social life was tough given my physical limitations. For example, I never dated in high school . . . how do you go on dates in a wheelchair? My mother did her best to make sure I had as many social opportunities as my peer group and she had access to quite a few guys who were more than willing to take Ms. V's daughter's to school functions. I had grown to know many of the students at my mother's program because I went to her after school hours and served as a tutor. You can only imagine the looks on the faces of my school administrators when I showed up to school functions with a student they had expelled and sent to my mother's school. I loved every minute of it!

When it came to college planning. My ACT high score was never higher than a 20; it was those math scores again—but I excelled in reading, English and again in social sciences. But, I found myself wondering, who would accept me? I applied to four state colleges; Bradley University, Eastern Illinois University (the closest to home), Illinois State University and Southern Illinois University at Edwardsville (SIUE). All four schools accepted me, but then I had to consider financial support and accessibility, both of which were deciding factors. After visiting all four schools, we found that SIUE was the most accessible; but it was also the furthest from home. But since I was (am) a true believer of God's Grace and Mercy, I knew everything was going to be OK.

After my graduation from high school, my grandparents wanted to visit my future college. So, we packed up and headed to southern Illinois. It was a fun time and I was extremely proud of my accomplishments. My grandmother, who was one of my biggest fans, reminded me that there was nothing I could not accomplish in life if I stayed focused and "prayed" up! And every time my family tells this story, we say, "God worked it out," because that is just what God did while we were on the tour. I was both embarrassed and proud because my grandfather spoke to every Black person he saw on the campus and told each and every one of them to watch out for his granddaughter! After all of my grandfather's "advocacy," I was encouraged to complete a leadership scholarship application in the end, I was awarded a four-year scholarship.

On August 15, 2000, the car was packed and we were ready to hit the road. My family was ready to take me to college, but I froze! I sat at the top of the stairs in my house and sobbed uncontrollably. I did not want to go. I felt as if I could not leave my home, my place of safety and familiarity, and my security—I was not ready. My body would not move. But, my mother came to the top of the stairs and we prayed. She reminded me that God had a purpose for my life and "he had not brought me this far to leave me." She reminded me of all the times she was scared; at my birth, which was 12 weeks early and when I weighed 2 pounds—but God! When she learned that I would never walk without assistance; but then found that I would never be limited in where I went and what I was able to do—but God! She reminded me of being left during the fire drill, but it was not a real fire—but GOD! There is so much more to the story that cannot be shared within these pages; but just know that my mother reminded me that I survived and thrived.

My family hugged me as I wiped my eyes and then said, "Let's do this"! So off to college I went. Academically, I did extremely well. I majored in

Health Education and graduated in four years. Fast forward: I returned home, but could not find a job in my field due to my physical limitations. I was college educated but underemployed. I was depressed and often felt hopeless. But, I sought counseling and regained my faith. I worked for two years as a teaching assistant for students with special needs and loved it, but knew I could never teach because I did not encompass two qualities that I thought outstanding teachers encompassed; organization skills and creativity—because they were not my strengths.

I loved talking to and helping people and I was often considered to be an "old soul" or wise beyond my years. I began to contemplate applying to graduate schools to study social work or school counseling. But then, I was given another reality check by my mother when she said, "Bri, you think you want to be a social worker because that's what you know (both of my parents were social workers), but think about what do you enjoy doing more than anything else?" "Reading and listening to music," I responded. "What job will let you be around books, movies and music all day?" "Mom, I can't be a librarian!! Did she not know how competitive the admission process would be? I had only known of two Black librarians. But, I went for it and defied the onslaught of low expectations by educators and professionals. I defied the odds! I, a gifted Black female with physical but not mental challenges began to find myself and started to fulfill my dreams. For example, the number one Graduate School of Library and Information Science in the United States, the University of Illinois—Urbana Champaign, was in my hometown—and I was admitted. Only 25 graduate students are accepted into this prestigious program each year, and I was one of them. I completed the program and I loved it! Plus, I am a really good librarian. How do I know? My middle school students validate it for me every day: they visit often, want me to read to them, ask me for book suggestions, and resource assistance; they never want to leave the library; it is always busy.

What can other Black females learn from my story of trials and triumphs? What can their mothers, fathers, families, and school professionals learn? Be open and honest with students and your children about their weakness and their strengths, while providing supports and resources for both. Don't wallow in tragedies and challenges. Find ways to overcome and succeed. My mother knew I sucked at math; so she provided tutors and never once fussed about my poor grades. She built opportunities for me to excel in areas of my strengths and talents. Also, surround gifted children with a circle of supports, with peers and culturally relevant support people, material and information. I was often "the only" in many settings—so we traveled across the country and into many communities so I could see other scholars, like myself doing well. Another thing that can be done is to teach parents about giftedness and what it means to parent a gifted child. I was fortunate—no, blessed that my mother got it and when she didn't understand, she had a network of other parents raising gifted children to turn to for advice. She understood my gifts and my special needs. Now, you may ask, how would I describe myself today? I am a Black educated, gifted and talented librarian in a wheelchair who rocks! How cool is that?

Vernessa T. Gipson, MSW, is a licensed social work, mediator, family advocate and community organizer. She holds a Master's degree from Eastern Illinois University in child Development and a Master's degree in Social Work from the University of Illinois at Urbana. For the past 30 plus years, Vernessa has been a Head Start preschool teacher, child abuse and neglect and adolescent caseworker, a school social worker, and the coordinator of day treatment school for adolescents with severe emotional and behavioral disability. Her frequent interface with the child welfare and special education systems regarding the development of comprehensive service plans and IEP's, lead Ms. Gipson to be appointed to the only jointly funded social worker/advocate position in Illinois. Ms. Gipson's volunteer work includes the development of Children's Defense Fund schools within the state of Illinois, grant writing to secure funds for the implementation of CDF Freedom Schools, Urban Policy Debate teams, a family advocacy center, and culturally relevant programming for 21st Century Learning Communities.

Brianna Morgan is a living example of what is possible when the statistical odds say otherwise. A recipient of special education services since the age of three, she is a graduate of SIU-E with a Bachelor's degree in health education. After returning to her home community of Champaign, Illinois and unable to find a job in her field, mainly due to her physical limitations, she spent three years as a teaching assistant for students with behavioral disabilities. She was a highly sought after TA. Brianna's love of books and reading, all types of music and movies and her ability to maintain lots of "trivia information" lead her to become a librarian. Brianna earned her master's degree in Library Science from the University of Illinois at Urbana. She is currently employed as a school librarian in Urbana, Illinois.

CHAPTER 22

I READ TO LIVE

Kristy Girardeau

Key Challenges: low teacher expectations, parental incarceration, parental low education, finances, parental divorce, teen pregnancy

---

Skipping rope. Eating candy. Continuous laughter.
Oh, the joys of childhood. Sugar and spice and everything nice.
That's what little girls are made of.

I read to live. I have three siblings; one sister who is older and two younger brothers. I was always the more responsible child. I loved school. I loved books. I loved learning. Where my siblings were rebellious, hanging out with friends, and challenging authority, I read. Books fascinated me, then and now. The ability to read words and imagine yourself in places and times that, as a child, you felt you could never go, was like magic to me. Books transported me from the realities of everyday life, to be placed into utopia without a care or worry in the world. I have always found books to be intriguing, mystical even. I was able to escape from negative things in my life.

As a child, I was not aware that my upbringing was different, abnormal even, from others in my community. I thought that this was how all families

Gumbo for the Soul, pages 131–135

behaved. I read to live. I grew up in a very religious home. My mom was an evangelist in the church and my dad was a long haul truck driver. He was absent from the home for weeks at a time, leaving my mom to care for us. My mother was very active in the church. We attended church five nights a week and all day Sunday. We had Easter speeches, were a part of the children's choir, attended Vacation Bible School, and any other function pertaining to the church. Church was literally our home away from home... something that I thought was a safe haven for most, became a catalyst for pain for me.

As a child, I didn't understand the choices my mother made. As a result, I internalized the childhood trauma I experienced and subconsciously blamed her for the state of home. I sought the comforts of school; the normalcy of school routines provided an escape from my reality. It was here that I had control over my life and the ability to shape my destiny. I worked hard in school, determined that education would change my life's trajectory.

I was always a high achiever. School was easy. I never studied for an exam or lesson. I recall sitting in class, listening intently to the teacher, capturing mental notes of the lecture and storing them away. I always sat in the front of the class so as not to be disturbed by others who chose to act out. My life was depending upon this education. My grades reflected my intensity. I was an A student in a low-income African American high school. I was unaware of gifted classes. I wasn't offered any. Those were reserved for the "special students," those that didn't look like me. I was labeled as one of those "ghetto" girls because I lived in one of the toughest neighborhoods in Decatur, Georgia. Those neighborhoods don't produce smart students. The only publicity we received was office referrals and suspensions.

I have learned as an adult that my mom and dad both were victims of generational thinking and circumstances. It is nearly impossible to pass on what you do not possess. Like my grandparents, they did not graduate high school. My mom left in the twelfth grade due to pregnancy and my dad ultimately received his GED in prison along with my two younger brothers. They never spoke about the importance of school and education. There was not an expectation to read nightly or daily homework checks. I cannot recall a time when my parents helped me with my homework, encouraged my participation in the spelling bee, or checked in with my teachers. School was a place to go because it was a requirement. In fact, my mom would state, "You are the child that I don't have to worry about. You are smart and you are going to be alright." I often wondered, as a child, how she arrived at that conclusion. Was it because I was compliant and took on the task of managing the household finances?

My mother and father were married. He was the breadwinner of the home. My mom worked outside of the home but she did not have to. My father took care of everything. I can vividly recall him returning home from a trip, exhausted and worn out. He would always enter the home with something for us. It is amazing how a child appreciates the simplest things in life, like a candy bar. It may not be much to some, but it was the world to me. He would hug each one of us, shower, and come to dinner. All he asked of my mom was to have a clean house, collard greens, black eye peas, and cornbread. He was oblivious to the day-to-day operations of the home. That is, until the lights went off, literally. I read to live.

My father began to come home and notice things were wrong. Lights were shut off due to nonpayment. We had food, but not what my dad felt we should eat. My mom would tithe 10% of everything she received. She would tell us that God receives his portion before anything. She did not care if the lights were shut off, rent was not paid, or there was no food; you paid God first. Her unwavering faith in God was something she deeply believed in and refused to change for anyone or anything. As a child, that left me confused and I often questioned how God could take what little we had and promised to "take care of us" and we still were evicted. I was around 10 years old. Our family was falling apart. I immersed myself into books to escape these problems.

My siblings and I became rebellious and began to challenge my mom. In essence, we were fighting back. We were fighting for normalcy. My parents began to argue constantly. The arguing turned into physical fighting. The more that they argued and fought, the more involved my mom became into the church. She would state, "God will see me through." One day, there was a knock at the door. It was the sheriff. My mom was being served with divorce papers. My dad left. At 10 years old, I did not know how to process this. I was angry. I was hurt. I despised my mom because I believed she chose the church over my dad. I began to hate her. Unbeknownst to her, I felt she hated me too. And then it began . . .

My mom did not know how to process the divorce. Since I am the child that most resembles my dad, she took her frustrations out on me. I constantly heard, "You're just like your daddy. He ain't no good. Your daddy don't care nothing about you. He left us." I did not know what to do with that, so I did nothing. I read. I read to escape what has now become my life.

As a result of the divorce, we began to struggle financially. My mom and dad played against one another. I felt that they both held out resources to see who would bend first. In the end, we suffered because of their battle. We moved often because we could not afford the rent. We did not have the latest shoes, clothes, or toys. We relied heavily on the church for resources. My mom finally found a place based on her income. We stayed there for a while, but my childhood was still far from perfect. We were not allowed to have friends unless they became a part of the choir (my mom started her own church in the home). She began to preach anywhere she could. She preached at the local mall and at the entrance of the apartment complex. She even preached on the answering machine saying that if anyone called the home a sinner, they would be saved by the time they hung up. We were the laughing stock of the neighborhood and school. I was embarrassed. Where my siblings fought anyone who laughed at us, but I used books, once again, to escape.

In the meantime, my father went on to live, what I considered, a life of luxury. He purchased a nice home and cars. He would pick us up, every so often, and boast about all that he obtained. We would have to ride around with him in the car while he picked up his freshly laundered clothes and get a haircut. We watched him flirt with women in his cowboy attire and pinky ring while wearing his finest cologne.

I became disgusted. Disgusted because we are struggling and he thought it was OK to live the lavish life. I began to act out in various ways. There were multiple times that I would refuse to go with him when he came to pick us up. My mom always insisted and reprimanded me for being "disrespectful". I did not know how to process that and thus felt alone. I would talk ugly and demand to be taken home. My daddy never responded to me but instead carried me back home to my mom. This continued until I became pregnant at 17 years old with my first child. It was at that moment that my parents said I was now grown and to go live.

Today, I am a mother of four and married. I have experienced many failures and setbacks as a result of my upbringing. As an adult, I now understand that my parents did the best that they could with what they had at the time. In spite of my childhood and generational circumstances, I am a first generation college graduate. I am currently enrolled as a PhD student at Georgia State University. I have had the opportunity to meet many wonderful scholars, many of whom I consider to be mentors and friends, who continually encourage me to be my best and to never give up.

My story is one of perseverance in the face of adversity, determination, and hope. I did not see failure as an option and therefore did everything to succeed. I knew education was the key to changing my situation. There are four things that I held on to, in spite of my circumstances, that kept me strong as I wish that it will do the same for you: trust your soul, for it will never steer you wrong; believe in the impossible; pray as that is direct communication to God; and have faith, for faith is the substance of things hoped for, the evidence of things not seen.

The journey to make it to this point has been filled with many ups and downs but in the end, I made it. As you enter new terrains and embark on new journeys, may my walk encourage and bless you to press into your dreams and imagine the unimaginable. Always remember to be kind, clothed with humility, and covered with grace. Ride the waves and finish strong, for in the end it is not what you have accomplished but how you handled and embraced the journey along the way! Take God with you always and remember NOTHING is possible without Him! The parents we were given were chosen for us. You determine the life you ultimately have.

———————————

Kristy Girardeau is a doctoral student in Early Childhood and Elementary Education at Georgia State University, where she received her dual bachelor's degree in Early Childhood Education and Special Education as well as her master's degree in urban teacher leadership with a concentration in reading. Mrs. Girardeau was the recipient of the 2012 National Council of Teachers of English Early Career Educator of Color Leadership Award and the 2013 Teacher of Distinction Leadership Award. Her research interests are literary practices of Black girls, the culturally responsive teacher, early childhood and urban education, and gifted education.

CHAPTER 23

THE DAY I FOUND PAIN

Derria L. Ford Glover

Key Challenges: parental loss, peer pressures, (over)weight

The reality of all minorities who have found success lies in the fact that we have all encountered some type of hardship that could have prevented us from being successful. I have learned over the years that every success has a story that embraces the struggle that parallels success. As a teenager, I never conceptualized what that meant for me, but in my wildest dreams, I wouldn't have imagined the amount of strength, faith, and perseverance it would take for me to overcome my personal tragedies. If I took a microscope and looked at my childhood, I was always classified as "different" which often comes with being gifted and Black. I was often teased and taunted by my family and peers because I wasn't your typical "Black girl."

As a child, I was gifted and talented. I loved to read and write, I took classical piano lessons, and I wanted to be an opera singer. I was known for making up stories and often walked around practicing classical songs that I learned from my weekly vocal lessons. My parents love supporting my ideas so I went to a school that emphasized creative writing. I took weekly gymnastics, piano lessons, sung in the classical choir, clarinet lessons, and went to musical

Gumbo for the Soul, pages 137–140
Copyright © 2017 by Information Age Publishing
All rights of reproduction in any form reserved.

summer camps so I could continue to craft my skills. Every year, my great aunt hosted a benefit concert and all of the kids in the family presented a talent as a part of the program. I remember singing loudly "My country tis of thee," and all of my cousins laughing at the top of their lungs. My great aunt always supported my song choices and told me to "sing anyway."

Not only was I interested in music, but I also had a passion for sports. Granted, I was overweight most of my childhood and preteen years, but I played anyway. My dad would tell me "Who said Big Girls can't be fast" and fast I was. I even stepped in and ran the 4 by 4 on the track team when one of my friends hurt herself before the race. My parents supported every passion that I had, so lack of confidence was not an option.

My life at home was much different from many of my cousins and peers. My parents worked hard to shield me from the evils of the world. Drug abuse, sexual abuse, and domestic violence were situations that were relatively unfamiliar to me, but very familiar to many of my cousins. As I grew older, I knew my home life was different, so I attributed most of their teasing and taunting to jealously. They envied my life.

Although my childhood was full of opportunities that could have wounded me, none of these situations I mentioned tested my faith as the day my life forever changed. As a college sophomore, I always anticipated some situation would happen that would test my faith, but I never expected my success story to be filled with so much anger, fear, hurt, blame, and defeat. I can't remember the exact date but I remember every detail of the moment. I remember eating Kentucky Fried Chicken for lunch, I remember listening to Kesha Cole in the car, I remember looking up at the clouds and making objects out of the big fluffy clouds, and I remember it being our first family trip. I was in the car with my father and mother . . . looking forward to a long overdue and needed vacation. Just us spending time together. Family vacations were not a norm in my family and this one was supposed to set that stage for many trips to come. It had been years since we had seen my oldest brother and we were all excited. My brother moved to Texas and it had been a couple of years since we had been together as a family, so my parents saved up and decided to take a 14-hour trip to put a smile on my brother's face.

We arrived at my brother's house late Sunday evening. We spent hours catching up, laughing, and sharing photos before we all decided we had enough and it was time to pass out. The next morning, when I woke up, I saw my mom and dad sitting at the kitchen table. My mom wasn't feeling well and my brother and father were trying to figure out what was wrong. My mom was a diabetic, so they gave her orange juice and fed her breakfast, hoping her blood sugar would stabilize. I remembered fussing at her. It had been five years since she had a stroke and she never fully recovered, so much of my high school years I dealt with her anxieties and depression that were rooted in her illnesses. We were inseparable and every friend wanted to call her 'mom' because she was so easy to talk to. Her mother passed away when she was 19, so she tried to give me the mother–daughter relationship she desired as a young adult.

I decided to step outside to talk to my niece and her friend who were sitting on the front steps and all of a sudden I turned around and started running in the house because I could hear screaming. As I entered the house, I could see my mother falling to the floor and my sister-in-law trying to catch her before she hit her head on the coffee table. We called the ambulance and it seemed like hours before they arrived, but in reality it was only a matter of minutes. By the time the emergency team arrived, she was non-responsive and not breathing. 1...2...3...shock replayed in my mind over and over again as we rode to the hospital behind the ambulance. I looked in the back seat, hoping I would see my mom sitting there. I was hoping this horrible moment was a dream—not real—but the sickness within my stomach let me know it was reality. When we arrived at the hospital, we were taken back to a private room; we waited and waited for an update. The doctor finally came in and told us my mother passed away.

That day my life truly changed and I felt the weight of the world on my shoulders. I could have quit all of the positive things that were going on in my life and hidden in my shell, but instead I decided to fight harder for everything. My mother spent years believing in me and it would be a disgrace if I did not continue to thrive. I surrounded myself around positive women and immersed myself in my own goals. I wish I could tell the world it was easy, but it was far from that. I spent years being paranoid about my own health; traumatized by the thoughts of suddenly passing away. I spent days crying in my dorm room shower because I started my junior year of college weeks after burying my mother. I turned my back on God because I could not believe He would allow me to lose my best friend. I smiled but I was angry and upset; my faith was broken and my relationship with my father was rocky. However, when you are determined to excel, there is nothing in the world that can stop you.

I lost my mother, but I never lost myself. I never imagined the impact and the challenges I would face, but a determined mind can't be defeated. I quickly learned it is not all about what happens but more importantly it's about how I *choose* to deal with it. For those who have lost a parent, a close loved one, I want to share how I coped. I coped by remembering the good times. I coped by staying focused on my goals as my mother expected. I coped by staying faithful, knowing there is a reason for everything; learn from the triumphs and learn from the trials, tribulations, and losses. Just know that life goes on and do all that you can to fulfill your dreams and those your parent or parents hold (and held) for you.

Derria L. Ford Glover is a Doctoral Candidate in Leadership and Professional Practice at Trevecca Nazarene University. Her research emphasis includes leadership development, organizational leadership, nonprofit leadership, emotional intelligence, transformational leadership, and leader efficacy. She is a grants professional and has successfully obtained and administered a variety of Federal, State, private, and foundation grants in the nonprofit and educational institutions over the past seven years. She has a clear passion for serving her community by advocating for the improvement of administrative policies that impact low income and disadvantaged individuals. She has a Master's of Business Administration and Bachelors of Science with an emphasis in Psychology, Industrial Organizational Psychology, and Business Communications from Middle Tennessee State University.

CHAPTER 24

THE DIFFERENCE BETWEEN GIVING UP AND MOVING ON

Jamye Hardy

Key Challenges: imposter syndrome, goal setting

For the first time in my life, I felt completely defeated. By November of my first year in graduate school, the accumulated effects of trying to beat the odds and the stereotypes of a Black woman who came from a divorced, working class family had finally broken me.

I have no memories of a time when I did not know the challenges of being a gifted Black female in America. My parents made sure that I was well aware of the obstacles that would be in my way, and I accepted the challenge with confidence. However, I do have several memories of my childhood setting me up for success. From an early age, I was involved in everything under the sun, from dance to Girl Scouts. My mother, a corporate non-profit business woman turned middle school guidance counselor, instilled in me the values of hard work, perseverance and the power of prayer. My father instilled in me the passion to learn, gain knowledge, and understand it all. But most importantly, I remember my Black culture and African heritage

Gumbo for the Soul, pages 141–144
Copyright © 2017 by Information Age Publishing
All rights of reproduction in any form reserved.

that was taught to me through dance, drum, story, and after school educa-tion. I knew that I had come from greatness and I had no intentions of achieving any less than my ancestors. Just as they did, I was taught to never give up. Under the influence of my parents, I consistently attended schol-arly, cultural, social, and artistic events that exposed me to successful Afri-can American role models. I remember telling myself that when I grew up, I wanted to be just like them. Black, successful, and most of all, happy.

With this in mind, from a very young age, I remember structuring my involvement and goals around beating the odds. I worked hard to excel in everything that I did, and that work ethic followed me all the way through col-lege. Awards here and leadership positions there, everything was set up just as I had planned. And once I settled into my social work major, aspirations to be become a therapist, a community organizer, and a university president fueled my fire. I found that the harder I worked, the greater I achieved. Against all odds, I never gave up. But somewhere along the way, I lost myself.

I began to question a lot of things that I had once been so sure about, like what my personal goals were and who I really wanted to be as a person. I had worked so hard that achievement became the focus of my life instead of my own goals. Then, seemingly all of a sudden, it was the middle of my last year in college and I had no idea what I wanted to do with my life any-more. I once was confident that I had a flawless resume and transcript, but I began to question whether it was good enough. So while in crisis mode, I went full speed ahead into the first opportunity that looked like a good idea. I found myself, again, chasing achievement and not my goals and what I truly wanted to achieve for myself. I was anxious to get my life "back on track" . . . whatever that meant.

Years later, grasping at whatever fleeting thoughts that came my way, I found myself in a master's program in a field that I had never been inter-ested in before, and at a school in an area with which I was even more unfa-miliar. I was six hours from my home in a town with four stop lights and not one familiar face. Sure, I knew that it was going to be an adjustment, but I had a "great opportunity" to get another notch on my belt of achievement, and I couldn't resist.

When my two best friends dropped me off at my new college, we cried bittersweet tears and reminisced about how far we had come together. When they left, their tears dried up, but mine did not. My tears flowed for days, which turned in to weeks and then eventually into months. I frequent-ly called my friends and parents back home, and they all reassured me that I was just going through a transition period. I wanted to believe them, but I knew that it was much deeper than that. By November, I was knee deep in course assignments and even deeper in sadness. The course work was not what I had expected, nor was it what I wanted. I had forgotten the things that I liked to do, along with any aspirations in and outside of school that I once had. It was nothing less than an out of body experience. For the first time in my life, I felt completely defeated.

I became angry with myself for feeling the way that I did. This was supposed to be my next stepping stone of achievement! I would tell myself that I needed to stop being so childish and weak. I kept telling myself that I was stronger than I was acting, and my frustration grew because it wasn't getting any better. I was embarrassed about how I was feeling, so I kept almost everything to myself. Every day felt like I had kicked a wall, talked myself out of the pain, and did it all over again the next day. At that point, I couldn't verbalize a single goal that I truly wanted to achieve. I had worked my whole life to beat the odds and to achieve. To go above and beyond. To surpass what people expected of me. But in the process, ironically, the one thing that defeated me . . . was me.

I had gotten so caught up in chasing achievements that I had lost my own goals along the way. This led me directly into a physical and mental space that was unsafe and that I never thought that I would be in. It wasn't until that experience that I realized that achievement is only worth the work if I felt personally fulfilled at the end of it all. And add to do this, I had to learn how to reflect on what I wanted, to validate my personal goals, and to truly believe that the accomplishment of my goals would contribute to the greater good.

For the first time in my life, I finally understood the difference between giving up and moving on. There are very few decisions that we make in life that are irreversible. If something doesn't work, we have to give ourselves permission to accept it as a learning experience and head back to the drawing board. When we give up, we retreat. We try to forget what happened and we get stuck in the mistakes of our past. But when we move on, we reflect on our actions and their outcomes. We forgive ourselves, and go forward with confidence.

Far too often, gifted women of color endure much more than the average individual. We are told that we have to be twice as good as men simply because we are women, on top of already having to be three times as good because we are of color. So we push ourselves to exceed expectations, known and unknown, because we know that we have to and because we know that we can. As women of color, we will encounter pressure to achieve whether we are ready or not. And though we are capable, how often and to what expense do we push ourselves, as I did, to the brink without considering the risk of losing ourselves and the consequences that entails in the search for achievement?

As a wise woman and friend so elegantly stated, "We must never strive for achievement for achievement's sake. Meaningless pursuit of ideals is unfulfilling, exhausting, and depleting." We must strive toward the achievement of our own goals because when we lose sight of our personal goals, we lose ourselves. And most importantly, we must never give up, but always give ourselves permission to move on. So how did I rediscover myself? I did so by talking to others, setting realistic goals that matter to me, and finding peace in just relaxing.

Jamye Hardy is a Counselor and Coordinator for 1st Year Programs at American Baptist College in Nashville, TN. She earned her bachelor's and master's degrees in Social Work at Western Kentucky University and is a licensed master social worker in Tennessee. Jamye was the recipient of the 2015–2016 Outstanding Graduate Student Award for the WKU Department of Social Work as well as for the College of Health and Human Services. Jamye was also the 2015–2016 recipient of the Young Woman of Achievement Award from the Bowling Green Human Rights Commission. Her current research areas of interest are benefits of undergraduate student volunteerism, mental health initiatives on college campuses, and improving access to therapy services for African Americans.

CHAPTER 25

NEVER PUT ROCKS ON AN EAGLE'S BACK

Breshawn N. Harris

> **Key Challenges:** extended family, single-parent family, poverty, deficit thinking

The eagle metaphor is used across many cultures as a symbol that represents courage, strength, self-actualization, and independence. When eagles fly, they soar high with spectacular ease and to heights unknown. The eagle metaphor can also be used to describe the characteristics of an individual beginning to carve his or her niche in life. As a teenager, I was that eagle who was attempting to soar to great heights, but life's challenges, disappointments, and heartaches made it difficult for me to see how I could spread my wings and fly.

I grew up in South Phoenix, Arizona. My father chose to live an unhealthy lifestyle and be absent from my life, so, my brother and I lived with our mother, but our mother's lifestyle choices forced us to have to live with our maternal grandmother. The transition to my grandmother's home was very difficult. Her income was fixed and limited, our resources were few

Gumbo for the Soul, pages 145–149
Copyright © 2017 by Information Age Publishing

and far between, and family dysfunction was the norm. As a matter of fact, the dysfunction was so bad; there were many nights that the police were called to the home. Neighbors witnessed the endless arguments and fights. The dysfunctional drama ventured into my school life as well—my schoolmates and teachers were privy to our dysfunction and negative "surprise visits" from my mother. The dysfunction and embarrassment became the norm for the next 11 years of my life. But there were people who served as blessings in the many storms that I endured—people who were committed to my success and dedicated to my spiritual development and the development of my character. These individuals saw something special within me and poured into my spirit, all of which helped me to combat all of the pressure and stress that I weathered as a result of my family life.

As a gifted student in middle school and junior high, I always earned the distinction of being on the school's honor roll. It was not uncommon for me to record superior grades of A's and B's in all of my classes, while playing sports, performing community service, and participating in weekly church activities. It was actually a breath of fresh air to be engaged in extracurricular activities as they served as a diversion from the stress of my home life. My elementary teachers were compassionate to my situation and understood my feelings, and they were not willing to see me fail. Whenever an opportunity was presented, the teachers encouraged me, stayed on my case, prayed for me, presented me with academic enrichment opportunities, and became cheerleaders at the sporting events my family members did not attend.

It is important to know that despite the hand one is dealt in life, it is how one chooses to play those cards to become and remain a winner in the game of life when even the hand given was "bad." So I made it my mission to surround myself with individuals who spoke positively to me and about me, nurtured my spirit, my mind, and fed my soul. I surrounded myself with friends and people who were also trying to defy the odds of their life's challenges to reach their personal goals. None of this removed the pain that I lived with at home. But, I refused to allow my situation to serve as a crutch. As a gifted student, I knew that I had the potential to go to heights that I can only imagine.

While in high school, the challenges and problems surrounding my home life intensified. The family dysfunction reached new levels when words exchanged between my mother and grandmother caused division and strife within the family. The stress often sent my elderly grandmother to the hospital and the resentment I had toward my mother served as another stressor for me. I felt like I was my grandmother's protector, so I would not allow anyone to jeopardize her health, happiness, and sanity, all the while, my grades never faltered and I continued to stay focused, so that I could plan a life that was different than what I experienced and was accustomed to. As time progressed, my love for sports and extracurricular activities increased, as did the time I was able to spend at home 'protecting' my beloved granny.

My volleyball coach told me that I was an exceptional player and in addition to my academic ability, my playing volleyball may assist in my earning a college scholarship. So, I knew I had to continue playing sports because, they served, not only as a diversion to the stress of my home life; they also served as advancement toward my future. My coach's statements also peaked my interest. Since the sixth grade, my number one goal was to attend Howard University, a Historically Black College and University in Washington, DC. But since I came from a financially meager background, it was close to impossible to afford four years of tuition at a private school more than 2,000 miles away from home. To achieve this goal, I made personal goals while in elementary school which included surrounding myself with those who saw my potential, spoke positively about my existence, and connect with individuals who believed in me. The balance was necessary to counter everything that was waiting at home.

As I continued my high school journey, I excelled academically, progressed athletically, and began to understand who I was as a young woman, but I continued to experience heartache on a personal level. During my four years of high school, no one in my family attended any of my athletic competitions or saw me participate in any school function. I longed for their support during competitions or extracurricular events. It was difficult, painful, and sometimes, embarrassing that no one from my family was in the stands to watch me play sports and receive awards during parent night. But thankfully, the individuals with whom I chose to surround myself stood in the gap and served as a surrogate family and cheered me on. At times, your family is comprised of those with whom you make a bond, who provide you with support, who love you unconditionally, and treat you like their own. Although you do not share the same DNA or share the same blood, it does not mean someone is not family. Family is devised by the unconditional love and support they give.

During the fall of my senior year, I communicated my college plans to my high school guidance counselor. With excitement and joy, I boldly professed, "I would like to attend Howard University in Washington, DC." I felt my grades were excellent and my academic background prepared me for the rigor of Howard University. My counselor had limited knowledge of Howard as she had only counseled one other student who enrolled in Howard University. Jay,[1] who graduated from my high school with a 4.2, dropped to a 3.0 during his freshman year at Howard. His GPA was .5 points higher than mine and my guidance counselor felt that if "Jay" made such a drop in his grade point average, then surely, I would do the same. My counselor attempted to dissuade me from applying because she did not believe my academic background was sufficient enough to be considered a prospective student at the institution. She went further to state that she did not believe my academic intelligence would survive among the ranks of the more academically astute students who possessed a 3.9 GPA or higher. Immediately, my self-esteem plummeted and without academic justification, she instantly devalued my potential to thrive at Howard University. I was hurt, stunned, upset, and felt worthless—my childhood dream of attending Howard was shattered in a matter of minutes. I went home, cried to my grandmother and told her what happened. I thought that she would go up to my school and tell my counselor a thing or two about the words that I felt were so unkind. But that did not happen. My grandmother did the complete opposite—she told me a thing or two... she said, "Baby, it doesn't matter what that woman tells you because she can never put rocks on an eagle's back. You are destined for greatness and nothing anyone says to you will prevent you from soaring high. You will use her comments in one or two ways. You will either believe what she tells you, or use her statement to help you get to your destination." At that time, I did not quite understand the wisdom and metaphor my grandmother shared, because I was too angry to comprehend the analogy. But years later, I realized that my grandmother saw me as an eagle; as a child and as a young woman. It did not matter what this counselor spoke for my life, because the rocks (i.e., the counselor's comments) would not stop me from achieving my goal.

In summary, had I listened to the words of my high school guidance counselor, the 'rocks' that she placed on my 'eagle back' would have prevented me from achieving the greatness that was already ordered for my life. By tuning out the counselor and listening to my late grandmother, I soared like an eagle to great heights unknown! This eagle (a) received a full athletic scholarship to play volleyball at Howard University; (b) made the Dean's List (minimum GPA of 3.5) three times while at Howard; (c) interned at Black Entertainment Television (B.E.T); (d) interned and worked for the Million Man March; (e) graduated with a BA in Communications; (f) interned and worked for the 1996 Summer Olympics in Atlanta, GA; (g) was inducted in Howard University's Athletic Hall of Fame in 2007 for volleyball (one of the first women to be inducted in the sport in the history of the institution); (e) graduated in 2014 with my doctorate in Higher Education Administration; and (f) in 2015 was enshrined in the Mid-Eastern Athletic Hall of Fame for volleyball. I was one of four inductees, three of whom were professional athletes, to receive this prestigious award.

In essence, life may deal you a pretty bad hand and you may question why things are happening to you. However, you must keep it all in perspective. It is imperative to remember, you are gifted, you are important, and you matter. Focus on the positive things, and make a plan to work hard and not give up. Surround yourself with people who support you, pour into your spirit, speak life into your soul, and see the greatness within you. Never allow your circumstances to be your crutch in life. Instead, use them as a source to propel you to great heights! People get what they expect out of life, so make high expectations and be relentless in your pursuit to achieve each of your goals. If opportunity does not knock, who says you can't build your own door? Greatness is in you as you are designed to soar like the eagle you are. Why? Because no one can ever put rocks on an eagle's back! You are that eagle!!

Breshawn N. Harris, PhD, is a scholar, educator, and advocate for HBCUs. She is a secondary educator and licensed professional school counselor in Phoenix, AZ. Dr. Harris has worked more than 16 years in education and has a passion to assist students to enroll, persist, and graduate from college, with an emphasis on HBCUs. Dr. Harris is the Founder of Legacy Educational Consulting where she consults with high school students to assist in their college planning. Dr. Harris's research includes: Black Male Achievement, HBCUs, first generation college students, academic and social integration, minority male mentoring programs, high school bridge programs, closing the achievement gap, and college career and readiness.

You have within you all you need to become the
GREATEST . . . like a rich, savory, pot of Gumbo,
stirred with love. In time, with every experience, you
will soon become the woman you were born to be.

—Joy Lawson Davis

CHAPTER 26

BENDABLE, YET UNBREAKABLE

Tiffany Hollis

Key Challenges: single-parent home, poverty, behavioral issues, underachievement, deficit thinking, first generation college, domestic violence

The saying "How you start is not how you end up" emphasizes that despite challenges and complexities one may face, their fate is not sealed and he or she can overcome adversity and live productive lives. According to the history of my family, I should not have attained the level of education that I have thus far. But starting life with disadvantages does not mean that one's destiny is defined and unchangeable.

My mother dropped out of high school and by the age of 21, she already had two children out of wedlock, by two absentee fathers. My mother worked hard to provide for us and even lived with her mother for a while until she was able to get on her feet as a young single mother with a limited education. We eventually moved from Connecticut to South Carolina to live with my great grandmother, who we affectionately called Big Mama.

Gumbo for the Soul, pages 153–158
Copyright © 2017 by Information Age Publishing

After a while, my mother made the decision to move out of the house with my great grandmother to show and prove that she could make it without the support of my grandmother and my great grandmother.

Although my mother worked hard, with only one income, she constantly struggled to provide the most basic needs—there were times when we didn't have any food, or the hot water was cut off. Like many others born into generational poverty, education seemed to be my vehicle to move out of poverty, but I knew that I had obstacles to overcome—memories of the sporadic, yet rampant incidents of domestic violence that my mother experienced at the hands of her boyfriend, the emotional un-attachment of my mother (although not intentional, she was dealt with so many of her own issues, she often ignored the grim reality), not knowing my father, and just sheer fear of the unknown as mom sought to provide a nurturing and caring environment in the place we called 'home'.

School became a safe space for me, but it also became a place where I felt invisible. Not many people paid attention to the young African American girl with an attitude, a smart mouth, and who would fight anyone (including teachers) if they even looked at her in the wrong manner. In fact, many teachers just wanted me out of their classroom, so the referrals and the suspensions added up. I would get suspended from school only to engage in risky behaviors within the neighborhood in which I lived. I was an angry girl who lashed out.

My mother worked several jobs and was often unaware of the things that I did, but she would eventually find out—every time. Yep, when you live in a small town, word travels. It was not until I met my mentor or should I say my 'match' that my trajectory in life began to change and I started to focus more on the role that education would play in helping me to overcome the obstacles in my life.

Having moved from the North to the South, I experienced racism first hand in elementary school. I remember getting into trouble in Kindergarten for 'talking too much'. I was able to read above grade level, but when I would ask my teachers questions, I would be scolded so would wait to ask Big Mama the questions when I got home. It was not until we switched schools after moving out of Big Mama's, house that I met Mrs. Terri Bridges. Mrs. Bridges was a God send—she listened to everything I said, hugged me every day, and even moved me to the third grade reading group to challenge me because once she noticed that I was just "too darn smart for my own good". She actually showed me that she cared.

I was classified as Gifted and Talented in third grade. The advocacy of several teachers, including Mrs. Bridges, ensured that I got tested and I spent most of my time in advanced classes from that point forward. My mom had no clue what went on at school because I would forge her signature so that I could participate in and take advantage of programs and opportunities. Mom tried to be as involved as she could, but the amount of time and energy she could devote to my siblings and me was limited. Mom was not at home much and when she was, there was often dysfunction and chaos due to domestic situations with her ex-husband (the father of my younger siblings).

Around the time when I was in fourth grade, I experienced the first turning point in my trajectory—things started to go downhill. I got bussed to the Gifted and Talented Program at Luther Vaughn Elementary School where Mr. Luscious Jones, an African American male, was the principal; He did not take any mess and was even harder on the African American children who attended the school because he had high expectations for us. I remember getting referred to the office because I argued with one of my White classmates in the Gifted and Talented program who laughed, made comments about me being poor and not being able to afford a trip the class was scheduled to take; my home school handled disciplinary matters, so, although I received the referral at Luther Vaughn, my home school dealt with my disciplinary consequences. I was suspended for being disrespectful and sent home. No one ever talked to me to find out why my behavior had abruptly changed or why I was getting into so much trouble. From that point forward, I got into arguments daily that eventually became physical. I even talked back and made threats to teachers but little did they know that I was crying out for help because the situation at home was getting worse and I lost focus. I began to get into more and more arguments and fights, which led to more and more suspensions. Despite my absences, I would come back, ace the tests and even be prepared for the next lesson because I had read ahead during my suspension, or as I liked to call it, my "spare time."

The fights, defiance, and disrespect continued well into middle school. It was as if my reputation preceded me because there were teachers who would write me off before I even opened my mouth in their class. I had been labeled as the "bad girl" with a "smart mouth" who was a class clown, but there were a few teachers who tried to challenge me and some who cared about me.

There was no such thing as Gifted and Talented in the middle school. Instead, one could be placed on either the college prep, or general track. Even though my behavior was atrocious, I still managed to make straight "A" honor roll, which stunned many of the teachers with whom I interacted. It soon became evident to them that I was smart and eventually, I was placed in advanced classes and became the only minority student in many of my advanced classes over the years.

In order to be successful, I had to conform to the dominant standards and start to embrace my "new" identity. My inner conflict continued as I struggled with being the honor student I *had become* during the day and the stereotypical student on welfare growing up without a father that others *expected me to be* once I returned to my home each day. During the next few years, I grappled with where I fit in—I juggled my workload at school, helping my mother with adult responsibilities at home, all while upholding my reputation of being that "hard" girl that did not take any mess.

I met my mentor, Dr. Cleveland, who was also my guidance counselor, while in middle school. One day, she pulled me out of class to talk with me because she had noticed that I was getting into a lot of trouble. I told her that I did not want to talk to her because I did not know her like that and that she should mind her business. But she didn't give up . . . she called me to her office the next day and offered to share a positive quote with me. She provided me with several quotes and suggested that I journal as a means of "getting things out". I would go to her office a few times each week to write, read, eat, and just listen to her talk. I did not say much at first—I even told her to just give up. She knew that I was used to people giving up on me, so instead she did the opposite and told me that she was not going to give up on me or go anywhere because she saw potential in me. She also told me that I was destined for greatness and reminded me that as long as I embraced whom I was and whose I was, that I could achieve anything despite my shortcomings.

At first, it was hard for her to break down the barrier that I had built around myself. She placed me in numerous after school activities and would take me home each day, so I no longer had the excuse that I did not have a ride. She also placed me into other events and activities and even went, as far as to place me into summer programs that she believed would nurture the potential she noticed. She even began to teach me how to talk to adults in a more respectful manner and how to convert my anger into positive behaviors. Most importantly, she taught me how to honor and respect my mother and the decisions that she made and reminded me that my mother was just that, my mother, despite the issues and decisions she made.

My mentor played an intricate part in my life as I matured and I began to slowly transform and become a better person. She gave me information about college preparatory programs, nominated me for awards, and often would register me for various contests and opportunities. She took a vested interest in me and helped me channel my anger into positive outcomes. For example, she strategically arranged an internship—with her, no less, through a program called YOU (Youth Opportunities Unlimited) at Limestone College in Gaffney. During the internship, I was provided with a summer job and given a stipend. Being at the school with her and the principal, Dr. Carol McFadden, who was also an African American female, allowed me to see firsthand how schools operated. Consequently, it also gave her a chance to keep me under her supervision and away from my 18-year-old boyfriend who was, at the time, a known drug dealer. Somehow, she knew I had been sneaking to see him and spend more time with him, than a child my age should.

At that time, I experienced another change in my life, but this time things were beginning to look up and my trajectory was being altered. This woman, who was strategically and divinely placed in my life, helped me to transform into the person that she knew I had the potential to be. It was during this time that I saw the "roots" being positioned to provide me with the foundational supports that I needed to become grounded. Being grounded reduced the likelihood of me drifting away from future goals and aspirations.

Dr. Cleveland was a clear example of a caring adult who invested time, energy, and hope in me because she believed in me. She worked with me throughout high school, placed me in activities, checked in and checked up on me, helped me process through tough situations, encouraged me to attend church, signed me up for plays, attended my awards ceremonies and events, and would take me places with her and her family. I longed and cried out for positive attention from a caring adult, and Dr. Cleveland provided what I needed. Over the years, she and I developed a strong bond. I slowly began to change and I no longer got into fights, got suspended, and I even got comments such as a "pleasure to teach" on my reports.

By this time, some of the aspects of my home life had improved, but it was hard putting on a façade and pretending that everything was ok. Home was the one place that was supposed to be full of love, safety, security, and support, but it just wasn't there. Furthermore, I still encountered negativity at school as well, but I still tried to maintain academically so that I could go away to college. College for me was the only way out.

It is my hope that this account conveys the strength, resourcefulness, and resilience of an African American first generation of college female and the obstacles and barriers that I encountered and had to overcome. I hope that it is through my account that youth realize that they can overcome obstacles and become successful. I hope my words will support, challenge, and motivate students to move beyond the obstacles and aspire to reach their goals. I am a prime example of how hard work and playing by the rules can defy the odds, even if you are a student from a low-income background who lives in a society in which the odds are steeply stacked against you.

I have learned that my professional identity and my personal identity cannot be separated. I realized that although I am still that young lady from the "ghetto," I have to think, act, and conduct myself within the *other* world because of the status and privilege that I now possess as a result of higher education. Who am I? I am more than just a female doctoral student. I am a first-generation doctoral student who is a potential role model for all children, showing them that anything is possible. I am a person who works hard to ensure that I make myself better by my own standards in hopes that my efforts will inspire others to overcome adversity and persist in spite of obstacles in their paths.

Tiffany Hollis is a doctoral candidate in Curriculum and Instruction with a focus on Urban Education at the University of North Carolina at Charlotte. She has a clear and strong commitment to diversity, equity, and social justice with over 13 years in the education setting as a social justice educator with a special education background. Her research interests include understanding the cultural and contextual (e.g., home, school, and community) factors and processes that contribute to resilience in economically, socially, and culturally diverse children and adolescents, and the families and communities in which they live. She has over 13 years of experience in addressing risk factors facing urban, economically disadvantaged adolescents of color, including homeless youth, youth in foster care and out-of-home care, youth in the juvenile justice system, youth who have mental health issues, and youth with special needs.

CHAPTER 27

BEING CALLED A NIGGER

Reflections as a Student in Teacher Preparation

Amina Humphrey

Key Challenges: racism, peer pressures, affective issues

I was bussed eight miles from my Black agrarian community of Oak Grove, Arkansas, plus or minus 75 folks, to Lockesburg, Arkansas, population 600. With one blink of an eye, you'd miss those two or three stop signs. But I never missed the context of the town or the local school that I attended, which was majority White, mainly conservative, and mostly racist. In elementary and middle school, most of my teachers were White, except for Mr. Talley and Mr. Forest. These two men were teachers who were both relics of segregation's past and present. They taught my father, aunts, and uncles in the old Black schools from the '60s–'70s.

But it's the '80s, and it's my time now! I like Public Enemy, George Clinton, Prince, Michael Jackson, Jheri curls minus the moisturizer, *Soul Train*, and African medallions paired with colorful spandex tights. I was also "colorful" in

Gumbo for the Soul, pages 159–163
Copyright © 2017 by Information Age Publishing
All rights of reproduction in any form reserved.

thought and action, and progressive in my youthful politics. I was a different kind of child; I knew it; I liked it, and I loved my Blackness! I wore this Blackness as my ideology, as a shield to openly defy the White supremacist context of Lockesburg and its beloved school, home of the blue darter.

Furthermore, segregation's past influenced the Black/White interpersonal dynamics of small-town Southern USA, but in spite of it all, I had much love for Mrs. Homes, my White and "make-up challenged" language arts teacher. She loved her tight-fitted Lee's jeans and her multiple shades of purple, green, and pink eye shadows. Her eye adornment was even outlandish for the gaudy 80s. But that's what appealed to me about Mrs. Homes, her use of color suggested, "I am beyond conservative small town USA folkways. I am an individual!" I laugh now as an adult at my romanticized childish views and subsequent assumptions, particularly as Mrs. Homes began peeling off her mask.

And Mrs. Homes taught my favorite subjects, anything to do with words! I excelled in her language arts and journalism classes. She knew I loved reading and writing. I was one of those kids who finished my work early, and then I would sit at my desk and read quietly until the bell rang. It was always some sort of classic. I relished Stamps, Arkansas' homegrown-mother-aunt-sister-in-my-head Maya Angelou's *I Know Why the Caged Bird Sings* or Alice Walker's *The Color Purple*. They were the "comfort food" for my soul with covers worn to oblivion and pages faded from "everyday use." The written word was my friend, my only friend as a child, tween, and teen.

In fact, Mrs. Homes knew about my passion for words. Whenever, I finished my work, she allowed me the "privilege" of editing the newspaper and yearbook copy. It brought me great joy to be the expert and to receive praise from that favorite teacher of mine, Mrs. Homes. (And based on my skills as a writer, I would later attend the Arkansas High School Press Association, win awards for copy, photography, and art, and meet our then-governor, Bill Clinton.)

And one day, Mrs. Homes announced in our English class that we would be reading *Huckleberry Finn* by Mark Twain. Now as someone who appreciated classics, particularly the literature of the South, I was not a fan of Mr. Samuel Langhorne Clemmons because I heard he used the word *nigger* in his writings. I am not a fan of the word *nigger* in general because my colonized, self-loathing, Black father and his ignorant, hostile, White German wife called me *nigger* at their leisure at home, and frequently in anger. I had and still have a contentious relationship with *nigger*, to say the least.

You can imagine my trepidation as Mrs. Homes placed us in literature circles, and we began taking turns reading *Huckleberry Finn* out loud. There were enough students for roughly four literature circles, with three or four students per circle, but since there were only three Blacks in the class; we were split as there was not enough of us to be represented in each group.

The books were passed out to each student. There was no context to reading *Huckleberry Finn*, the protocol for the day and every day until the book was finished was "sit down; grab your books; get into your circle; take turns reading, and answer questions for homework." This was robotic pedagogy, but the mundaneness of it all did not deter my feelings of anxiety on day one and each subsequent day of having to listen to my White non-fluent classmates as they struggled to read Twain. As a matter of fact, it was painful. I will never forget as Aaron began to read, trying to blend the word *nigger*, and once he comprehended the meaning of the word, he looked at me with a sheepish-grin, as if to say, "I'm sorry." At that moment, I felt beyond awkward as I had to listen to the prolonged reading by Eric and others. I kept sending mental signals to Mrs. Homes to intervene, to just do something to stop this lesson . . . do anything but to continue it. But Mrs. Homes sat in oblivion at her desk, graded papers, and prepped for her favorite class, journalism.

I remember the day in great detail. We finish the first reading of *Huckleberry Finn* in our literature circles. The bell rings for recess. Frank races outside to play kickball. Unlike me, he does not love to learn, but he loves his country music, his confederate flag, his deer-hunting rifle, his chewing tobacco, and he absolutely loves the word *nigger*. Mrs. Homes adores him, but I don't understand why.

On the way to the playground, Frank stops suddenly and calls me a *nigger*. He sneers, snorts, and laughs sarcastically. I stand stoically as he and the other White classmates just laugh and run excitedly to the field to play kickball. In that moment, I experience the residuals of Twain's Huckleberry Finn's *nigger* in a White supremacist educational context.

And on that day, my love for Mrs. Homes ends. I "hate" Frank, but I "hate" my English teacher Mrs. Homes even more. She let this happen! Frank makes no apologies for his words or for being a racist, nor does Mrs. Homes. Silence and dismissiveness emanate from her. The realization is overwhelming for this 12-year-old girl. Mrs. Homes condones the usage of *nigger*, towards me. I thought she gave a damn about me!

This was one of the greatest educational lessons I ever learned from childhood, this experience from over 30 years ago. Mrs. Homes peeled off her mask, including that "beloved" gaudy purple, green, and pink eye shadow, to reveal the ideology and power of White supremacy. To her, I was a *nigger*, and her silence confirmed it. And I suffered with silent reverberating admonitions of "Fuck you, Mrs. Homes! Fuck you, Frank! And fuck you too Mark Twain Samuel Langhorne Clemons by default!"

Frank was not punished for calling me *nigger*. His White privilege was supported by Mrs. Homes, the school, and the town. Furthermore, to reinforce the status quo, they approved of White supremacy as a tool for learning as we continued to read Twain, one of the "greats" in the literary canon. My raced and gendered position was to know "my place," while simultaneously having to develop the resiliency to not allow the pain of White supremacy to shift my heart to hate.

CRITICAL REFLECTION AND TRANSFORMATION

They say when you know better, you do better! I cannot speak on Homes or Frank and their evolvement as critical and reflective learners, but I can speak about mine. I no longer say "fuck you to Homes, Frank, or Twain." Everything serves a purpose. What did I learn from this experience? How will it help me in the future?

Fast forward and 30-plus years later, I am now an English, journalism, special education teacher. I am now a master of African American studies. I am now a PhD with a race and ethnic studies focus. I am now a qualitative researcher. I am now a professor of African American studies and education who has trained hundreds of teachers in graduate teacher education programs in Southern California over the last decade in the areas of social justice, race, diversity, culture, inclusion, and racism. I am no longer in Lockesburg, Arkansas, hearing the word *nigger* on the playground. As I walk the halls of schools in South Los Angeles, I hear the word in classrooms. I hear students refer to each other as *nigga*, and they sometimes refer to the teacher as "my nigga."

I have flashbacks to my childhood, the experience with Frank and Homes, the 12-year-old girl who experienced racial injustice. But the word is now pervasive . . . transracial, transcultural, global, but consistently problematic. This incident from over three decades ago is always in the forefront of my mind as I train teachers on how to address sensitive, controversial, and diverse issues in public schools, particularly the word *nigger*.

In my post-observational debriefings with in-service teachers, I ask them, "Why do you allow students to use this word?" Their answers vary, but the most common answer is "that's just how students talk." Teachers feel like they are racial and cultural outsiders, and they don't have a right to correct students, particularly African American students. But as a racial and cultural insider, I am still the child who was called and labeled *nigger* at school. What would the child in me want teachers to know? Thus, I began addressing the word *nigger* in my curriculum, as a part of courageous conversations about race and racism. In preparing for this lesson, I merge my identities, the child who was called *nigger*, the former English teacher, and the professor who now teaches African American studies and in-service teachers. What have I learned as my experiences have grown personally and professionally? How do I teach about *nigger*? What I do know is that context, discussion, criticism, and reflection are essential. I offer these suggestions for teaching:

1. Analyze the origin of the word;
2. Provide context for how the word is being used during specific time periods;
3. Discuss the historical and contemporary usages and meanings;
4. Facilitate critical discussions and reflections;
5. Describe personal experiences with the word beyond the assigned text; and
6. Critique systemic forms of racial oppression in America and the emergence of *nigger.*

In conclusion, I do not offer a forgiveness tale about Frank, Homes, or Twain. I do not offer you a critique of Twain and his rationale for using *nigger* in his writings. I offer no stance for the familial, social, and/or cultural usage of *nigger* or *nigga* in American society or the global community. But in providing my own experience with the *nigger* from childhood to teacher education preparation programs, I do offer insights about the (a) pedagogical considerations of this word; (b) its effect on children; (c) those who continue to use curricula as a tool for White supremacist pedagogy; and (d) the role that teachers play in mentoring and supporting children's emotional growth.

Amina Humphrey, PhD, is a writer, artist, activist, English and special education teacher, qualitative researcher, and Visiting Assistant Professor in the African American Studies Department at Loyola Marymount University in Los Angeles, CA. She is a graduate of UCLA's African American Studies Department and the Graduate School of Education and Information Studies where she completed her MA and PhD. Dr. Amina Humphrey has worked in teacher education preparation in Southern California for over a decade and educated hundreds of pre-service and in-service teachers, administrators, and doctoral candidates in South Los Angeles in the art of teaching and researching for social justice. Her social justice research agenda is race, gender, sexuality, qualitative research, and the social and cultural contexts of education. This includes: art as pedagogy and activism, culturally-relevant pedagogy, home and school literacy practices, critical media literacy and African Americans, social reproduction and the school-to-prison pipeline, teachers and participatory action research, African Americans and rural education, racial and gender socialization of Black girls, Black women and education, and Black women and sexuality. Dr. Amina Humphrey is the founder of African Diasporic Activism with an emphasis on Sub-Saharan African refugee children's rights.

CHAPTER 28

LIKE A LEAF IN THE WIND

Growing up Gifted in Turkey
Without Privileges and Capital

Zeynep Isik-Ercan

> **Key Challenges:** poverty, low teacher expectations, behavioral challenges, lack of academic challenge, procrastination, time management, language as ELL student

In this narrative, I discuss my experience as a gifted child growing up in 1980s Turkey and later as an adult in the United States. I write about how my young adulthood and present day exceptionality have been shaped by my personal traits as well as challenging socioeconomic and sociocultural contexts. I describe the role of nurturing adults and other opportunities encountered along the way. These opportunities helped pave the way to success, despite the lack of an organized plan or clear path to academia. Today, I am an accomplished associate professor of early childhood education at Rowan University in New Jersey.

Gumbo for the Soul, pages 165–170

I was a child who uttered her first words—"Chai!" (I want tea!)—at 6-months and walked as a 9-month infant. My mother always told the story of my early "giftedness" with awe. One day, returning from school, my brother found me crying in front of the apartment. He realized I had found my way to our apartment by crawling and passing a small street. At that time, I was 7-months old, and my babysitter had left me sleeping alone while she went to do shopping. An exceptional beginning was clearly seen. However, life for the younger child of two working class parents in Turkey in the late 1970s and early 1980s did not present many opportunities for my parents or me. Gifted education as a field was too new and was mostly in the form of private education. Usually, only the children of highly ranked officials or rich people in urban hubs like Istanbul, Ankara, or Izmir would be privileged enough to have access to private schools or instructors. Both my parents grew up in a small village by the Black Sea, and their parents were farmers. With their parents' support, they managed to get a public high school education—among first in their village—and they eventually landed two officer jobs with the Ministry of Finance. Yet, they struggled with finances and survival as two young parents with rural backgrounds, and dealing with health issues and raising two young children added more stress. Given this context, there was no clear academic path set by others for me or my brother to follow.

Because my parents kept getting new appointments or promotions, we moved across the country several times. My parents had to find full-time care for me during school hours, but babysitting was a low-level, insulting job to many back then, so many mothers just stayed home to care for their children and most of the babysitters kept neglecting me, and eventually, they were fired or quit. As a result, unlike many of my peers, I went to a preschool when I was 3-years-old. The school was the first preschool in the small Black Sea town we lived in and had a hefty tuition.

As a toddler, I always showed excitement and initiative for everything. I was always pro-active because I did not recognize my underprivileged background. This, at times, created tensions with teachers. In my annual report card, one teacher wrote, "She always wants to be the leader, is jealous and capricious." However, children from more privileged backgrounds were treated differently. The privileged children in the preschool were often given chances to perform poems and talks at state events, national holidays, and parades. For one national holiday ceremony, the teachers' favorite students failed to memorize a long poem. When I jumped in and recited the whole poem, which I had learned just by listening to the others practice, the teachers gave me the opportunity to recite it publicly. I was the tiniest of the 4-year olds, so that day in the ceremony they had to place a stool under my feet so I could reach the microphone. I remember being applauded by the crowd, among them, a tourist shouting: "Bravo, Turk!"

I remember my mother always supporting my autonomy. I was never encouraged to be a submissive future wife and, as a girl, I found both my parents absolutely determined that I would further my education. They raised me to be a strong-willed person, and despite class based limitations and financial struggles, I never was made to feel as if I were unworthy of a bright future.

My love of reading began incidentally. I would play with and tear off the pages of my older brother's alphabet book when he began first grade at age seven, which was the expected grade level for reading in Turkey. One day, after I turned four, I made a nurse's cap from scrap paper and showed it to my parents. They liked my cap but were shocked to notice that I had written "Hemesipe" (an incorrect version of hemsire or nurse in Turkish) on it. They discovered that I was already reading and writing! I was immediately given newspapers, book pages, and bills to "verify" I was the one who wrote that. I was able to read them all and even upside down! That day changed my life.

At the time, Turkey did not have a big children's books market or well-functioning public libraries; thus, children with high reading abilities would read serious works by intellectuals, with few or no illustrations, and non-fiction. Encyclopedias were also popular. We had big, heavy bound copies of all sorts. At the age of six, I vividly recall reading about the sequoia trees in California and imagining visiting the Taj Mahal and the Pyramids.

Due to lack of finances for child care, my brother and I would spend our summers with our grandparents and would rarely see our parents during those three months. Lonely summers in the village were perfect for soaking up the books that belonged to my uncle, who was a teacher and stored his unwanted books in my maternal grandmother's house. Yet, whenever I stayed with my paternal grandparents, who did not own even one book and were in their late 70s, my grandmother often got anxious seeing me reading books all the time. She would say, "You are going to have mental retardation from this many readings!" To her surprise, when I went to wedding receptions, I would read. When I went to picnics or hospitals, I would read. Books always came in handy when I felt extremely sad over missing my family. Reading was the only thing that lifted me and showed me other worlds and possibilities.

Two weeks into kindergarten, I was bored with the naked classroom with its rows of long tables and sight words. Drawing lines and circles became mundane, and I began writing stories in class. Surprised, my teacher took me to the principal's office, and with my parents present, the principal determined I would be sent to the second grade classroom, a leap of two grade levels. This decision, while recognizing my exceptionality, caused me to be the youngest and always smallest child in my classes. I also missed the formal language and content knowledge instruction provided in the lower grades. All of a sudden, I, an ever impulsive and talkative child, faced increased social and behavioral expectations. Needless to say, I caused some problems.

As the youngest in class, I could never sit still. After five minutes of sitting in my desk, impulsivity would hit, and I would feel as if I were being suffocated. When I craved more extracurricular activities and became restless, a teacher offered me the opportunity to sing into a microphone in the principal's office during recess. The teachers were patient. They switched seats when I became too talkative. They observed good progress even when the product was not there. And they trusted my abilities when I seemed detached from any goal or organization for my studies. As I reflect on my presence in class, I think I would have been placed in a special education class for a learning disability if I were attending school in present day Turkey or the United States. Instead, I had teachers who attributed my impulsivity, talkativeness, and attention problems to high intelligence.

While my teachers' flexibility accommodated some of my needs, their care did not address the vulnerabilities hidden behind my achievement level, such as the tendency to make careless mistakes from rushing the work—grammar, spelling and handwriting difficulties stemming from grade acceleration; forgetfulness; and difficulty with organization and planning tasks. I often procrastinated because I struggled with structuring my academic studies, goal setting, and time management.

Sundays were always stressful. It was the time when I remembered my missing homework, realized that I had projects due the next day, discovered I had lost materials that would be checked by teacher or that there were torn or worn book pages. I often dragged my feet when faced with work and would usually begin studying Sunday late afternoon or early evening. My parents would say, "If you work hard and achieve success, this will be because of your determination and work. We will not spoon feed you." As such, they rarely checked my homework. My overly hardworking and organized mother did not empathize with my situation; after all, my brother was the tidiest, most organized, most careful child a parent could want.

During the majority of my school life, including college, this pattern continued. I would lose everything, forget my homework, and avoid work until the last minute. To this day, I remember the sense of embarrassment I felt every Monday morning in fourth grade, my fear of an angry math teacher's reaction to my negligence, and praying for a miracle so I would be passed by when the teacher was checking the homework. Yet, I would be able to perform well in school due to my memory, reasoning abilities, verbal strengths, and my enjoyment of tackling timed tests.

While testing usually prevents many gifted children from accessing opportunities, my love of multiple-choice tests opened some doors in the Turkish context. Based on the results of a centralized placement exam, I was placed in a boarding high school in Ankara, the capital city. The school focused on finance, and besides taking 17 classes—some of which were occupational—I also attended the college preparation school in the evenings and all weekends. My parents paid for the preparation school, and the government paid for the boarding school tuition. However, due to the lack of academic guidance, the choices I made for the future were never intentional.

I soon realized I did not want to deal with tax law, accounting, or finances. I thought I was going to apply for law school, which was my father's aspiration for me. Instead, as I was trying to select a major in teaching Turkish literature, with a slight mistake during making choices, I found myself in a social studies education department. Yet, like many things I encountered before, I soon developed a liking for history and social studies, and I loved my teacher-in-residence program. At that time, I also earned my elementary education certificate. Despite not doing well in regular college exams with content knowledge, I earned a very high score on a centralized multiple-choice exam that tested overall cognitive abilities. My score qualified me for an interview in my own institution's selective Master's program. Due to my high score, I was placed there, replacing some people with stronger networks. That year, I also taught third grade in an Ankara public school.

One day, another encounter opened the door, which resulted in my being where I am today. A classmate in my Master's course mentioned a government scholarship for graduate studies in the United States. Again, in my usual unintentional and unplanned way, I applied based on my high exam score. Six months later, I received the scholarship. I participated in an intensive English language program for a year before I applied for graduate school in the United States.

The Ohio State University was the first institution to provide me with an acceptance, so I immediately jumped at the opportunity. During my graduate work and the new cultural context of the Midwestern United States, I once again struggled with everything from time management, to understanding and performing the Midwestern accent, to structuring my life and setting long-term goals. The context in the United States required one to be utterly extroverted, ambitious, and determined. I had to have specific goals and plans for the future if I wanted to gain the attention of academic advisors. Yet, I did not have any family history in respect to higher education, nor did I have cultural capital within the world of academia or the competitive corporate world. Even today, I am the first and only one in my entire family who has a doctoral degree and is in academia.

While my story is a unique case that began in Turkey, there are several ways that this account is applicable to the U.S. context. The two countries have different cultural structures; yet, my experiences and those of gifted children in the United States are comparable. While my story turned into a success story, gifted education is often used as a gatekeeper for children in different social strata and blocks them from accessing high quality curriculum and challenging academic content. Therefore, many gifted and talented children face barriers such as poverty, disability, social class, and race. How can we open the doors to children with potential for inventions that can save us from nuclear trouble, global warming, or who will enrich our lives with seminal works in history, literature, or philosophy?

Many times during my life, I have felt like a leaf in the wind, going to any open door that could take me somewhere instead of following a carefully planned academic plan developed during my precious early years. When I visit schools in poverty-stricken areas, the general pattern is that the majority of children do not have clear visions for their future or for what they want to be and could be. Like me, many of these children have been unaware of the potential opportunities, possible early successes, and the ways to effectively plan sustainable academic pathways. Along with social and institutional barriers, the lack of structure and early planning for the future are important elements that impact gifted children's success. This was something missing from my childhood, but that does not need to be the fate for all children. We need careful eyes that will pay attention to details in a child's developmental potential. We need to train teachers in the ways they can better understand and shape children so students can build on their abilities in sports, music, drama, science, nature, communication, movement, and spirituality as well as the conventional subjects.

Zeynep Isik-Ercan, PhD, is an Associate Professor and the Program Coordinator for Early Childhood Education program at Rowan University. She has an MA and a PhD from the Ohio State University in Early Childhood Education and Curriculum & Instruction. Her research agenda focuses on culturally and linguistically diverse children, teachers, families and communities within the field of early childhood education (ages 0–8). Some of her recent research projects include the educational experiences of children and families from unique immigrant communities such as Turkish and Burmese. Dr. Ercan examines how innovative pedagogies and practices such as incorporating technology and science/literacy inquiry projects can respond to the needs of culturally and linguistically diverse classrooms. She provides professional development and mentoring in the areas of diversity, curriculum, best practices, STEM integration and project approach through research partnerships.

CHAPTER 29

TO THINE OWN SELF BE TRUE

Stand Tall

LaShonda M. Jackson-Dean

> **Key Challenges:** peer pressure, self-esteem, school challenges, perseverance

I always was tall for my age, standing 5' 7½" at age 15. I accepted and enjoyed being tall and wanted to be taller. I deliberately walked as upright as I possibly could, even as a young child. With my height and confidence coupled with my assertive demeanor and intelligence, others in my age group perceived me as being different. This difference was not always in a positive or affirming way.

Being an only child and very intelligent, I wanted desperately to have playmates. I availed myself to anyone who would talk to me. It quickly became blatantly obvious that I was not the so called cup of tea for many of my classmates. They would shun me by not acknowledging me when I spoke, by unanimously disagreeing with my ideas or suggestions, and collectively disapproving of my appearance. I was shunned for being more physically

Gumbo for the Soul, pages 171–174
Copyright © 2017 by Information Age Publishing
All rights of reproduction in any form reserved.

developed than my peers. Having a more physically developed body and an overly developed personality, along with being smart, made it difficult to fit in. The philosophy I lived by was to not stress myself trying to fit in when I was *born* to stand out.

The way I was treated did not bother me a great deal. I coped rather well. Although I wanted to have friends and be a part of the popular crowd, my "big" personality often overshadowed the personality of others, and I refused to be disrespected by my peers. Simply knowing my *worth* and that I *deserved* better prevented me from accepting anything less. It did not matter how nice I was or what I said, I was always socially isolated. How do I describe social isolation? I describe it as rejection and exclusion from the ones you feel you should have some connection. I refused to compromise myself for acceptance just to be rejected. My philosophy was that everyone must have the opportunity to be themselves and should resist being anything different just to be accepted. This same philosophy has motivated me to remain true to myself throughout my lifetime.

What child and teen does not want friends—or a least one good friend? But I had limits to how much or how hard I would work to get friends. I wanted friends and wanted to be a friend to others, but I had personal limits to what was acceptable and what was unacceptable for friendships. I was nice, complimentary and accommodating, but not weak or desperate for company.

I was always one who would give and give but never really received much back. I was fine with not receiving much in return because I did not go into a "relationship" looking for anything more than a surface-level friendship. Although, it would have been great to actually develop lifetime friends, it didn't seem that this would be my fate.

I was a secret friend or more like a confidant to many. They would come to me when they wanted to be real. They would come to me when they needed someone to listen to them, to air their personal, family, and school frustrations, problems, and wishes. They would come to me when they needed a shoulder to cry on. I was everybody's "friend" in that sense, because I was always the one giving the advice or being a comfort to others. I was there. I listened to them. I reassured them that things would be fine. However, in my giving (and not taking), I would always fall in the same trap of thinking that, now, we would be friends, but it was never the case. It was seldom reciprocal. I would be there for them and when they were better, they would walk past me with their real friends, without even speaking to me. And, I was there for them when they came back.

I was raised by my mother and stepfather, both very confident and independent individuals who taught me to be the same. I spent the bulk of my childhood and adolescence being a friend to the friendless. The funny thing about that is, when I got a friend, others then saw their worth. One by one, they would pull my new friends away from me, to leave me, in a sense, alone. I could have gone to my faux friends and demanded an explanation, but falling into playing futile games like that would only turn into a vicious cycle of disappointment and sadness. I did not worry because I was never alone due to my parents and families, and there was always a friendless person available. A person with less confidence would have suffered from insecurities, self-esteem issues, as well as a crisis with her identity. I never felt shaken or fearful because I knew who I was and who I was to become.

As I walked alone, I could see influences all around me. Although classmates tried to isolate me, did not want to include me, refused to talk to me unless they needed something, they walked a little straighter when they saw me. My perception of them was so important that they had to create an image they thought I would notice, rather than be who they actually were. Even in my youth, I knew it was better to be myself and to accept others for themselves.

I was not afraid to walk alone because I knew, in some way, that I *was purposely* different. Different in a good way, in a way they could not understand. While disparaging me, while rejecting me, I think that they wanted to be like me—intelligent, proud, confident, compassionate, forgiving, and tall. My stature spoke volumes.

All of this has taught me that we all must take the opportunity to get to know ourselves—the person that is distinctly you. You must learn what you want out of life and what you do not want in life. Discover yourself! When you know who you are, the real you, you are no longer afraid to be alone; you are no longer afraid to be different, and you do not internalize rejection and seek the comfort or presence of underserving and unworthy peers or 'friends'. When you know who you are, the real you, you are never alone because you are your own company.

In this life, we *all* have a purpose. We all have a journey to experience, and whether it is individually or collectively, it is still a journey. Although we may start our journey with others, it does not mean we will remain at the same pace, make the same turns or even finish together. Many will make the journey alone so, it is very important to know who you really are in order to manage standing tall and alone. When I think about my journey, Shakespeare's character's Polonius comes to mind. He once told the tragic character Hamlet, '*To thine own self be true*'. This is how I have focused my energy—to always be true to myself. In my life, *tall does not mean height*, it means to carry myself with pride, self-assurance, and dignity. I stand tall because I stand by my beliefs and values. I refused, as a child and teen, to compromise myself. I stood tall, firm, and unwavering in the face of rejection.

To accomplish our personal and purposive mission in life, we may need to go on a self-designated journey. As in any journey, the best trips are carefully planned. When you are unsure of how to get from point A to point B, you research for directions or use a navigation system or GPS. Think of your goal as the address to your destination and your current status as your starting point. The move from your current status is the scariest because you are moving from the known to the unknown.

As you travel along your journey, there will be different turns that may lead to you to better places. There will also be some turns on your journey that may lead you to some unsavory places and people. When you discover you have made a wrong turn on your journey, reroute yourself and get back on course. Remember your capacity to stand tall and alone so that when you have to go it alone, you can. Stay the course, be aware of your surroundings, and you will eventually hear "you have reached your destination." Stand tall, regardless of your stature; standing tall is not just physical; standing tall is mental! Be a friend to others, but first be a friend to yourself. Forgive others for their identity issues and give them the support and then the space to learn about self-love and pride. Continue to help others, but do not become help-less and defeated in the process. Stand tall and be true to yourself.

To ensure you learn the lessons life has intended for you, remember, to "thine own self be true."

LaShonda M. Jackson-Dean, PhD, author and philanthropist is the founder of Jackson-Dean Investments, Jackson-Dean Professional Solutions, and JDI Business Scholarships. Dr. Jackson-Dean, an Air Force Disabled Veteran, provides coaching services through Jackson-Dean Professional Services for Veterans, entrepreneurs and those who inspire for greatness. She is an adjunct professor for Cornerstone University. Her research interests include Under-representation of African American Women in Corporate America, Wage Disparities, African American and Women Studies, Veteran and Disabled Veteran Marginalization, Entrepreneurship, Project Management, Transformational Coaching, Organizational Leadership and Whole Being Wellness. Dr. Jackson-Dean received her Bachelor of Science in Business Administration from Wayland Baptist University, her MBA in Management, as well as her Doctorate in Management, specializing in Organizational Leadership from University of Phoenix. Professor Jackson-Dean is a sorority member of Pi Eta Delta and a committed community advocate.

CHAPTER 30

FIGHTING THE GOOD FIGHT AS AN AFR-RICAN LEADER

Patricia Jahaly

Key Challenges: racial identity, biracial, racial isolation, academic identity, poverty/financial challenges, single parent

I am a talented and intelligent, Afro-Rican school leader. It has taken seven years to say those words out loud, with a smile, and with conviction in my heart. This is a journey that started on an elite liberal arts college campus where I was less than three women of color in the education department.

In the fall of 2007, I began attending Sarah Lawrence College's Art of Teaching program fully funded by the Regina Arnold Scholarship. This hefty financial burden lifted off of my shoulders came as a great blessing as it would enable me to work within a field that I knew I would dedicate my life work to. I could not fathom the years of discovery and self-reassurance that needed to happen in order for me to stand tall as a leader. Zora Neale Hurston once wrote, "there are years that ask questions, and years that answer" (Hurston, Z. N. 1937, p. 21). Prior to this acceptance, I was pregnant with my first child, unemployed and unmarried (if that truly means

Gumbo for the Soul, pages 175–178

anything), I had also been laid off from my job in advertising and grappled with my next move in my career. Here I was 26 and clueless. I found myself attracted to the Art of Teaching program at Sarah Lawrence because of the philosophical alignment as well as the kindred spirit of my professors. I knew I could learn great things at this school. It was under the large weeping willow that sat in my view from my class in an old mansion that I found myself being "the voice" of every Black and Latino/a man, woman and child and every plight known to the urban education scene. I don't know if this was my perception or my reality, but the two merged into a gelatinous encumbrance that became too much too bear.

As the daughter of Puerto Rican parents whose life began in Spanish Harlem, I felt indebted to them to spread the word that every family in the hood was not every ounce and grain of what Kozol wrote about in Savage Inequalities. I began steeping myself in Lisa Delpit, Christopher Emdin, and Gloria Ladson-Billings to name a few, but most importantly I found Paule Freire and bell hooks. I realized that within the context of these texts and dialogues, I didn't have a strong identity of who I was but instead what I wanted for students of color. How could I work in service to others without knowing how to work within me.

When I began working in the South Bronx in 2009, my mission became actualized and confirmed, my work within the urban setting would be my life work. I stayed late and burned myself out in order to make sure that students were receiving that which they deserved... a high quality education. This narrative consumed me. In retrospect, I see how myopic my vision was, not because it wasn't what is good for students; because it's large vagary that lacked an aspect of authentic pedagogy within me. I began to search for me. Who was I within this work that I felt so deeply rooted in all that I valued? Where could I point and say that aspect of me is in this part of my work and did not simply regurgitate mandates and curriculum? And lastly... where was the Afro Rican whom I embodied?

When I became a leader within a school, I knew that I would continue to fight the "good fight" and demand equity and a relevant education for my students of color. I began to identify for and more with my Latina heritage and discuss the African ancestry in me that curled my hair and colored my skin—a skin that I began to say was nothing short of beautiful in its brown and golden glory, but still said this in a whisper. I didn't shy away from it when I was with my students. A false bravado only shown in the face of students doubting themselves and worth. Perhaps, my cry out loud was through them as I never wanted them to feel that doubt that I felt—the doubt that filled me like Pecola was found in "The Bluest Eye." As my narrative began to grow and I settled in my deep melanin skin, a new change would present itself and true challenges and internal battles would be waged.

Despite the fact that my colleagues would ask about Puerto Rico (a place that is my second home in location, first in my heart) and seemed to be intrigued by pedagogy (as if my authenticity was a novelty and necessity in order to validate their assertion of what Black and Brown children needed), I felt the need to diminish my identity once again. I didn't know it then but my success in leadership became synonymous with the notion of whitening my profile. It wasn't necessarily that I felt the need to physically conform, but rather that my intellectual and conversational base was around European tenses, ideas but never beliefs. I was me at home, talking to my Mom in Spanish, lamenting about my grandmother's farm in Vega Baja or the curious nature of congrejos that had begun to creep into her backyard. She would build and cement my foundation by talking about her work with Angela Davis and Malcom X, but again . . . where was I? At work, I was Patricia. Strong, bold and in desperate need to conform. Years later, I see this tension as not only interesting as I work in the urban setting but as a detriment to my self-worth.

When I accepted a position as Director of Curriculum and Instruction at a new charter school in Harlem, it was under the eyes of many White people that I felt an even stronger need to convert. Conversion in my eyes was to emulate the White femininity that I had seen in other principals or school leaders. In my eyes, that is what I defined as success. I stopped listening to hip hop in my office, I even stopped talking to children about the neighborhood goings on and current events (something that was a hallmark in my teaching...the relevant and authentic connection that defined me even if at times I felt like an imposter). I wanted to preserve myself in the eyes of those watching that I could be that which they found valuable because that was after all what leadership looked like. This glib notion fell to the floor one day when I was in an exchange with a co-worker and the tables had turned. I began to feel attacked and when I rebutted, they looked at me with horror. I became "the angry Black woman" devoid of intelligence and ripe with emotion. I was perplexed as to how I landed back into this space of selflessness, after years of making sure they knew I could communicate with them. This sacrifice of my self-worth left me with little pride and lots of doubt. Shortly after, during a meeting when I mentioned the great Zora Neale Hurston, a question arose from the group that if we picked this figure would the Black leaders of Harlem refer to her as an "Uncle Tom." It was at this time I knew I had ventured too much and lost myself. I needed to find me, a consistent mantra that weaved in and out of my persona but that now needed to be solidified and grounded in.

Over the next six months, I began a journey of finding myself. I began to converse again with those leaders and mentors that spoke to me when I was a beginning teacher. I began to steep myself in Afro-Rican culture soaking up every ounce as if drinking with a thirst that could never be quenched. I remember going to Puerto Rico four times in one year studying and taking in my heritage as if rehydrating the depleted resources of my core. This was my home . . . this was mi orgullo. . . . This was my home and it could live symbiotically with my leadership style, status and purpose. Reflective thoughts poured out from me like water from a spout. I asked myself rhetorical questions that only I could answer. It was through these words that I saw all those questions about my life years ago begin to find snippets of answers. The realization happened the last time I was in Puerto Rico. I was drowning in self-doubt. Could I be my authentic self as an administrator and leader? Could I be the powerful leader I had envisioned for myself and it was as if the resounding "YES!" came from the oceans surrounding me. How was now the question I had to explore in order to fully liberate myself.

True liberation has come with much self-reflection and acceptance of who I am. My identity is rooted in my Afro Rican-ness, but also my ties to the urban community that nurtured me when I was young. It is the struggle that I know my family went through and continues to go through that continues to make me unapologetic when I question the intentions of those around me and their intentions for the Brown and Black students they serve. This is not to say that you are only entitled to feel this connection if you have been through a struggle. Your narrative is not defined by a certain set of characteristics but instead how you improve upon them and come through with a liberated sense of who you are. In my mind, liberation became acceptance. I accepted myself, the complexities and simplicities and stopped apologizing for that which was a part of me. I lean into who I am in order to be truly authentic to me which is what I owe myself and is the most liberating. In the setting of our world where Black and Latina women are underestimated, underrepresented and undervalued it is only me who can provide the liberation from the shackles of conformity in order to be who I need to be in order to serve those that I work for and with . . . the students within my schools. It is no longer necessary to apologize for every misstep but instead to act and clarify later because I am a talented, intelligent, Afro-Rican *liberated* school leader.

REFERENCES

Hurston, Z. N. (1937). *Their eyes were watching God.* New York, NY: J.B. Lippincott.

Patricia Jahaly is an experienced urban educator and leader who has worked for a decade in public elementary schools. Patricia establishes high expectations for student achievement and classroom practice. She currently is the Principal for an all girls Charter School in the Lower East Side of NYC. She is a graduate of Sarah Lawrence College and Bank Street College.

CHAPTER 31

PEOPLE COME INTO OUR LIVES FOR A SEASON

Donna M. Johnson

Key Challenges: sexual assault, career choice challenges, loss of friend/friendship challenges

I remember the first time that I saw her. It was a bright day in April, with a hint of Cleveland's winter coolness still in the air. Tracey was sitting in the back of the bus along with a group of other students, singing an a capella rendition of Heatwave's, *Always and Forever.* Dressed in a navy Calvin Klein three-fourth length coat, Tracey led the group, which sang a rocking rendition of "Boogie Nights" next. I'd entered the bus and looked for a seat in the back. Moving past a line of students standing in the aisle, I grabbed the last seat, two rows in front of Tracey. Other students, decked out in black and gold for School Spirit Week, continued to chatter over the roar of the engine and its vibrations as we sailed toward home.

I met Tracey at the first girls' book club meeting the following week. We became fast friends. Tracey was the only person I knew who had been diagnosed with a photographic memory. She would devour books quickly and discuss them with full page recall. I'd won a city-wide writing contest sponsored by our local newspaper at age five, and had a natural gift for literary criticism. Our opinions often contrasted, however, I saw myself in Tracey—a 14-year-old African American girl attending a predominantly White mid-western suburban high school—who was funny and smart. We were two of five Black students in the ninth grade honors program; the remainder were boys, who only talked to White students. Tracey and I often studied together, and regularly spoke to each other in Spanish, which is why we always shared the top student award given by Señora Ramos, our favorite teacher. We would do the *Walk Like an Egyptian* dance whenever we got good grades, and hang out at Randall Mall.

Tracey was popular, with friends from various cliques, while I hung out with a small group of nerds. I spent my time outside of school with family. Tracey, a dancer, spent most of her out of school time at a community theater. We both loved the Jackson Five, and fantasized about traveling to California. Tracey wanted to dance on Soul Train and I wanted to take a picture in front of the Hollywood sign. We vowed to achieve great things in life. Our friendship would last 30 years.

Life was pretty good until I was assaulted by a man while walking home from the library one fall evening during my junior year. A driver saw the attack and began honking and flashing his car lights until the man ran away. The police arrived and escorted me home. The attacker showed up outside of my school a month later, which terrified me, and caused my grades to fall. There are no words to describe this horrible time. Whenever I walked alone on the street, I would almost fall apart at the sound of anyone walking behind me. At the end of the school year, my mother relocated me and my brother to San Diego, where my grandparents lived. My father paid for the relocation and drove the moving truck. San Diego's sunlight, palm trees and ocean air helped me to heal, and would do the same for Tracey.

Two days before our senior year began, Tracey came to live with my family in San Diego. She'd been engaged in a summer relationship with an older married musician at the theater, which caused a scandal and left her broken-hearted. When Tracey arrived, she was different in so many ways. She seldom sang or danced. Her once expressive brown eyes were empty, her normally border-line curvy and athletic frame was gaunt, her beautiful honey-colored skin was dull, and her shoulder-length hair was in desperate need of a beautician. Tracey also slept often, and sat in silence for months, until her blues went away.

Senior year went by fast. There was a lot of pressure about grades, SATs, and prom. Tracey and I couldn't wait to get our drivers licenses. I got a job as a cashier at the Naval Training Center, while Tracey went to work on creating sets at the Old Globe Theater in Balboa Park. I was determined to achieve my goal of reading the entire twentieth century literary canon of African American female writers before leaving high school. I read every

Toni Morrison book published at that time aloud to Tracey during her blues period. Every time that I read for her she would ask, "Did you know that Toni's my girl?"

We proudly walked across the stage in our caps and gowns while some of our classmates streaked at our high school graduation. Tracey surprised everyone by announcing that she'd enlisted in the Army, and would be stationed in Germany. I enrolled at San Diego State University. We wrote each other often. When she returned three years later, Tracey left the military and settled in San Francisco, where she studied textiles. I was still living in California, so we saw each other often. As we'd fantasized in high school, Tracey got her chance to dance on Soul Train and I took pictures in front of the Hollywood sign. We both danced under the Catalina moon, sang "It's a Small World" at Disneyland, and biked across the Golden Gate Bridge. We also dipped our feet into the salty Pacific Ocean, while bearing our bikini-clad bodies on California beaches, and drank wine on Sunset Cliffs in San Diego, while listening to jazz with our dates, and watching the sun fade.

I left California the following year to enter a master's program at Howard University in Washington, D.C. Tracey moved to Philadelphia to attend the University of Pennsylvania a year later. We visited each other often. The mutual confidence that we had in our relationship made it possible for us to achieve academically and in our careers during that period. Any accomplishment one achieved felt like a personal accomplishment to the other. We'd witnessed every major event and milestone that the other had achieved since we were teens. We documented each with specialty cards, gifts, photographs and hugs. We were fortunate. Tracey moved back to Cleveland after five years in Philadelphia, started working for a start-up film production company, and rented an upscale downtown apartment. Her mother was over the city's film office; her relative was a judge, a prominent journalist, and a congressional representative during this time. I moved to New York City to complete my doctoral program at Columbia University and working as a school principal. Tracey lured me home two years later with talk about us raising our children and being old church ladies together.

We met for breakfast at our favorite restaurant in Shaker Square a few weeks after I returned home. Tracey was dressed in a cream colored Adrianna Papal dress, complemented with a Prada purse and Christian Louboutin shoes. Her hair was bone straight and dyed a warm honey blonde. I wore an Ann Taylor lavender jersey dress that I found at an outlet store on the drive home. My auburn dreadlocks sat regally on top of my head. We were no longer the 14-year-old Black girls who used to dream of success in high school. We were successful women.

Sitting across from each other at our small round table under the natural light from the window, I recognized Tracey's distance immediately. Our relationship had changed, and although we talked often, I had not noticed it until that moment. We struggled to find our voices that morning; it was awkward. I made the regular inquiries, but Tracey responded with one word answers that limited conversation. When she did speak, Tracey talked with a newly acquired European Blaccent about the help, low-income people, and the distressing "ghetto aesthetic" that is Hip Hop. I made a statement about how oddly difficult the conversation was, to which she responded, "I know. Huh." After lunch, we hugged and quickly went in separate directions.

We hung out only a couple of times over the next two years, although I regularly saw Tracey on television at high society events and with celebrities. I was busy building my career, and was happy for her success. Tracey then reached out to me one week to help her to cook a meal for a famous actor who was filming a movie in our city. She'd done the casting, and wanted to impress the cast with a dinner party. I arrived early on a Saturday morning. We talked and laughed like old times while I prepared a five course meal for 20 people, and she prepared her apartment for the party scheduled to take place later that evening. When I finished, Tracey informed me that I would not be able to attend the dinner, as there were too many invitees. This hurt and confused me, but I left without saying a word.

I moved back to New York City the following year and reconnected with old friends. A few years later Tracey called to tell me that her mother passed, the company she worked for had closed, and that she was struggling. I sent her money to cover her rent and to travel for job interviews. She finally took a job in Princeton, New Jersey, and I helped to pay for her relocation. Tracey contacted me when she arrived but I never heard from her again. I tried reaching her several times over five years. It was a painful experience, made worse by the reality that because of our friendship, I'd neglected to make other close friends along the way. I moved on, but still wondered about Tracey sometimes. I found her Facebook status revealed that she was married with a daughter, living back at home, and had founded a successful literacy program.

I was never told why my best friend threw our 30-year relationship away, nor why she left me alone to pick up the pieces. This was a hard reality, a betrayal, and a painful experience that I had to work through. I remember my grandmother saying to me when my grandfather passed, *"Honey, people come into our lives for a season and a reason. Change is the only constant. This is the cycle of life."* I never understood her until now. People enter and leave our lives for reasons beyond our control. A season can last a day or several years. We don't always get to choose. When this happens, it is best not to take it personal. I coped with rejection from my friend by engaging in regular prayer, meditation and self-reflection. I also went to counseling to become more self-aware, and focused on my physical health. I refused to allow the fear created from this rejection to get in the way of my moving forward. It is important to remain open to self-love, positive relationships, and new beginnings.

Donna M. Johnson, EdD, is an activist—scholar, educator and founder of Bright Future Youth, LLC. She is also a licensed teacher and school and district administrator. Johnson's research interrogates the formal education experiences of African American girls in grades P–12. Dr. Johnson has worked for over a decade to increase awareness regarding the educational needs of African American school girls, as well as to advocate for their empowerment in U.S. schools and gifted programs. Dr. Johnson's research interests also include teacher education and professional development, school leadership and reform, and multicultural and Black education.

CHAPTER 32

FROM "SMARTY PANTS" TO SCHOLAR

A Personal Journey of Self-Acceptance

Jennifer M. Johnson

Key Challenges: peer pressures, acting White, social isolation, poverty

The thing that makes you exceptional, if you are at all, is inevitably that which must also make you lonely.

—Lorraine Hansberry

"Yay!" I exclaimed, "I'm finally going to school!!"

I am ready! Like a flash, I begin to run towards my new bus stop at top speed. My head is filled with images of all the things I will get to see and do now that I'm finally old enough for kindergarten. Reading, counting, writing . . . I just can't wait to be one of the big kids. My excitement won't be contained! It's finally my time to learn and grow and become an independent woman at the ripe old age of five.

"Wait!" Shrieked my mother. "Stop! Catch her!"

For some reason, Mom was yelling at me to come back to the house. What's wrong? Well, apparently, there were a couple of problems with my eagerness. Here I am, running full speed up the street and not only is it the middle of summer, but I was also headed straight towards the *city bus stop!* LOL—I am so thankful my uncle was able to snatch me up before I ran right into oncoming traffic.

To me, this memory shows that although I didn't really know what school was, I knew it was where I needed be. Sometimes, I have vivid flashbacks of that young, eager, bright-eyed version of me. I was short for my age, with big bangs and two fluffy ponytails. I remember being very confident and self-assured. There wasn't anything I couldn't do! According to my mom, I was full of sass, independence, and a bit of impatience. Occasionally, I would wait with her at the bus stop with my older brother Eddie and waive to him as he headed off to this magical place called "school." When he got back, he always had such great stories of the things he learned or experienced with his teachers and friends. I wanted that, too! So, of course, I was ecstatic once it was my time to go. School would be the place where I would go to meet new friends, get "smart," and discover answers to all of the questions I had about the world.

"You are now in the red reading group."

Although I did not have a lot of money or resources growing up in Buffalo, New York, I did have the privilege of attending good public schools. Good schools with caring teachers who took the time to validate my burgeoning skills and encourage me to do my very best. While I can recall several fun activities and experiences from early elementary school, I first remember "learning" in the third grade. That's when we were put into small groups for reading, and we had the opportunity to read aloud from the pages of our readers. Remember those? Each reader and workbook was a different color and there was a kind of internal pressure to move to the next one as soon as possible. I was put in the red reading group with a small group of students and we got to read from a workbook one level higher than the class. I was so excited! It was everything that I thought school was about...become your very best and learn everything about the world... I was so happy! Little did I know that from that moment on, I was set on a trajectory that would influence my educational opportunities for the rest of my life.

"Why do you talk like a White girl?"

We knew this was coming. No one ever called me "gifted" but I was frequently labeled as "smart" or, more frequently as a "smarty pants." In some spaces, this was a good thing, other times it made me a target. My elementary school was racially diverse but I would most often hear these nicknames from my Black (mostly female) peers starting in the fifth grade. Before then, everyone relished in his or her intelligence; by middle school years that began to shift. Along with being singled out for my smarts, my peers began to question my "Blackness." How? By asking me why I "talked like a White girl." Not surprised? Clearly, I'm speaking to my soul sister! If you were anything like me, a bright Black girl from a working class neighborhood, you were called out or teased for "talking White" or "acting White" on more than one occasion. It even happened to my younger sister. As a result of these experiences, I began to retreat into myself. I was no longer as eager to speak up, more resolved to just move though school unnoticed to avoid any taunting. How could I explain that I wasn't trying to talk or act like anyone other than myself? Why couldn't I just be accepted for who I was?

Unfortunately, I experienced a good deal of social isolation from my Black peers that continued through High School. Some of it was self-imposed. It wasn't like I was constantly bullied or people were blatantly mean to me, I just found it hard to make connections without feeling pressure to justify myself all the time. When I was focused on getting good grades and staying involved in student activities, others were concerned with fashion and dating. I found myself trying hard to navigate various social cliques while not stepping on the land mines of vicious gossip or teenage pregnancy. I began to retreat socially and focus on the life I wanted for myself in the future. To maximize my opportunities, I became an overachiever—I got involved in leadership activities to stay "friendly" with my peers but never had any close friends. Additionally, I began working two jobs to help support my family, doing everything possible to avoid any distractions that could take me off my next step—college. I was hopeful that there, I would be able to finally find where I belonged, gain validation for who I was, and discover the person who I was truly destined to become.

"What do you want to do with your life?"

Well, the good news is—my story has a happy ending! Even though my early years were a bit of a struggle socially, the opportunities I had to gain a strong academic foundation propelled me into the life I enjoy now. I earned a partial scholarship to college, and met an amazing group of women who remain my closest friends today. Don't misunderstand me; I faced troubling times in college also. It was an eye-opening experience—being in a new environment where I found stark differences economically and socially from my peers, but in that same environment, I found my voice again. I found a sense of acceptance that I had not experienced before—I was able to be all of me, all of the time, without apology. The independence gained in college helped me see again why it's so important not to be defined by the opinions of others. Deep down, I knew who I wanted to be and now I had the space to become that person. I just had to be brave. Slowly but surely, the real Jennifer, that eager, bright eyed, and confident person I had lost touch with, emerged. That Jennifer not only graduated from college, but went on to earn a doctorate in education by the age of 30. It felt good to be her again.

Maybe you're like me in some ways. I can't say that I had a terrible childhood; but I certainly faced tough times. Oftentimes, I had to rely on my inner strength or "grit" to make it, but I also had a few people I could look up to as role models along the way. Even if I wasn't comfortable with sharing my story with them, somehow they knew, and their implicit or explicit support helped me in ways I cannot even articulate. Today, I am an educator; nearly exclusively support Black students as they navigate to and through college. I try to be the type of role model I needed in my life coming up. This is my message for you. I want you to know that even if it seems like right now no one understands you, or that you are ignored and isolated in your experiences, you are not alone. There have been others who have had similar struggles and we have made it. I believe that for you too. You are exceptional, you may at times feel lonely, but you are beautifully and wonderfully made. You too can find where you belong by having the courage to first accept yourself and be that unbridled dynamo you are destined to be!

Jennifer M. Johnson, PhD, is an Assistant Professor of Education at Bowie State University. Her research interests include pre-college access programs, historically Black colleges and universities (HBCUs), students in science, technology, engineering and math (STEM) programs, and high-achieving students of color. This scholarship explores the ways race, gender, and class intersect to shape the educational experiences of students across diverse institutional contexts.

CHAPTER 33

FROM HEARTACHE
TO HEAD UP

Charemi A. Jones

> **Key Challenges:** single-parent family, poverty, abuse, violence, perseverance

As you can imagine, expectations are always high for that smart girl with "all the talent." "Momma's favorite," my sisters always said. I was the middle child who believed in following the rules. That was how I lived, and doing what I was told kept me safe from punishment.

I don't remember when my parents separated, but their divorce had a lasting effect on my life. My parents met on a military base, and married during the height of the Vietnam War. My mom told us stories about how they lived in Germany for a short stint, but returned to the United States when my father was stationed in North Carolina, the state where he was born.

The lure of war apparently beckoned my father. He 'volunteered' for three tours in 'Nam. My dad lied about his age in order to join the Army. He told the Army recruiter he was 18, but he was only 17 when he enlisted. He met my mom four years later, and although my father was raised by

Gumbo for the Soul, pages 189–193

both parents on a farm in North Carolina, the Army forged who he would become as a man.

My mom says that when my dad returned from his tours in Vietnam, he had changed. Every little thing would set him off and his anger was often unbridled. She added that shouting and yelling accompanied most of his conversations with her. His violence against her left her with bumps and bruises. One of my dad's punches loosened mom's tooth and that was the final straw. Mom left my father. She packed us up and moved to Chicago, where we still reside.

It would be years before the divorce was finalized. In the interim my Dad would occasionally call us. He promised to send gifts and money. But, after a while, my sisters and I would laugh when we got off the phone with him because *we knew better.* I later learned that my Dad did not re-enlist in the military because he didn't want to pay child support. I remember my sadness at this revelation and wondered if taking care of his family, his children, was that bad?

For a while, I was happy with my small family: mom, sisters, and me. I did whatever I could to make certain my mom didn't have the stress of taking care of home and worrying about the well-being of my siblings and me. I learned, early on, the importance of keeping a clean home, getting my homework completed, prepping and cooking meals, helping my sisters, and being a support for my mom. I often saw her struggle, but thought that if I continued to I excel, especially in school, I would reduce her burdens.

Perhaps the "perfect daughter" accolades my mom and I would frequently receive from people were a stretch, but at times, it became a type of burden for me. Expectations were abound. My sisters grew to expect me to "take up the slack," especially when my mom gave us instructions, and I was the only one who completed the tasks. Each one of us knew that if mom didn't have a good day, or was just really tired; an unclean house, incomplete homework, or not having dinner prepared was a surefire way of either not getting an anticipated treat, or a butt spanking.

My sisters and I were latch-key kids, meaning while mom worked or attended school, we were responsible for our egress and entrance to and from the apartment. We would look with anticipation from the living room window when the time for our mom to come home neared. I remember one time when my mom's car was not working, and she had to take the bus to work. She arrived home late, and I could see that when she entered, she had been crying. She explained to us that while she was standing, waiting at the bus stop, someone grabbed her purse and ran. It was payday and rent was due. While things weren't as expensive then as they are now, it was still a lot of money. For me, I didn't know which was worse—the fact that the several men who were also standing at the bus stop did nothing to help, or that along with her paycheck my allowance was gone.

Soon after that my dad contacted us. We hadn't heard from him in a while and I don't remember what we talked about, but I do remember him saying he would send money. In the past, my sisters and I would laugh at his false promises, but when we finished talking to him, he asked to speak to mom again. He told her to look for the money in the mail. All I knew was that mom was running a little short on money and school was starting in a couple of weeks. So, the money would be a godsend. My mom took us shopping for school supplies and clothing. I am not sure where she got the money from because the money from dad never came.

About two years passed before we heard from my dad again. This time, he wanted my sisters and me to visit with him for Christmas. We hadn't been back to North Carolina since moving to Chicago, so mom thought that it would be a nice trip because we would have an opportunity to see family we hadn't seen in a while. That year, Christmas was okay. We spent time with my dad, our stepmom, and younger stepbrothers. We even got a chance to see our grandmother and other relatives, but we were ready to go home.

A few days after Christmas, we wanted to talk to our mom, but, my dad wouldn't allow us to do so, so we started writing letters. When dad found the letters, that angry persona re-emerged. He was extremely angry. He wouldn't mail the letters, nor would he allow us to talk to our mom. Two weeks later, I was in panic mode; we hadn't returned home, so we weren't in school. A month later, my dad took us to our grandmother's house and it was not until March that we were finally enrolled in school. We had missed three months of school! I was terrified. Even at that age, I knew that missing that amount of time would affect my grade point average. Nonetheless, being a smart girl had its privileges. I passed the fourth grade. I was a very smart and high-achieving student, so I was able to do well. However, cumulatively, that year affected my ability to become valedictorian or salutatorian when I graduated from elementary school.

Later that year, in mid-July, on a hot summer day, I remember sitting on my great-aunt's front porch watching cars drive pass. A familiar car drove by several times and finally stopped in front. I remember screaming, "Momma," as I rushed from the chair, and jumped off the porch, running towards my mother. My mom talked to my great aunt, who by then had called my grandmother, who worked at the daycare center down the street.

My grandmother was never a really an affectionate woman, and was often very abrupt when my mother tried to talk to her. She said she would call my father. My mom, who had full custody of my sisters and me, let my grandmother know that she had full intent of taking us back home to Chicago, but would wait until she got off work. My grandmother scoffed, and walked back to work. My Mom loaded us in the car, with clothes on our back, and we began our journey back *home* to Chicago.

It would be another 12 years before I saw my father or grandmother again. By then, I had accomplished so much. I performed well in high school, therefore, I had the opportunity to attend any school in the State of Illinois on a full scholarship. But I chose to attend a small liberal college in Oakland, California. I wanted to get as far away from Chicago as possible because my mom had remarried and my stepfather was abusive.

It was so hard seeing the woman I loved dearly be treated so cruelly by a man who didn't seem to love himself. I really don't know if that is true, but what I do know is that I just wanted to get away. Curiously, he was always nice to me, but I felt so bad and confused!

I remember my mother crying as she got into the cab after dropping me off at the airport so that I could fly off to college. But her tears brought her strength. She returned home and successfully divorced my stepfather. In the end, he actually apologized to her.

During my first year of college, I was not focused and found it difficult, at best, to sometimes even get out of bed to go to class. As such, my grades suffered, and I returned home to Chicago. By then, I, who was so smart, had lost confidence in myself because of my failing grades. I had to regroup and redefine myself. I spent the next year attending a community college until I could receive a financial aid package and return on the journey to completing my Bachelor's degree. Within a year, I received my Associate's degree, was admitted into the Phi Theta Kappa National Honor Society, and accepted into Illinois Institute of Technology (I.I.T.). I graduated three years later with a Bachelor's degree in Biology.

Now, my story doesn't have a fairytale ending, because I came face-to-face with a common phenomenon called "falling in love" while I was at I.I.T. Suffice it to say, I had a rocky journey on my completion of this degree. But I realized something; it was okay to change the trajectory of my life. I ended up meeting different people and coming into myself from a totally different perspective. My keen sense of justice took priority in my life. As a result, like many of my relatives, friends, and my mother, I became a police officer.

"What the hell?!" you may ask. Well, all I can say is that I am very content with my life and am a leader in my field. I train people to use their knowledge and lived experiences to help others. Not only did I complete that Bachelor's degree, I returned to school and obtained an MBA (Master of Business Administration), MPM (Master of Project Management), MEd (Master of Education), a terminal MS (Master of Science) in Education, and will soon complete my EdD (Doctorate of Education).

My mom followed my lead, returned to school, and obtained her MBA. When I complete my doctorate, she wants to return to obtain hers. She says she looks up to me! And I have completed my doctoral degree, graduating in 2016.

Charemi A. Jones, EdD, received her Bachelor of Science in Biology from Illinois Institute of Technology, Master of Business Administration and Master of Project Management from Keller Graduate School, and her Master of Education and EdD from DePaul University. She is an educator whose approach to education is based on the S.E.A. Paradigm: A multi-disciplinary approach to providing authentic and relevant education imbued with service and advocacy constructed through the multi-dimensional lens of intersectionality. Dr. Jones is a 20 plus year law enforcement officer and instructor.

Every experience, like the ingredients in Gumbo,
combine to enrich your life, each ingredient was
valuable by itself, but in combination, they enriched
my life, just life Gumbo!

—Joy Lawson Davis

CHAPTER 34

PASSION AND PURPOSE THROUGH PAIN AND DYSFUNCTION

SaDohl Goldsmith Jones

> **Key Challenges:** family transitions, verbal abuse, physical abuse, sexual abuse, neglect, self-worth, overcoming, underachievement, misdiagnosis

Through the years, I have discovered my passion and purpose in life. The funny thing is that I think everything I have experienced was preparing me to be who I am today, although I get nervous when I think about the possibilities that lie ahead. I grew up in New York, where life wasn't always the best and I remember, while in high school, being told "I was never going to be nothing" or "I would not graduate from high school.

Don't get me wrong, my parents were the best, they were loving, caring, encouraging and great providers. I have good memories of being a kid in the Bronx, with my parents. But the memories I have that aren't so good, stem from family friends taking advantage of a working family and a young girl.

Gumbo for the Soul, pages 197–200
Copyright © 2017 by Information Age Publishing
All rights of reproduction in any form reserved.

One summer, when I was 10, my sister and aunt came to visit. I was told I would have to go "down south" for a little while, which wasn't too unusual because I went down south most summers to spend time with my mother's family... I loved visiting Georgia. I had tons of cousins and I got to play outside all day. However, this summer was different. My parents didn't go with me and when I left, it felt very permanent and I later found out that it was. That summer marked the last time that I would live in New York. The settings reversed and I went "home" to visit in the summer and went to school and spent most of my time "down south." It was tough being 10 years old and not being with either of my parents. Instead, I lived with my sister who was more like my mom. She was and still is awesome! She took care of me and treated me like her own daughter and we are still extremely close to this day.

During this transition, I learned a lot and also spent a lot of time alone. My sister thought that I was anti-social; all I did ever wanted to do was read and watch TV. The ironic thing about that was when I lived in the Bronx and came to Georgia to vacation I loved being outside, but when I moved to Georgia to live, I didn't want to go outside at all. The running joke used to be that, when I got into any trouble, my punishment would be to go outside... since I enjoyed being in my room alone so much. In reality, the transition was emotionally difficult for me, which also affected my academics. Also, I was bullied so much while in the fourth grade, I dreaded going to school and hated lunch. When I entered fifth grade, I was labeled with a behavior problem and by the time I entered seventh grade, I was placed in a lower level math class and remained in the remedial math class until my teacher realized that I was bored and had me placed in advanced math and reading classes.

By the time I entered high school, I was used to being doubted by others and not taken seriously, so I began to "go through the motions." I was active in band and cheerleading, and I had a good group of friends. At the time, I trusted my friends more than I trusted most people in my family. As a matter of fact, I moved out of my family's home and began to live with family members of my best friend. This was a choice I made because I didn't feel like anyone in my family wanted me around except on their qualified terms. It did something to me as a young lady to hear negative things about myself on a constant basis, especially when the things weren't true and came from the people who should encourage you the most. I remember sitting in a room and listening to other adults in my family say how much they "couldn't stand me," that "I was not going to graduate from high school," that "I would never be anything," and "I would be pregnant before I got a diploma." I did not feel protected or safe, so I subjected myself to the unnecessary stress of living with other people's family, just to avoid hearing negative things about myself. I could not wait to get out of Georgia, away from everyone and *never* wanted to come back.

I felt alone, so I learned early to depend on God and myself because people failed me. I remember wishing that my parents would send for me, but that never happened (and I am not sure it would have been the best idea, either). So, I decided I would "bite the bullet" to get through high school and go to college... I worked hard in high school; excelled academically and applied to college.

The summer before college, I had the opportunity to spend time at home in New York, like I did every summer since I was 10 years old. But this time, when I left Georgia, I knew that I would not be back to live with my family in Georgia, so I packed up my room in preparation for me to pick them up after my summer break to take to college. Upon the completion of my summer visit to New York, as I was on my way back to Georgia to pick up my belongings, I received a phone call from my family in Georgia telling me that all of my belongings were placed in trash bags...all of my awards, trophies, high school accolades—everything—discarded as trash and placed "in an outhouse." I was devastated and hurt. I felt as if this was how they had always seen me...as something in the way—that they wished they could just discard...just like they did my belongings. As a result, I had to start college without any of my own clothes, because most of them were ruined, placed practically outside for months in the elements, so they were un-wearable. I never mentioned this to my parents' nor did I complain; it was just another piece of the puzzle that would motivate me to prove them all wrong. I was not trash; I was not dispensable.

I didn't have the best start to college. My past family situations and transition to a new setting caused me to struggle during my freshmen year. I persevered and after my sophomore year, I decided to continue my college career and rent a room in a boarding house and work to make (and save) money. I was very excited!

During the first week in my new living quarters, I fell asleep while watching a Black history movie (one of my favorite pastimes). I was alone in the house, but I was awakened by a very loud banging noise. I thought it was someone banging on the front door for one of my housemates, so I peeped over the top of my covers. It was then that I realized that the banging was coming from *my* door! Someone was trying to kick in my room door—and they succeeded. I laid there and prayed that male intruder didn't see me, but I realized that he did and as, he came to my bed, I remember thinking, God please save me...and while I will not go in to details, I will say this "incident," as I now call it, changed how I thought of life and others.

You see, this was not the first time someone had taken his or her own "liberty" with me. I had blocked out the other times and somehow pushed through; however, this time was a bit different. I couldn't "push though." I became extremely paralyzed; however, I didn't want anyone to know what happened to me—I wanted to appear "normal," and while I looked normal on the outside, inside I was completely dead. I then came to the realization that I could use the abuse that happened to me: physical, sexual and verbal, to help others—I finally realized the purpose I had in life.

During the times that I was experiencing abuse, I remember wishing that I had someone who would understand and speak for me, because I did not know how to speak for myself and for that reason, I chose counseling women and children as my career path; I conduct research to be a voice and an advocate for those who otherwise would not be considered. Through my faith and through counseling, I was able to finish undergraduate and graduate school, and graduate with honors. I then went on attend one of the top universities in the country and obtain my PhD Now, I own a business that allows me to help young girls and women, who need a voice, to find their purpose and passion in life. I now know that God has always had a plan for me. I remained faithful and focused, so I got to where God wanted me to be. Does this mean my life is perfect? NO! But it does mean that I know that there is something bigger than me that guides my life and as long as I use my life as an example for moving through pain and seeing the possibility of you reaching your purpose, I am living in my purpose and my passion.

SaDohl Goldsmith Jones, PhD, LPC is a Counselor Educator and License Professional Counselor. Dr. Jones received her BA and MEd from Clark Atlanta University and her PhD from the University of Iowa in Counselor Education and Supervision. Her research focuses on social justice advocacy in gifted education, twice-exceptionality and mental health counseling. Dr. Jones is the owner of Jones Counseling and Consulting, LLC, where she consults with school districts, and provides psychotherapy and clinical supervision services.

CHAPTER 35

MY LIFE BEGAN TO BLOOM AT FORTY

Tammy D. Lane

> **Key Challenges:** parental loss, aging process (e.g., late bloomer)

Who knew life could begin at the age of 40? Similar to a savory gumbo laden with powerfully seasoned stock, meats, and vegetables, my life became flavored, savory-seasoned at the age of 40. In the year 2004, unexpected and instantaneously, the direction and trajectory of my life and future changed. With a pinch of humility, a cup of resilience, and a handful of grace I was able to accomplish what seemed like a lifetime of goals as well as fulfill my last daughterly duties. My two favorite young men were all grown and I entered a transition. During this transition, I experienced a series of phases that carried me in, out, and through many vicissitudes.

Over the course of 12 years, with no break in between programs, including summer, I attained a Bachelor of Science in Elementary Education, a Master of Science in Higher Education, and I am eight months away from earning a PhD in Educational Leadership. While completing my undergraduate degree, I was blessed with the strength to take care of my ailing

Gumbo for the Soul, pages 201–204

mother in my home, work as a paraprofessional in a public school, and to excel academically. I would later get married, relocate to a city that I had visited once as a 21-year old, and acquire an administrative position in higher education. I am now a published researcher within months of entering the professoriate. Although I thought my goals were far-fetched as life happened, it has become obvious to me that my soul never gave into worldly things that could have very well obstructed my destiny. An essential part of this story is my feeling of renewal, grit, and love for Black students. Who says life ends at middle age?

After undergraduate graduation, my own educational endeavors and passion to educate and inspire students were finally coming to pass, and to keep the academic momentum going I promptly enrolled in a graduate program. With all that had emerged, I was riding on cloud nine, not knowing what was lurking in my immediate future. Two months after celebrating undergraduate graduation, I lost my best friend, my mom. I mourned deeply the thought of eternal separation from the woman who taught me so much about the benefits of education and life in general. In fact, it was an agonizing thought.

In the mist of my pity, her sweet spirit spoke to me in a dream. Like the wings of a bird, hearing her voice made my heart flutter. She said, in her authoritative voice, "Mourn no more for me for I am immersed in the pinnacle of glory, and so let me rest! My work is done, and yours has just begun". You see, she had always told me not to focus so much on her being ill because God's plan for her was already in progress, and that I should refocus my attention to the Black boy or girl steadily being denied equal opportunity to learn due to the idiosyncrasies of a skewed educational system. She often reminded me of the morose reality that because of the color of skin, many educators cowardly sited the perceived hindrances of genetics, lived-experiences, and self-destruction as an excuse to give up on Black students. Mom was passionate about the students she taught for over 30 years and would have wanted nothing more than for me to carry on the fight for equal justice in the classroom for Black students. So, I channeled my grief into changing the narrative for Black students.

Embarking on a new life with a former high school sweetheart, I married, relocated out of state, and continued working on a Master's degree. In order to fulfill a course requirement, I sought an internship and was fortunate to land the position in the student affairs engagement department at a historically Black college and university. The position was the beginning of a change in paths from elementary to postsecondary education. Wow, what a difference! Not only was the trajectory different, the narrative was new.

This was my first time being in a predominantly Black environment and I valued it. The cultural familiarity was like nothing I had ever experienced. Even though the population was predominantly Black, it was so rich with a conglomerate of cultures. As time went on and I became familiar with many of the students and began peeling back the layers, I realized many of the students who had come from failing public school systems were actually talented and gifted. Many of them were not afforded the opportunity for their gifts and talents to be recognized and supported. Unfortunately, many of the students failed to graduate high school with grade point averages that could have possibly resulted in merit scholarships to cover the cost of college. Finally, they were being educated in an environment that cultivated giftedness and talents, but the new threat was not being able to finance a college education with the possibility of dropping out. My question became: What can I do to ensure that these students succeed?

As the stars aligned and due to the divine intervention of God, a position in the financial aid and scholarships department became available, at the same HBCU. I applied and was hired. I was able to counsel many students and as such, a great percentage of these students obtained resolutions to their financial woes and if not already, are positioned to graduate from college. During this period, I graduated from my Master's program as well. My efforts and need to serve as an agent of change in education grew. I applied and was accepted into the PhD educational leadership program at an HBCU.

The doctoral journey opened my eyes to a plethora of possibilities and avenues to change the narrative for the students that I am so committed to. The possibilities to research, publish, and contribute to the body of knowledge that leads to change for the Black student is exhilarating. Although I am proud to acknowledge that I have excelled in the program, I find it more rewarding that I have written and published research addressing the problems and stresses of attaining a college degree when finances are meager for students. In fact, I have addressed several areas of concern for Black college students. Whenever, I am asked to speak on issues regarding higher education, I am always ecstatic. It affords me the opportunity to enlighten others on the many quandaries as well as victories of Black students.

I will graduate with a doctoral degree within months from now and will continue to propel issues plaguing Black students to the forefront. As doors continue to open for me, I will work to close the sundry doors of inequality for the Black student. Additionally, my intention is to highlight the endeavors of Black students and historically Black colleges and universities. Furthermore, after graduation I will enter the professorate. Becoming a professor is a significant accomplishment and responsibility because I am charged, just as my mom was, but at a different level, with educating the next generation of educators and educational leaders. I am delighted about the responsibilities of training students to be just as enthusiastic and passionate about having a positive effect on the lives of their future students. This responsibility teaches the students to be reflective and profound educators and leaders. *"Changing and enhancing the lives of students"* is my mantra.

There are infinite possibilities for making a pot of gumbo just as there are infinite ways in which to change or enhance our own lives as researchers, professors and administrators, and also the lives of students. There is never an inopportune time to feed our souls and to rejoice and reflect on stimuli that have lead us to motivate and inspire others, specifically our students. My story is meant to inspire those who are at a crossroad in their lives. Until the last breath in our lives we are assigned a purpose and it is our duty to discover and diligently work to pursue that purpose beginning at any stage of life. The selfish me wishes that my inspiration, my mom, was here with me. However, I understand that she is in a place of peace and she could not be more proud of me, which turns the agonizing thought of her passing to joy as she continues to inspire me. The children of Israel wandered for 40 years meaning that biblically the number 40 denotes a period of testing, trial, and reflective learning. Forty years later, at the perfect time and place for me, I accomplished a lifetime of goals academically and spiritually, and the unsurpassed part of my story is that I am changing the lives of Black students. As I aim to reflect and inspire others, my soul endures renewal 12 years later because as I write this story, I realize that all along, I was gifted.

Tammy D. Lane, an Asa G. Hilliard III and Barbara A. Sizemore Research Institute Scholar, is a guest lecturer and a third year Educational Leadership PhD candidate in the dissertation phase in the Whitlowe R. Green College of Education at Prairie View A&M University. Also, Ms. Lane is a Scholarships Coordinator in the Office of Financial Aid and Scholarships at Prairie View A &M University. Ms. Lane holds a Bachelor of Science in Early Childhood Education from Kennesaw State University and a Master of Science in Higher Education and Student Affairs. While Ms. Lane's research agenda focuses on student/faculty affairs issues, her dissertation focus is LGBQT equity in an HBCU context. She is the author of several publications, research, writing, and presentations.

CHAPTER 36

THE PERILS OF BEING
TOO YOUNG TO BE GROWN

Tonya Leslie

> **Key Challenges:** peer pressure, behavior issues, under-achievement, anger

I started working at 16 years old. Not because I had to, but because I wanted to. I always wanted to be a grown up—to make my own money and make my own decisions. I remember when I got my first credit card—a JC Penny's card. I was proud that I could secure a line of credit.

I started my professional life working at a shoe store in the mall, first as a cashier, then as a sales person. During the 1990s, before shoes were the 'thing', I was known for my crazy collection. I had dozens—plastic over-the-knee boots, neon green suede loafers, red cowboy boots, metallic-studded rock star platforms . . . you name it, I had it. When I became a sales person, I worked on commission and thought I was raking in the dough. I thought; if this is what it means to be grown up, give me more! I spent my money on the material things that usually appeal to teens such as clothes, friends, movies, a beeper, a private phone line and finally a car. I thought I was living the life.

Gumbo for the Soul, pages 205–209

I also thought that part of being grown meant having relationships with boys, but in my case, they were men; I entered into situations that were probably beyond my emotional ability to handle. After spending my childhood and early teens living a life behind thick glasses and badly combed hair, I began to blossom in my 16th year. My new physical self, coupled with a salary that enabled me to afford regular visits to the salon and all the drug-store cosmetics I could buy, meant that I suddenly had a lot of attention—from boys and girls alike. I took on an all-knowing countenance about all things related to sex, which was mostly gleaned from my older sister and her friends. But I regularly shared that knowledge as my own while in the high school bathroom with the girls who hung out and smoked between classes.

Even though I conformed in the most stereotypical ways to all fashion and flavor that the late 1980s and early 90s had to offer, I thought I was different from other teens. I shopped in vintage stores and wore ironic t-shirts. I blared hip hop and the music of Black rock bands through my car stereo when I drove to and from school and as an ode to some of my favorite 'Lisas' (Lisa Lisa from Cult Jam and Wendy and Lisa from Prince and the Revolution), I shaved off one side of my hair.

Most of my friends looked like me—we were Black and children of Caribbean immigrants. We knew a lot about being different and feeling left out—especially since we were all bused out of our community into a predominately White school because we were gifted and high performing. While there, we banded together and began to craft a new identity for ourselves; mainly one that included cutting class and hanging out in New York City. We saw ourselves as the alternative to our classmates. I even received accolades in the high school yearbook for being "village-y," which was a nod to Greenwich Village. At the time, it seemed like the epicenter of alternative cool because I was *sassy* Just like the title of my favorite magazine.

Yet, I was struggling. It was my experience that parents who were Caribbean immigrants could be easy to fool, and since my older sister was causing her own havoc in our house, my daily dramas were easy to hide with silence and carefully chosen stories that highlighted the good stuff. Against the weight of others' traumas and challenges, my issues seemed almost miniscule and it turned out, Cindy Lauper was right—money could change everything. Once I had access to my own cash, I rarely had to turn to my parents for money and because of that, I gained the upper hand. In many ways, I stopped asking for permission and just assumed permission. I recall a time my mother tried to stop me from going out once by stating, "Give me your car keys!" I responded "Why? You don't pay the bills for it. It's not yours." and out to the club I went.

I found myself pushing my parents away when, in reality, at this time, I needed them the most. But I thought they just didn't understand. They came from countries where the sun shined all the time and everyone knew each other. They didn't know, any more than I, what to do if a man on the subway flashed them or someone tried to jumped them and steal their bag. In many ways, I felt like I had to protect my parents from the realities of the life that I was living. How could I reveal to them that the young man that brought me home was a notorious drug dealer who asked me to carry a bag of crack vials for him one day? How could I explain that the young White friend, who dropped me off, did so in a car he had stolen earlier that evening? As a matter of fact, in the shadows of Long Island suburbia, he taught me how to break into a car, using a slim Jim to open the lock, and a slide hammer to break into the ignition. (He eventually got sent away to Juvenile center or "juvie" as we called it). I worked hard to shield my parents from the fights I got into with girls at school because they thought I was dating their boyfriend. I walked the line between being bold and being scared.

Yes, I had my own car, my own room and my own telephone line, proudly purchased and maintained using my own money, earned from my own job. I was performing "independence." I was making choices and decisions that I knew weren't the greatest, but I was still young enough to think that the consequences wouldn't catch up with me.

I was also academically resilient. My grades were good enough. As one of the few Black students in my high school, the expectations were low. I knew that if I tried a little, it would go a long way. So I did just enough to get by, but also read voraciously on my own for my own pleasure. Still, I knew how to "do" school. My teachers liked me, so my teachers and parents gave me a lot of freedom. As long as I got moderate grades, everyone was happy and turned a blind eye to the other things that were going on. Even when I got into a fight in the hallway with a female classmate, everyone gave me the benefit of the doubt that I didn't really deserve.

Once you start performing, it's often hard to go back on your own drama. It is hard to admit you are all bark and no bite. I was nothing like I was pretending to be. I wasn't a 'slut', even though someone wrote that about me on a classroom chalkboard. I wasn't 'tough', even though I talked in provocative ways that surprised even me. I got myself into situations that I loath to admit, even now—the shame of some of my actions is overwhelming. *Who was that girl?*

By my senior year in high school, I felt like I had created a reputation that I didn't really want, but my reputation had taken on a life of its own. Every day I felt like I was performing for a show that I could not figure out how to get out of and away from. I didn't think I could talk to anyone about how I felt and I didn't know how to ask for help.

And then I decided. I would leave high school. Now, leaving high school wasn't really an option. Not with my parents. There was no way I was going to be allowed to drop out. Still, I knew I had to get away from the person that I was becoming in high school. I sensed that I would get to a point where I couldn't take some of it back. Many of the girls' lives in my circle changed irrevocably—one's face was slashed and several became pregnant. I knew that college would provide me a space to be a new, better self, but that seemed too far away. I needed a change . . . quickly! So, I reached out to my guidance counselor, did some research, and found that New York City offered alternative programs for high school students. One program allowed high school students to complete internships rather than go to school and still graduate with your high school diploma. You were not required to return to your home high school. Needless to say, I signed right up and I landed an internship as a student reporter at New Youth Connections, a magazine for teens by teens that was distributed throughout the high schools in New York City.

Getting to the office at the New Youth Connections meant a 90-minute commute each way, each day. To say that my life changed when I became a student reporter would be an understatement. As a teen reporter, I was given the freedom to pitch my own stories, do my own research, and write my own articles. I suddenly understood that being grown meant having responsibilities beyond hanging out and spending money. The internship provided me with the opportunity to ask meaningful questions, to start a project and see it through to fruition, and to write my own stories. I had to earn the trust of the editors to prove that I would do what I promised. The more they trusted me, the more projects I was assigned, and the more perks the teen reporters received, like when we were given tickets to go to a concert with the new and upcoming rap group A Tribe Called Quest. I was also able to meet the rappers, Salt and Pepper and Kid and Play—I was on Cloud 9.

I made new friends at New Youth Connections—friends who didn't know who I was and didn't care what I'd done. Friends who liked me for me. Friends who turned into my college roommate and friends who became colleagues and peers 20 years later. The editors and staff at New Youth Connections talked to me about my life and helped me make decisions. They also helped me to verbalize the challenges I faced and offered to help. When I told them that I didn't get into the college of my choice, they wrote letters of appeal. Years later, when I couldn't break into the publishing field the way I wanted, they arranged an interview with a company with which I stayed for 10 years. In each instance, I was surprised at how much help and support came my way once I opened my mouth and asked.

To date, I still keep in touch with New Youth Connections. I go back to reunions and communicate with the staff that started the organization and those who still serve as employees. I learned so many things that served me well while working there. I learned how to type (on a typewriter) how to conduct an interview, how to listen and respond to someone's story, and how to take myself and my work seriously. After finishing my undergraduate degree, I went on to earn a Master's degree and have finished up a doctoral degree—and all of this from a student who didn't really "apply herself" (a common comment from my teachers). Most of all, I learned that it's never too late to change your own story. Every day is a new opportunity to change direction, take a new path, and start over. Sometimes, you need help to get out of a hole you dug yourself into, but I learned there is always someone who will meet your reach. And sometimes one small step in a different direction propels you down a long road to self-discovery. You just have to be brave, believe in yourself, think outside the box, and find people to talk with. You have to ask questions and have a vision of a better future. You have to admit your mistakes and then do better to make wiser choices.

Tonya Leslie, PhD, is the Vice President and Publisher of Family and Community Engagement at Scholastic Inc. Her doctorate, from New York University, is in teaching and learning. Dr. Leslie's research interests include resilience, culturally responsive pedagogy and family and community engagement. She is also the author of several children's books.

CHAPTER 37

PUSH BACK AND STAY IN THE GAME

Life Goes on After Mistakes

April J. Lisbon

> **Key Challenges:** peer pressure, rejection, self-esteem, identity, perseverance

Times of old and times of new. I can think of many days when I would tell myself 'how cruel is life to you'. It wasn't that I did not have love and support of friends and family or that I felt alone, I simply felt like it was easier to be dumb than be young, Black, and gifted—after all, this is what the world expected of me. Now, as I sit in my room listening to the wind beat against my window pane, I am reminded of a time when life's games were cruel and no longer worth living. I remember the days when I simply wanted to 'get my head out of the game'.

As a teenager, I was identified as a gifted student. I was filled with pride and excitement in knowing that someone recognized how smart I really was. My mom and other relatives always told me that I was smart and could do anything if I put my mind to it. However, there were events in my life when these words simply fell on deaf ears. I've had my fair share of earth shattering events ranging from being removed from Advanced Placement classes to earning Cs in math. Oh, I can't tell you how many times I hit my fist against my head reiterating the phrase "you're so stupid" or "you're just dumb!" The level of psychological warfare these experiences created internally set me on a path of uncontrollable sadness. There was a level of sadness that led me to devalue and even hate the person I was—an intelligent Black female.

Honestly, I found myself despising my intellect even more as a teen. It seemed as though *smart* girls were never chosen to hang out with the popular kids. It seemed like all of the girls in my social group always dated the popular guys at different schools or on campus. Yet, I, the ugly duckling, never found anyone that wanted to be with me. I found myself in a place where I felt I had to portray being loud and obnoxious in order to be noticed by others. I allowed myself to believe that smart girls never won and I acted my school life accordingly, even if it meant earning grades well below what I knew I was capable of attaining.

Eventually, my grades began to slip and I started believing that I really was dumb. I recall in the middle of my eleventh grade year as an AP English student having my classes changed to regular English because I simply wasn't giving it my all. That schedule change shook me to the core. I questioned 'how did I allow myself to let it get this bad'? I guess my desire to fit in with the cool kids was more important than being the gifted and high performing student I knew I could be. I kept telling myself that if I wanted to fit in, I had to underperform, rationalizing that smart kids were never accepted. Rehearsing such negative thoughts for several years, ultimately led me to engage in risky and unproductive academic and social behaviors, which almost cost me my life.

My mental state didn't change after graduating from high school. I carried the same attitude of "dumb is fun" when I began my undergraduate years at a well-known university in Florida. I remember scheduling classes around ratchet television shows and pretending to be studying at the library when, in reality, I was too sleepy to do anything after partying at night.

My freshmen year in college came with many highs and lows. I finally established relationships with people who appreciated me for me, regardless of my level of intelligence, because we were all in school for one purpose—to get a degree and a job. However, the high school girl in me, the one who was still searching to be admired by the *fine* brothers, found herself in a relationship with a very attractive young man who was emotionally toxic. I found myself trying to find love in all the wrong places, as the cliché goes, and that *one* relationship changed my life forever and not for the better.

The reality is that I was involved in an unhealthy relationship at the age of 18. In my need to fit in, I failed to see all of the warning signs. I chose not to see that the person who I was dating had a violent past; I felt I could never find another attractive Black male to date again. My self-esteem was really low during this time in my life; I never saw myself as being pretty. Having someone whom I perceived as being *fine* desiring to be with me made me *feel* like I was pretty. If I had not said 'yes', I felt like no other Black man would have wanted me because I had convinced myself for so many years that darker skin girls were not pretty. Warped perception I know, but it was still my perception of who I was as a person—unattractive. I remember telling myself that he would never hurt me because I was smart enough to know better. However, when you think you can change someone for the better, you realize that no matter what you do, your best simply isn't good enough.

In the end, I found myself the victim of domestic violence but simply blew it off. I made myself believe that what he did to me wasn't as bad as the other girls he had dated. I knew this because one of the girls he dated lived across campus from me. When I learned what he did to her, I convinced myself that I *must* have been his main girl. In time, it simply became too much and in the end he left me for someone else. All I could think about was how stupid I was for getting involved in such a relationship. I remember speaking negative thoughts about my life daily to the point where I felt like I no longer had a life. I simply felt my life was useless and I didn't want to live any longer. I was ready to die.

For many years, I battled thoughts of ending my life as nothing seemed to work out for me as it had for others around me. I felt like the world could be a much better place if I were no longer in it. I believed that death was my dearest friend. Thinking in this way meant I no longer had to fight my internal *demons*. I no longer had to think about being young, Black, and gifted! I was afraid that if I continued to exist in the world that I would continue to be a failure—a failure to my family, friends, and my unborn children—if I lived to have any. It simply seemed like committing suicide was the right thing to do. I was a disaster waiting to happen, or so I thought. I can laugh at my pain now as I eventually realized that those thoughts and feelings never profited me anything because the fighter in me could never die. I realized that I was born to live, even when I wanted to die.

In hindsight, I really don't know how I survived it all as I never shared my hurt with anyone. I always kept a smile on my face to masquerade the pain. What kept me grounded was my belief in God that eventually my life would turn around as I knew there was a reason for my existence. My mother instilled in me that 'God's got a purpose for you, if you'll let him have his way.' I always kept these words in the back of my mind, even while going through the toughest times. I was blessed with amazing friends in high school, cousins, and church friends in college who helped me focus on the future while living in the present moment. I also had my poetry. I used the words from my pen to release the anger that brewed inside of me. My poetry kept me sane during those dark hours.

If there were any takeaways or recommendations I would make as a gifted Black woman, the first is that you should never allow anyone of any race or gender make you believe that you are not smart enough or not good enough to excel in life. Your intellect does not define you but is another component of your being. It is your personality and your character, your gifts and talents, and your existence that will help you succeed. Your intellect simply allows you the opportunity to achieve beyond average. My second takeaway is that when you feel like you have come to the end of your road, talk with someone you trust. Never allow your hurt, as I did, to take control of your life. Finally, give back to other young Black and Brown gifted girls and young ladies like yourself. Mentor them. Support them. Share with them your stories as they matter. Let them know that it is very common for young ladies of our caliber as well as ground breakers in society. Remind them of how special they are and that you applaud their ability to make differences in their lives, their families, and their communities.

To be young, Black or Brown, and gifted is a beautiful combination when you *choose* to believe it. Simply hearing it from other individuals will not help you excel in every area of your life until *you* embrace your personhood. As you read these stories from your fellow gifted women, I want you to realize that you must stay in the game. Push back even when you feel life is throwing obstructions in your way. Seek help from others who want to see you excel and allow them to carry the loads that are too much for you to bear. Your survival matters. Love yourself, believe in yourself, live for yourself. You are young, Black or Brown, and gifted. The world needs to see *you* shine.

April J. Lisbon, EdD, is a School Psychologist with the District of Columbia Public Schools. She received her BS in rehabilitation services from Florida State University, her MS in Counseling and Human Systems from Florida State University, and her EdS in School Psychology from Florida State University. She also earned her MBA in Management from Tiffin University and her EdD in Education from Northeastern University. Dr. Lisbon's research centers on special education and school psychology including over-identification; identification and assessment; underachievement; learning disabilities; and special education leadership as well as ethical issues in education reform.

CHAPTER 38

LEARNING TO LOVE MYSELF AFTER SEXUAL ABUSE

Arleezah Marrah

Key Challenges: sexual abuse, self-concept, overcoming and resilience, Christianity, forgiveness

---

I am not sure how old I was when it happened, but my mother's boyfriend sexually abused me. It was the night that changed the way I felt about myself. My mother's live-in- boyfriend was always a little odd to me, but I figured, if my mother trusted him, then so could I.

It was a normal night; nothing out of the ordinary. I was unable to fall asleep in my own bed and I wanted to be comforted by the smell and the feel of my mother. As I did numerous times before, I got out of my own bed and searched for my mother's room to go to sleep in the bed with her. However, this night was different because my mother's boyfriend was in the bed with her, also. At first, I hesitated at the sight of my mother's boyfriend sleeping in the bed and thought it was best to go back to my own bed. However, I wanted to be comforted by my mother. She awoke when I approached her slumbering form to ask if I could sleep in the bed with

---

her. She then asked her boyfriend to leave the room so that she and I could sleep in the bed together. He obliged and left the room.

A little while later, I was awakened by the feel of hands rubbing my butt. My first thought was "what is going on?" When I realized it was my mother's boyfriend, my next thought was "why is he doing this?" Then I thought, "Why isn't my mother doing anything? Does she not know what is happening to me?"

I was so fearful that I remained perfectly still as if I was asleep. As he continued to fondle my young body, I squeezed my eyes tightly so that I could not see what was happening to me. I looked up briefly and validated that it was indeed my mother's boyfriend who was sexually abusing me, all while my mother was asleep. My mother was peacefully asleep while her boyfriend continued to inappropriately touch my body.

I am not sure when the horrible ordeal ended that night but I knew that it was not right and I needed to tell someone. The next morning, I told my older sister what had occurred and she stated that she believed me because he had approached her in a similar way; however, he was unsuccessful in his attempts. With all of the courage that I could muster up and with my sister at my side, I let my mother know what happened and how her boyfriend had touched me while she and I slept in her bed. As the words were leaving my mouth, I thought that this was it, I was going to be vindicated, and my mother's boyfriend would have to leave and never come back into my life, our lives. However, my mother and her boyfriend agreed that it was a mistake and that it would never happen again. All I got was a sorry apology from him. I was floored! I never imagined my mother not taking up for me and kicking her boyfriend out of the house. I imagined her screaming; yelling, or physically attacking him, but never in a million years did I think she would ask him to just apologize. I was her baby girl and yet in that moment, I felt so shameful and vulnerable. My mother, the person that was supposed to protect me from all harm and danger had let danger sleep in our home and simply apologize for violating me in an unspeakable way. In that moment, I had learned two things; I was not safe being a girl and that my voice and what I had to say didn't matter, even to my own mother.

Weeks later, my mother's boyfriend begin to sexually abuse me again. I cannot remember how long it went on but I know that I begin to accept it and even began to enjoy being touched by him. I didn't even bother to tell my mother, as I knew it wouldn't change anything and I learned to deal with it. Eventually, the relationship ended between my mother and her boyfriend, but shortly thereafter, I started to become angry and bitter because I realized that when he left, he took many pieces of me with him. I swore that if he ever came back, I would kill him. However, as time went on, many details of the sexual abuse begin to fade away. As I got older, my relationship with mother began to get back to "normal." But, I carried the burden of shame throughout my mid adult years, because I had held on to the feeling that deep inside, there was something wrong with me.

Eventually, I tried to move past the abuse and ignore the painful memories that popped up in my mind. However, I quickly found out that I could not keep ignoring the brokenness inside of me. During high school and college, I found myself constantly questioning who I was, was I good enough, or was I worthy. I also questioned the beauty and pureness of my body. During the times I was abused, I disliked everything about my body. As time progressed, I developed the feeling that my body never really belonged to me and that it was okay for others to invade my space.

In addition, I did not trust my voice and often found myself questioning everything I said or thought. The constant second-guessing and self-mistrusting exhausted me. I become envious of the "woman's intuition" of which so many of my female friends and family members raved. That guiding little voice that provided insight and warnings to women all over the world was something I never experienced. Everything that I admired about being a woman; the beauty, pureness, and femininity, was something that I did not have for far too long.

Eventually, while in my doctoral program, I finally built up the courage to seek professional help to assist me in processing and dealing with the sexual abuse I experienced as a child. At the same time, I began to serve in my local church and developed an intimate relationship with my Lord and Savior Jesus Christ. It was painful to deal with the scarring memories that I had suppressed for 30 plus years, but I could not continue to live with the bitterness in my heart and on my mind. So, I made the decision to forgive both my mother and my abuser; and with that choice, I began to see others and myself the way that Jesus would want me to see them; as broken people who needed a Savior. I began to understand that my mother did the best that she could at the time and that my abuser was a broken man that needed prayer. Through this process, I found both peace and joy; however, most importantly I found love for myself...the self-love that I had longed to have for such a long time.

Even though I still struggle with the memories of the abuse and the anger that accompanies the memories from time to time, I am able to take a deep breath and know that I am more than my past. I am not a victim but a victor and my past is just a platform for my testimony. My testimony can be used to encourage women who have also experienced sexual abuse and to let them know that they are not alone and they will overcome. I know that my story and my voice will touch someone's life and give them hope that they too can learn to love themselves—despite their past.

Arleezah Marrah, PhD, is an Assistant Professor of Counselor Education at Barry University. She holds a master's degree in counselor education from the University of South Florida and a doctoral degree in counselor education from Old Dominion University. Her research interests include continuous trauma among marginalized populations, research mentorship for women of color, and standardized testing.

CHAPTER 39

I'M NOT AN "OREO."
I'M FOCUSED!

Renae D. Mayes

> **Key Challenges:** racial identity, acting White, racial discrimination, isolation, negative peer pressure, first generation college student

In the middle of my sixth grade year, my family picked up everything and moved from our racially and culturally diverse community in Albuquerque, New Mexico, to a small suburb of Tulsa, Oklahoma. Initially, I was filled with excitement. While I would, of course, miss my friends, this also meant that I would be much closer to my dad's family. I would get the chance to play with my cousins and spend more time with my grandma and grandpa. It was going to be a dream.

The dream quickly changed to reality when we settled into our new home in Sand Springs, OK. I remember enrolling into school and being flabbergasted. In New Mexico, sixth grade was considered middle school and I wore that honor with pride. In Sand Springs, sixth grade was elementary school, so I knew something was up with this place.

Walking down the cobblestone hallway to the sixth grade wing, I saw colorful displays of art and student work. But what the school had in vivid

Gumbo for the Soul, pages 219–223

displays of colorful art was also what the school lacked in terms of people. Walking down that hallway, I noticed stark differences between how I looked and how practically every other person in the school looked. I was that lone chocolate chip in the sugar cookie. I am Black and I refused to be boxed in.

As a sixth grade student, I began to experience my racial identities in different ways than before. The students immediately embraced me in my class, at least initially. They readily told me who I should be, who I should talk to, who I should avoid, who was smart and who was not. Interestingly, they never engaged me or asked me about what I thought because they believed it was their job to teach me their ways. I quickly learned that there were other Black students in the school, but they were all related and had been in the small town for ages. Initially, my new peers thought I was a part of that family. But, when they learned that I was not and I had just come from New Mexico, I had to answer more questions about my background, making sure to note that although I was from New Mexico, I was not Mexican.

Things changed when they saw that academics were easy to me, especially in math. I saw math as a puzzle that once decoded, gave me a sense of satisfaction and even power. I felt like I conquered something great and in some regards, could speak a secret language that others struggled with or couldn't comprehend. While I never felt this contention with my aptitude, it became the subject of conversation with my peers. They admired how I could understand and even teach my peers math, especially the sixth grade girls in my class. The sixth grade boys felt that they needed to compete with me to prove that they were better and smarter, but they failed every time.

The playground was no different. I played games and did physical activities like tetherball and four square with the boys. I became known as a rough and tumble tomboy who was the one to beat. My peers would line up and try, one at a time, to take me down in tetherball and four square. Some would even team up and strategize on how they could defeat me.

Once my sixth grade peers saw my aptitude, I could feel a shift in their interactions with me. Some gravitated toward me and we built incredible, supportive, and long-lasting friendships, while others distanced themselves, made fun of me for arbitrary reasons, and spread rumors about me. I distinctly remember both my gender and my race being called into question with comments like "you're an Oreo—you know, Black on the outside and White on the inside" or "you're not really a girl." This was the beginning of the constant narrative of which I would have to push back against to define my identity.

These types of comments from my peers became more frequent and dare I say, creative with time. In junior high school, I was in all honors and advanced classes and was the only Black female student, let alone student of color in each class. I stuck out like a sore thumb and was the easy target of slights and insults from my peers. While I never told my family about these microaggressions, I came up with some clever responses by the time I hit junior high and even more so when I was faced with additional phrases that challenged my Black womanhood. Most times, I would just ask a person to explain to me how one can act a color and if they could act purple.

More hurtful than the comments was the isolation I experienced when I began junior high school. On the outside, I appeared to have many friends, but I distinctly remember the groups of students that made it a point to push me to the margins. For example, I was a member of the basketball team comprised mostly of White girls . . . they made it their point to exclude me. They would often get together outside of school and exclude me and another girl on the team who happened to be my best friend. Another instance took place when a teammate made goodie bags for everyone, which included snacks and samples of make-up products. When I opened my bag, I realized that the make-up products within the bag were not for people with my skin tone but they were appropriate for my White teammates. When I brought the matter to the attention of the teammate who made the bags, she didn't flinch and was less than apologetic. Nor did she make an effort to remedy what could have been a harmless mistake. I never knew why they disliked me so much, but the message they sent was clear—I did not belong.

High school was much of the same for me. I was well aware of the cost of being different and made it a point to focus on that of which I had control over—academics. I took as many Advanced Placement classes as I could and loved the challenge of each. I felt that even in the subjects in which I struggled, if I worked hard enough, I could get over any barriers. I even challenged myself to participate in statewide mathematics competitions at a local university and coincidentally, I placed third in my first competition. I looked for every opportunity I could to grow my academic skills and started looking into leadership as well. I joined every organization I could, sang in choir, performed in musicals, played volleyball, and mentored elementary school students. I did as much as I could because I believed in my ability to do each well in spite of the naysayers.

And there were plenty of naysayers. They never seemed to go away. Several stuck with the typical "Oreo" or "you're not Black" comments, while others added that it was permissible to be my friend—but unacceptable to date me. The latter was much more of a surprise as I was never really interested in dating the people who made the comment. Yet, once they shared their race-based criteria, it was much easier for me to move forward without them as friends.

Like most students in their final years of high school, I started looking for the next step in my educational journey. I knew I was going to college, but was less than familiar with the process. The process of going to college was often a challenge for first generation college students and I was no different. While my parents had limited knowledge, I benefited from being the youngest in my family with two siblings who were currently in college. Interestingly, no one in my high school, school counselor or teacher alike, ever sat down with me to talk about college or career planning. My family and I were left to fend for ourselves.

When I look back, I realize that I was narrow with my future career goals. I wanted to be a teacher because I had a lot of exposure in that field and felt confident in my abilities. Although I was strong in math and science, I was unaware of the careers that I could pursue in science, technology, engineering, and mathematics. When it came time to apply for colleges, I considered one in-state university with a reputable teacher education program, but was encouraged by my mother to go to a larger, out-of-state institution. I eventually conceded to my mother's advice and applied for early admission—to one school. Fortunately, I was accepted.

When I graduated from high school, I never looked back. I chased my educational dreams and realized new dreams. As I reflect on my experiences in K–12 schools, I realize that although I experienced difficulties, they made me who I am today as a Black female with a doctoral degree. As a gifted Black girl who attended predominately White schools, my identities were always in question. I could easily be picked out in a classroom full of people who didn't look like me or shared any of my experiences. There was always a narrative of Blackness with aspects of gender that were cast onto me rather than defined by me. In fact, I would go as far to say that I spent most of my time during K–12 trying to shed those narratives rather than define what each meant as it pertained to me, but I never let the naysayers halt my progress. I ultimately figured out what my identities meant and I knew that I was smart and I needed to pursue my joy of learning.

Eventually, I began to explore and critically reflect upon my Black womanhood at the end of high school and at the beginning of college. That focus got me through and created more opportunities than I ever could have imagined. As a professor in the field of education and an active member in the community, I think about students who may have similar school experiences. I commit myself, my work, and my time to making school a place where students of color can be celebrated and supported in ways that respect and nurture their identity development and challenge the stereotypical views of race, gender, and class.

Renae D. Mayes, PhD, is an Assistant Professor in the Department of Counseling Psychology and Guidance Services at Ball State University, where she also serves as the Director of the School Counseling Program. Dr. Mayes is a

National Certified Counselor and a licensed professional school counselor in the state of Indiana. Her research interests include: academic achievement and college readiness of gifted African American students, intersectionality in gifted education (race, gender, and disability status), and school counselors' role in school, family community partnerships.

CHAPTER 40

THE DARK SIDE OF GIFTEDNESS

A Hidden Curriculum of Rejection

Heather Cherie Moore

> **Key Challenges:** bullying, isolation, acting White, racial identity, self-esteem and self-concept, low expectations, academic challenges/rejection

Before dismissal, my second grade teacher asked me to come speak with her at her desk. As a gifted student, I was never in serious trouble socially or academically, so I was curious about why she wanted to speak with me. She said, "Heather, I received this letter from the teacher in the honors classroom. I know you really wanted to be in that class for third and fourth grade, but you didn't make it." Feeling dejected, I took the letter and walked back to my desk.

Rejection has been an intimate part of my educational experience. The concept of rejection is not an idea that you would expect to hear from someone who grew up gifted. But being both gifted and rejected from various

Gumbo for the Soul, pages 225–228

communities taught me how to never expect that my giftedness would save me from ridicule. After this experience in elementary school, I developed an obsession with rejection letters. I collected them, posted them on the walls, read them repeatedly, and would always keep in mind why I was not accepted into certain classes or programs. This moment was the first of many where I felt isolated because of my giftedness.

Looking back at my K–12 education, I would contend that my experiences as a gifted, working class, Black girl were a bit non-traditional. I was not recommended for a specialized gifted program. But my teachers identified me as a student who was "smart," "bright," "a pleasure to have in class." These comments appeared on my report cards, told to me, and shared with my family. I clearly remember being acknowledged by teachers as a model that other students should follow. But as I got older, I found that there was a noticeable hierarchy between students who were marked as gifted and those who were deemed on or below grade level, and as a young girl who was deeply rooted in the struggles of the working class, I learned that gifted students experienced their own hardships along the way. At times, it was difficult to find allies who didn't chastise me for my unique educational traits (or characteristics).

I will never forget the moment when my giftedness marked me as inferior and where I felt a strong disconnect from my Black, working-class (low income) peer group. It was during this moment where individuals closest to me critiqued my giftedness. After the first day of high school, I rushed home to start my homework. I was particularly interested in my Accounting class, a subject that I'd only heard about because of my mother's background with bookkeeping. These types of classes were never offered at my junior high school; there were very limited opportunities to take advanced or honors coursework. So my first day in high school was full of a set of new experiences. I was one of the youngest in my class because I started school early. And for the first time, I was in an all gifted cohort who were required to take two Advanced Placement courses in our sophomore year and multiple International Baccalaureate classes during junior and senior year.

I still wanted to stay connected to the people at the junior high school I left behind. I called a close friend and told him how excited I was about my Accounting class. He stated, "I see you are on the *White* train now." In that moment, I felt rejected by a predominately Black community that I believed I belonged to. Sure, I was bullied in junior high for being too smart, too poor, and too naïve. But I still desperately wanted to belong somewhere. After speaking with my friend, I remember asking myself: *Was it my fault for enrolling in a school that would challenge me academically? Should I not go to a college prep school because it would force me to turn in my "Black card to my peers?"* Looking back, I see how my giftedness as a young Black girl disconnected me from communities I so desperately wanted to belong to. Not only was giftedness something that was deemed "acting White" in predominately Black circles, it made me a target. After the first day in high school, I learned that while my giftedness positioned me well academically, it was at the expense of being ostracized by my Black, working class peers.

By the time I was a sophomore, I suffered from a teenage identity crisis. I knew I was smart but I had no idea who I was. As a girl from a large working class family, I felt the divide between my own educational experiences and those of my relatives. While I attended a prestigious high school that had a 99% placement rate to four-year colleges, my extended family members were in neighborhood schools that barely prepared them for citywide testing. This made me an outsider amongst my cousins—not only was I divided from the Black community in my junior high school, but I was pushed to the margins by my relatives. Quite frankly, I didn't feel like I belonged anywhere. I was different. I wasn't gifted in the traditional sense, I wasn't Black enough to belong in my peer group, and I wasn't supported by my extended family.

In my junior year of high school, I experienced a breakthrough. I figured out how to embrace the multi-faceted dimensions of my educational and personal identities. I learned how to unapologetically accept every facet of my identity, including my giftedness. My first hand experiences with rejection were centered upon a resilience narrative. I began to look at my rejections as my testimony. I became obsessed with constructive criticism—always asking my teachers, "How can I write this better? What does it take to *be* better?" In my feelings of rejection and isolation, I learned how to rely on *me . . . on myself.* Over time, I created a self that was informed by the leftover fragments of rejection.

My familiarity with rejection throughout my K–12 education helped me develop a useful identity that relied on resilience and was informed by my constant struggle to thrive in tough circumstances. Since I always felt like an outsider, I didn't always have a group to identify with. But this perspective helped me adopt a set of survival skills that helped me smile in the face of adversity, rejection, and isolation. As a young girl, I wish I knew that my gifted classification would place me on the margins and make it difficult for me to find communities to be part of. But these worthwhile experiences as a young Black girl prepared me for the unforeseen battles I have had as an adult in college and as a professional. I learned the importance of self-love so that I would not overly rely on the approval of others. I learned that even people close to you may have problems with your success. I learned that you must stay focused on your dreams and goals; value your gifts and use them to support others.

Heather C. Moore, PhD, is an Assistant Professor of Community and Justice Studies at Allegheny College. She received two Bachelor of Arts degrees in

Educational Studies and American Studies from Trinity College. Her MA and PhD are from the American Studies program at Purdue University. Dr. Moore conducts research on the representations of Black male students in American popular culture and teaching Justice learning in college classrooms. She has forthcoming book chapters on the hit television series "The Wire" and on the lack of voices of color as part of service learning courses in higher education. For the past 15 years, she has served as a mentor for gifted students of color in both urban and rural areas throughout the United States.

CHAPTER 41

THE GREATEST GIFT OF LOVE

Shondrika Moss-Bouldin

Key Challenges: divorce, family cohesion, father–daughter relationship, self-esteem

My dearest daughter,

I know you don't understand why we made the decision we did but I hope you know that I still love all you kids. You are my first born and I love you. Even though your Mom and I are no longer together, I still plan to be in your life. I hope we can talk soon. I love you so much. I even keep a picture of you inside my police cap.

I love you.

Love, Dad

I was in my early teens when my parents announced that they were getting a divorce. I had a mixture of emotions, but mostly of relief and anger. Even though my parents tried to hide the fact that they were not getting along, they didn't do a good job. During the day, they pretended everything was fine. But at night, I remember hearing their angry whispers when they thought my brothers and I were asleep, or even worse, being awakened by their quiet but heated conversations—more like arguments.

Gumbo for the Soul, pages 229–233
Copyright © 2017 by Information Age Publishing
All rights of reproduction in any form reserved.

The day my parents announced that they were getting a divorce, I did not say a word. But my five-year-old brother, who was the youngest of the three children exclaimed, "why are you doing this?!" I love you both!" My parents looked very uncomfortable at his reaction and my mother was noticeably sad.

I thought that it was interesting that my brother felt that he had to choose between my mother and father, because they never encouraged us to do that. Both of them always communicated that they loved us both, but I had already jumped on my mom's bandwagon. I had decided that my father was the bad guy, so I wanted no parts of him. I didn't need to know the details of my parents' divorce. All I knew was that my mother was hurting and, in my eyes, my father was responsible for her hurt.

I tried to avoid as much alone time with my father as possible. But the more I tried to avoid it, the more my parents countered my unsuccessful escapes with "family time," which included everyone: my Mom, Dad, and my two younger brothers. I began to wonder why they decided to get a divorce. And questioned myself with "Weren't divorced families supposed to do everything separately?" I soon realized that this was not the case with my family.

As a student, I was very smart and pretty perceptive, I took note of a lot of things. My mind keep questioning what was going on. It seemed as if my father came over every day, be it to see how we were doing in school or just to check on our well-being. I also realized that the divided homes of my parents were actually functioning as one; if one of us were on punishment at my Mom's house, then my father made sure that the punishment was enforced at his house. In fact, oftentimes, my mother and father created the punishment together. We were not able to 'play' our parents against one another, so we were unable to go over to my father's house and escape punishment.

Even when my father attempted to spend his time with us separately from my mother, as, fate would have it, we would inevitably end up spending our time as a total family unit. For example, I remember the first time we went out of town for a family reunion without my mother, my youngest brother became very ill and the next thing I knew, my Mother was there and we were spending time as a family unit again.

Being in this two family household that really operated as one family, affected my school experiences. When I was a teen, I made the decision to live my own life and not wallow in their problems I didn't want to become what society called a victim of divorce. I decided to follow the advice of my parents and participate in school activities. They encouraged me to do whatever made me happy, so while I was in high school, I joined every group that I possibly could. As a result, during my senior year, I was Secretary of student council, Editor of the school paper, a very active member of SELF (Self Esteem Lasts Forever), drama club, the Caller on my drill team, and a member of the National Honor Society.

Both of my parents were almost always there for me during pivotal moments in my life. It was a rare occasion that both of them were not. I recall an evening when I was performing during half with my drill team. When I looked into the stands, my parents were sitting next to one another cheering me on with pride. And that meant something to me; they were there, together, and I appreciated the fact that they never brought anyone that they may have been dating to our activities. It was if they collectively decided that our events were a "sacred space" and my siblings and I were appreciative of their decision.

It became easier to accept that while they may have divorced one other, they did not divorce us. The more time we spent together, the more my anger towards my father decreased. My parents made sure that they created a cohesive and supportive unit for my siblings and I to grow and be successful. And we were successful. All of us earned college degrees, and in fact we all went on to obtain Master's degrees. I went even further and continued with my education to earn my PhD from Northwestern University and now realize that my father's decision to work hard so that he could finance the best education possible for his children (in this case, a private school) and my mother's unwavering support actually helped build the confidence that I needed to attend and graduate from an excellent university.

My mother was determined that I was going to be an early college applicant. So, she made me finish all of my college essays and applications during the summer before I began my senior year of high school. Her determination (and mine) paid off and I was accepted with an early decision to Northwestern University and Spelman College with scholarships to both schools. I eventually chose Northwestern University and again, my parents came together to make sure that I was OK. They both helped me move into my dorm. But this time, things were a little different and it was very apparent to me that reconciliation of their marriage was inevitable. And at that moment, I realized that I was completely over my anger and I was happy for them.

During my freshman year of college, my parents called to inform me that they were going to re-marry but I wasn't surprised. I knew it would eventually happen, I just didn't know when. When the summer came around, my siblings and I all stood at the altar with my parents as the wedding party; I was the maid of honor and my brothers were groomsmen. I still remember shopping and selecting my dress; we were so excited. During the wedding, I realized that my parents were re-marrying one another, while also strengthening the bond between all of us and I finally recognized that the bond was always there, but it was stronger than ever before. That was one of the best days of my life.

My parents showered me with love and unwavering support throughout my life. They always encouraged me to aim high and were there for every monumental occasion of my undergraduate career, my master's recital, my defense for my dissertation, and all of my graduations.

Now that I am married with children and I have a family of my own, I appreciate the many gifts my parents gave me. They taught me that family is everything—never give up on your children, and never sacrifice being a supportive unit, in spite of your personal differences.

I know that there is no escape from my memories; they are buried deep inside of me. But, I rarely think about the negative aspects divorce had on my relationship with my parents during my teenage years. Ironically, the relationship that I have with my father is a lot closer than the relationship he has with my brothers.

As I write this piece, I smile because I remember my son playing in the ocean with his Granddad (my father) and his Me Ma (my mother) with the biggest smile on his face and a sparkle in his eyes. If any of us had held on to the past, none of us would have experienced that memory. I'm so thankful that my children have an opportunity to spend significant time with my parents and I know their love will impact their future relationships in a positive manner. There is no denial that their relationship has taught me a lot about love and the importance of family support in order to achieve my goals.

Most people are fascinated when I tell them my parents were once divorced but have since re-married and have been so for a combined total of over 40 years. Many find it hard to believe that such a strong couple once had a broken bond. But, this is my reality and although I don't appreciate it the way I should have as a child and teen, I can't imagine it any other way. I'm so happy that my parents found their way back to each other . . . back to love; and in the process, they taught me the power of love through reconciliation. Most importantly, they taught me that forgiveness is one of the most generous aspects of love. Anything is possible if you believe in love. When I think about them, I always remember that if you really love someone, you never give up on them. You never give up on love.

Shondrika Moss-Bouldin, PhD, is the co-founder of Soulploitation Creative Works/Acting Up! an artistic production company (fine and performing arts) based out of Atlanta Georgia and Los Angeles. Dr. Moss-Bouldin also works as an independent artist and scholar who earned all of her degrees from Northwestern University (BA, MA, and PhD). She received a Fulbright in 2006 to study in South Africa and has taught and/or directed at several universities and presented at numerous conferences. Dr. Moss-Bouldin is a member of The Lincoln Center's 2012 Director's Lab. Some of her previous artistic and consultant work include Disney Theatrical Productions, The Kennedy Center, Kenny Leon's True Colors Theatre Company, Horizon Theatre, Synchronicity Theatre Group, Creative Arts Team, Cobb and Atlanta Public Schools, Chicago Shakespeare, Georgia Council for the Arts, The National Black Arts Festival, and The National Black Theatre Festival. She has directed, produced, and choreographed several projects.

*Gumbo is a mixture of all that is great
about Black womanhood—our resilience,
our brilliance, our identity, strength, and the
beauty and multiplicity of our being.*

—Yolanda Sealey-Ruiz

CHAPTER 42

FEAR IS NOT AN OPTION

Barbara Mullen

> **Key Challenges:** decision making, fear of failure, imposter syndrome, self-efficacy, academic goals, career challenges

From the time I could understand the concept of fear, I held a healthy dose of fear. The irony is that my actions often demonstrated that I was fear*less*. Perhaps, internally, I was courageous and didn't even know. I would create a grand scheme, be afraid to accomplish the task and them tackle the task regardless of how I felt.

The first career choices that I can remember having as a young girl were becoming a fashion designer and a shoe maker. When I was older (circa late '80s, early '90s) I wanted to be an archeologist. I thought I'd grow up to hunt down relic thieves, (with a whip and a fedora) and bring prehistoric reptiles back to life in an amusement park. Sometime during high school, I imagined I'd go into advertisement and work for beauty brand, which I am sure happened around the time I was old enough to watch the movie *Boomerang* on repeat. But, when I entered college, I finally fell into public relations no thanks to any real direction regarding my career. I'd been to some journalism camps and so I thought media was the way to go

Gumbo for the Soul, pages 237–242

and it really was; I just didn't know what I was going to do with media, but I decided to focus on public relations (PR).

Pause. I was tired of school. I was tired of learning, being in college, and being broke. I wanted to do broadcasting but I was *afraid* I'd be in school a second longer.

Rewind. In college, I pledged Zeta Phi Beta my freshman year, flunked all my classes, and was promptly snatched home by my parents to attend community college. I then transferred to a state school, but I felt that I had something to prove and I still graduated "on time" because I didn't want to be delayed by changing the area of focus.

Play. By the time I considered PR, it was my junior year. I came to learn a year or so later that I should have had an industry internship every summer that I was enrolled in college. But that was not something the Black PR students were told. We also were not told to join the National Public Relations Society, that a Black Public Relations Society existed, nor that a department mentor was a necessity or that their were events in Chicago that were geared toward students in the PR field. I had very little guidance so my self-efficacy grew tenfold my senior year.

After I graduated, I didn't have any internships lined up. I then had the bright idea that I wanted to go to law school, but I bombed the LSAT and decided to stay in the PR field. That summer, I took a call center job at a huge company and I'd still be there today had I not been bored one day at work and began to search my high school's website. In between disgruntled callers, I searched the school alumni page and noticed a famous alumna worked for Black Entertainment Television. I can't even remember her name, but I sent her an email and told her I wanted to try to get my foot in public relations and entertainment. She responded quickly and shared that she knew the publicist for the Los Angeles office, and that they were neighbors. I applied for the fall internship and before I knew it, I was on my way to LA to intern with BET.

Pause. BET did not pay their interns, but I made a little money that summer in the call center and planned to live off of my earned wages. But I was wrong. I had a hold on my school account for parking tickets and they would not release my college transcript without settling my debt. Ironically, it was just the amount I had saved, almost to the penny. Two days before I left, I met the man who would eventually become be my husband. Nonetheless, I ended up going to LA with only two hundred dollars in my pocket.

Play. When I look back at the fall of 2006, I'm always amazed at the fearlessness I exuded. At the age of 22, I had a great job, but I left that job in the dust for a once in a lifetime experience to work in for a major television network in LA. I didn't have any money or family in LA. I just left. I also met a great guy right before I left, but I wasn't charmed into staying in Chicago. I was pretty naïve.

Spoiler Alert. LA didn't work out very well. I ended up not liking the Hollywood life. I had a lot of fun knowing that I didn't have to look a certain way—to an extent, but it's very superficial there. For example, during my first week, the entire office was on a liquid diet. Still, I had the chance to see the entertainment industry from a very different perspective than I would have had I gone to "make it big" as an actress. In the end, I knew it wasn't a good fit for me. I wasn't really ready to strike out and make it as a Hollywood publicist. Instead, I hoped to do something more.

At times, I wonder how life would be had I stayed in LA. Some of the relationships I made while there were awesome, some of which I still have today. I view the Facebook posts that they share that tell about the various award shows they worked and the selfies that they have taken with celebrities. One woman I worked with is now the director of communications for a major network in her own right. Sometimes I think, "wow, if I wasn't so afraid of struggling in LA or not being pretty or small enough, I could have been great!" I honestly don't know if that would have been the outcome, but I often wonder "what if?"

Rewind. I have had a nagging fear of choosing since I was at least 8 years old. In the third grade, during a holiday Christmas party, each student was tasked with bringing a gift for the secret Santa exchange. My teacher lined up us diplomatically and we each had a chance to go to the stack of gifts and pick one. When it was my turn, the teacher was confused as to who was next because me and another little girl were both standing next to each other. I was raised right, so I let her go first. She picked a gift first, and then I followed. When I opened my gift, I saw that it was a delightful Aladdin stationary set. But when she opened her gift, my heart sank. It was a Tinkerbell make up set with three tubes of lip gloss, a compact case, two bottles of nail polish and eye shadow. All of the colors hideous and not remotely similar to my shade of beautiful brown, but you couldn't tell that to my 8-year-old self. I never regretted anything as much as letting my classmate go first during that gift exchange. Since then, choosing has paralyzed me because I have a fear of regret and making the *wrong* choices.

Play. A turn of events required I go back to school to finish up one class. I completed a graduation audit and was able to walk across the stage during graduation. But, I later found out that I was short three credits. I realized that they didn't tell Black kids when they are short three credits. Instead, we were allowed to audit and walk across the stage in blissful ignorance. But, because I was short credits, that meant that I had to go back to Chicago. By that time, the cool guy I meet right before I left for LA had become my cool boyfriend. When I finished up that one class, I did all of the things in the Chicago PR scene that I was *not* encouraged to do as a student. I secured an apprenticeship with a theatre company, I landed another internship with one of the leading PR agencies in the world and finally landed my dream job as an account specialist with a Black owned PR firm in the Neiman Marcus building downtown. I was living. I took the leap and I never looked back. I was even able to freelance for BET when they came to town. Those milestones made me realize that fear wasn't really something that held me back, no matter how uncomfortable it made me. I was quite proud of myself.

Pause. In retrospect, I'm very proud of 22-year-old Barbara. If I were to meet her today, I may even look up to her and ask her about her secrets to success.

Play. Just when I thought I was getting in a groove, I was sabotaged by a nasty co-worker and as a result, I lost my job.

Pause. That's not entirely true. I was fired because I wasn't really good at my job. I was in love with what I thought I could do in my job and I was fired because I didn't perform. The real reason I left LA, the theatre company, the big firm and the little firm was... I didn't really like public relations. But, my coworker was nasty about how she actually fired me.

Play. Getting fired was really my fault. But as a result of me getting fired, I was living with my fiancé (at some point in 2007 he upgraded from boyfriend to fiancé) and unemployed and I didn't know what to do next. By that time, I moved back to Chicago, which was a PR town and I could have found a job in a few days or even a few months. I was a competitive candidate because I worked in top, highly sought after positions, but I didn't want to go back into PR.

I felt like I needed to be work toward something more rewarding. When I told my dad that I didn't have a plan of action, he suggested that I obtain a basic skills certification so that I would be eligible to substitute teach in the district. The suggestion made since because both of my parents were in education and they didn't want me to be in a position where I would have to call and ask for money. So, I began to research how to go about obtaining certification. While doing so, I came across an advertisement for an alternative certification program. Within the advertisement, what stood out the most was the phrase, "start teaching in the fall." It peaked my interest, so I attended an information session, sat quietly, and took notes.

At the conclusion of the meeting, as I walked out of the door, I was stopped by the director who asked, "What do you think you'll teach?" " I don't know, what's the need?" I replied. She stated, "Special Education." And I responded by saying, "Put me down for that." And I walked out. I haven't thought about that conversation from the summer of 2008 since it happened. But at that time, it was so easy and so effortless that it was a bit alarming. I decided to transition into a totally new career path with very little hesitation. I was Fearless.

I called my mother to share the good news. "Guess what mom? I'm going to be teaching special education, just like you!" The way she responded would make you think that every one of her students were her children, not me. "Why?" She asked. Do you even want to be a teacher? You better not teach it if you don't mean it and if you aren't going to help those children." I thought she'd be proud and gush with joy, but she didn't. Instead, she gave me a warning: If I messed over those children, I'd have her to contend with. I hung up the phone and soberly contemplated if I really wanted to do this, but I knew that I didn't have a reason not to.

I pursued the program and started graduate level classes the next week. While attending classes, I attended a teachers fair and was hired on the spot and was placed in a classroom within the next month. According to my mother, I was a "warm body" who would be able to sit in the classroom with 17 yes, 17 students with special education just so that the school system could report that the students were being taught. I don't know if it's a testament to my skill as a special educator or the inhumanity of the district in which I worked, but I knew the moment I stepped in the classroom that the students had never had a strong teacher and unfortunately for them, they didn't to get one that day either. My first year teaching consisted of things that legends are made of, so much so that I don't have enough room to write about those experiences. I had a terrible my first day and an awful my first week. I was passable after my first marking period, however, by the second semester, I was a pretty impressive teacher, even when I place my performance against my current standards.

Today, I'm hard on first year teachers at my school. I remember how hard it was and I remember not knowing the questions to ask and how to meet the needs of every student. Now, it is doubly hard to be a first year special education teacher in a self-contained classroom located in a poor neighborhood where people expect your students to fail.

Pause. I seldom think about my life's work, but when I do, I think about what I would have accomplished had I not been afraid. I also think about the students I served my first year of teaching, but I only know whereabouts of one of my inaugural students. She's a senior at a great high school who has been accepted Spelman. I can't say that I was the greatest teacher in the world, especially since she was in my class during my first semester. I did not get a chance to teach her my second semester because I recommended that she be removed from my class. I found out that she was placed in special education classes the year prior, but when I taught, I noticed that she squinted her eyes a lot. So, I recommended she get an eye exam which the school paid for. She was then reassessed and indeed, she needed glasses. I was afraid to say anything for about three weeks after this revelation. Although I was a first year teacher, I knew that there were tests that accounted for variables like vision and hearing, but I feared that I would look like an idiot to assume those things were overlooked. As it turned out, there was an oversight and because of the oversight, this student was in an environment that was not appropriate for her. Therefore, the school and the district were all out of compliance.

Play. These days I'm managing things well. I work with students, families and teachers to try to save starfish. I call students starfish because of the anecdote about the little girl who sees starfish washed up on the shore. The little girl attempted to throw every starfish back into the water as a means to save their lives. A man who saw her throwing the starfish into the water asked, "Little girl, what are you doing? Surely, you can't save them all." To which the little girl replied, "but to that one starfish," (referencing the one she just threw back), " I can make a difference."

Rewind. I spent the latter half of my twenties, enjoying my husband, (I married that cool guy I met before I moved to LA) and having his babies. I followed him across the country from Chicago to Seattle. We eventually moved to Houston and I am currently working on earning a PhD in special education leadership. But, every time I felt fear creep up I would throw caution to the wind and leap head first into a challenge. For example, I ran a marathon (while working on my doctorate) and had two babies. I moved, changed jobs, and dealt with racism in the schools and districts all while fighting for my little starfish.

Play. I still experience fear. Still. I'm no longer 22, but I am an expert in my field and I know what it takes to save Black children with disabilities. I also know what it takes to make good teachers become even better and the better teachers to become great for *all* students. But, I fear that I won't happen under my watch. My lingering fear is that all of this time and the decisions will add up to nothing. Children will still be mistreated, schools will continue to be mismanaged, and teachers will still not know how to teach. Currently, I am suffer from imposter syndrome, because the more I accomplish and the more I learn, the less confidence I have. But, I'm learning to look in the mirror and tell myself that fear is still not an option. When women turn 30, they are supposed to be more confident and have it more together. But I don't feel that way at all. I feel like there is more to lose and less to gain. I feel the pressure but I also feel the privilege. I get to come to work and truly impact lives in a way that I would have never imagined. I've achieved the sense of purpose I longed for in my twenties. So the question now becomes, what is really holding me back? There is no easy answer to that question. On any given day, I could be immobilized by a multitude of things. Still, I have to get up each day and push through thoughts that seek to make me stumble as I pursue to continue with the good work. I can't spend my time looking back at my 22-year-old self with jealousy or even resentment. I can't ask her why she didn't chose certain paths and why she let some dreams go out the door. She is not here; I am. And I am the woman I've always wanted to be. But, I do think my 22-year-old self would be proud.

Barbara Mullen, PhD, is a special education administrator in Houston, TX. She currently serves as a Senior Program Specialist, over inclusion for Houston Independent School District. She is also the founder and lead facilitator of Secure Your Oxygen Mask First, a teacher retention and professional development consulting firm. Dr. Mullen received her bachelor's degree in Public Relations from Northern Illinois University, her Master's degree in Special Education from Quincy University and her Doctorate degree in Special Education and Organizational Leadership from Capella University. Her research interests center around instructional practices and programming that positively impact academic achievement for students of color with learning disabilities in inclusive settings. Dr. Mullen is also the author of *Secure You.*

CHAPTER 43

THE GARRISON FINISH

Learning to Live on Purpose, Not Just on Time

Janice Nix-Victorian

Key Challenges: scholar-athlete, rural living, illness/disability, extended family, value of faith

As a young girl growing up in Southwest Louisiana, I had all the necessities—family, love, but, above all, I had the indelible wisdom of grandparents. Dad vowed to his father on his deathbed, when he was 18, to care for his mom. Thus, Grandma Louise was "grandfathered" into our household, literally. She lived with mom and dad from the first day of marriage until she was in her early 80s. Daily, she enthroned in the center of our kitchen, in a wooden rocker. Pressed and prim, face powdered, lips colored red, her black hair in an upswept bun atop her head with a white cotton apron that adorned her dress, as she prayed in Creole three times—morning, noon, and night. Our names were petitioned one by one, to God. Grandma Louise had modeled my first life lesson—prayer, it was priceless, yet free.

Gumbo for the Soul, pages 243–247

Daddy bred, trained, and transported racehorses to derbies and spent time on the road. I was never "old enough, yet" to travel with him, but was captivated by his tattered roadmap and the notion of travel through his storytelling. By way of his stories, my world expanded in comparison to the small-unincorporated community of Plaisance, Louisiana—population not even measured. Reared on the horse farm, I pretended to train with the racehorses when daddy harnessed the horses' reins to the steel carousel bar that rotated counterclockwise on its platform. I wrapped my legs around one of the inner bars and hung faced down, out of harm's way with my hands extended downwards into the loose sand. I envisioned the starter gate, the silver farm racetrack posts aligned on a 45-degree angle. "Ils sont partis," (They're off and running) I said when the carousel turned. My hands patted in the sand, one, and then the other in a walking motion and quickened to a trot in sync with the horse's pounding hooves.

Momma had her hands full with the seven of us. The two eldest were girls, then four boys in a row, and there I was, number seven. Overshadowed by four boys at the time, I learned how to be tough and to run brave and free like that little filly that lived inside of me. "Janice Marie, stop being so rough with your brothers, you're a girl," my mom regularly scolded. *I'm a racehorse*, my subconscious screamed, while my mouth whispered respectfully "Yes mamam." I knew I was a girl, but my everyday quandary was competing in a boy's world, while wearing my brother's snug and fitted hand me down jeans, patched at the knees.

We moved off the horse farm when I was nine. No more horses to ride, except an ungentle pony named Dynamite that grazed Pappy's pasture. Pappy purchased me a purple bike with a pink and white basket, and it had training wheels. I unreservedly accepted the bike but refused the training wheels. No baby's bike for me, I was a big girl. "Get up and do it again because every time you do, it will get easier" he instructed each time I fell, with fresh new bruises to show for it. My Pappy's lap was my new carousel, where I snuggled and I cried away my little girl hurts. With him I also laughed and rehearsed my bigger than life grown-up dreams.

Mom Lorena was a gardener who made me remove the weeds from the soil. She was a tall, olive skinned lady whose stern and serious eyes pierced beneath her straw hat she wore to block the sun. Her "yes" was yes, and her "no" was no. I addressed her accordingly. I always felt distant from her, yet connected to her in an uncanny kind of way. She passed away when I was 14 years old.

In high school, I was on the girl's track team. At 17, I was soaring through my junior year of high school. I was a smart, high achieving student throughout school. I excelled in most of my classes. I was athletic. "Unstoppable," one might say. I was training for the cross-country competition. One day, I strode into dead man's curve and came in for the home stretch, the stopwatch ticked on, second by second. I was not sure what time the coach had in mind, but I knew I had to beat it. "Bring it in Nix; come on, push," Coach Pete yelled! I lifted my head to open my breathing, relaxed the tension of my arms, right foot lifted and suddenly my shoulder plowed onto the black turf as I tried to break the fall in a roll. "What the hell just happened?" Coach questioned in the distance. Embarrassed, I pulled myself up to my knees and replayed the fall. I found no riposte as my eyes met his, "I don't know; I just lost my balance." After a few weeks of practice, my falling to the atrocity of dead man's curve became my new normal and my excuse was no longer tolerated. "Damn it, Nix, I need you to go to the doctor. Don't come back on my field until you are cleared! Do you understand?" "Yes Sir." I walked slowly to the locker room, wondering if this would be my last home stretch; saddened and isolated from the team, and concerned for my well-being.

Months raced by, the doctors were clueless, and all bets were off with the coach. Teams of specialists tested and searched for answers to the problematic hip. Hunches of lupus, cancer, multiple sclerosis arose, but all of the tests returned negatively. Eight months later, and with over 64 joints inflamed, I was bedridden, and whether or not my legs would sustain me was like a flip of a coin each day. Bizarre stuff began happening to my body, even chewing food was suddenly an issue, and my weight dropped from 125 to 100lbs. My pants size tumbled from a 7/8 to a size zero. "Is that even a size?" I argued with the store clerk. I refused to wear size zero pants. Elastic waist pajamas girthed my tiny frame and became my all around attire for home and doctor visits. Eight months later, the rheumatologist diagnosed me with Juvenile Rheumatoid Arthritis, and prescribed 15 aspirins, 8 muscle relaxers, and 3 anti-inflammatory drugs daily for five months to manage the pain and swelling. Life as an energetic teen, as I knew it, suddenly slipped away into my new medicated arena, no more track meets, no more skate nights, no more dancing, no more anything.

Not only were my day-to-day activities gone, but so were my dreams for going to college. Since the age of 15, I knew I wanted to go to college and get a PhD I was going to be the first in my family to do so. I had BIG dreams, and my senior year was now approaching, not to mention senior prom. My dreams rushed to a halt, obstructed by the intense flames that corralled my joints, keeping them hot and inflamed, stalling my racing spirit. I could not even write my name as my pen felt as if I was holding a brick and my joints hitched in excruciating pain.

Senior year in 1982, I attended school for all of two days then enrolled in homebound schooling. I felt alienated from both school and life in general. I wanted friends around, but at the same time, I was angry and my pride did not want them to see my condition. Over time, with my best friend's assertive support, I was resolute to march at graduation with my class. On that day, mom let me skip my meds. It was worth the severe pain, because I was able to make my parents proud.

During that time, I used over 30 different medications, sometimes I felt like they caused more destruction than good. My mother, a spiritual woman, cried out to God, and at night her plea took precedent over my pain. In the next room, she asked God to give her the pain instead. The night of my graduation invoked a paradigm shift in everything, as I knew it. With my future on hold and my present desolate and disqualified, all I had to grasp from was the grandstands of my past. Nestled deep in my soul, I heard the routine prayers from the old rocking chair that Mom Louise chanted. Those prayers kept us all, day after day. In time, I began to pray for myself unceasingly, trusting God to heal me above the doctors.

By the time I was strong enough to attend college in the fall of 1986, my high school classmates who had gone off to college had graduated. Unfortunately, Pappy transitioned to glory during my freshman year. On his deathbed, I promised him I would finish college. On many occasions, I was so discouraged that I pitched my textbooks into the wastebasket and phoned my mom, "I want to come home; it's too hard to manage it all." Momma said, "Take a warm shower, say your prayers, take your meds, get a good night's rest and call me in the morning if you still want to come home." With the sunrise came the memories of my falls on my purple bike that rallied ever so loud "get up, do it again, never quit even when it hurts, it will get easier." By God's grace, I retrieved my books with just enough tenacity to fight the snares of the naysayers. The odds were against me, but God takes pleasure on the longshots.

Finally, I became cognizant of a third lesson. Like Grandma Lorena, I had to incorporate a "Yes, God could do it attitude, without wavering." Deep inside, I felt my spirit race again and I would purposefully declare, "*Mind over matter. If I don't mind the pain, it won't matter.*"

Accomplishing simple tasks sometimes took longer to realize, but with every goal met came an increase in the measure of my faith. I graduated in fall 1990 from the University of Southwest Louisiana, transferred to Southern University, and earned a master's degree in 1993. In 2007, momma died of pancreatic cancer, before I earned my PhD in 2010. While those who knew me revered my obtaining the degree, I could only reverence God, who granted those same hands that could not hold a pen to complete a 470-page dissertation.

"Now amazingly, Janice, your inflammation level is in the normal range. The rheumatoid arthritis has burnt itself out," my rheumatologist said at a visit in 2012. My body did not ache and swell anymore, except for my degenerative hip that was partially in the socket and partially out. I had a left hip replacement in 2013 and recovered quickly. Finally, there is no pain. Life's challenges have kept me humbled. God's purpose for my life keeps me racing in strength not of horses or men (Psalm 147:10). Each time I look at the deformities of my hands, I am reminded of the power of faith. In the pursuit of competing and completing, in the arena of education, I was least likely to win, but won in the end—despite the challenges. I am reminded of the 19th century jockey, Edward R. "Snapper" Garrison, who initially lagged behind in a race but still managed to win. My solace is awakened! As I continue to pursue my career in education, I hope to encourage others to live on purpose, not just on time.

Janice Nix-Victorian, PhD, is Director of Student Support Service, at Louisiana State University Eunice. She received her PhD, from the University of Louisiana, Lafayette. At Louisiana State, Eunice she is the Coordinator of Grants development. Her research interests include poverty and education, sociolinguistics, second language acquisition, early immersion, and language planning and policy. She is level one certified in cultural intelligence.

CHAPTER 44

I AM NOT ALONE

Overcoming Abuse and Rejection

Quinita Ogletree

> **Key Challenges:** sexual abuse, suicide ideation, self-esteem and self-concept, anger management

1 out of 10. I am not alone. Somewhere near the end of high school and the beginning of college, I began researching the statistics about the sexual abuse of children. Something in me needed to know, and to believe that I wasn't alone, that I didn't cause this. I needed to know I wasn't abnormal or different. The scars of the abuse tore at my soul. I knew I was gifted, but it wasn't enough to protect me. Being smart didn't stop it from happening to me. I had already hid myself in a blanket of fat to protect me from unwanted attention. I was trying my best to find a reason to live each day. Trying to understand why this had happened to me and why I was still here.

The first time I remember trying to commit suicide was in junior high school. I was probably 12 or 13. For some reason, I believed one of the older boys who abused me liked me. It was probably a rationalization for

Gumbo for the Soul, pages 249–251

what was occurring in my life. However, I overheard a conversation between him and two others and realized he didn't like me at all. I went home and that night and dissolved Tylenol in hot water to be able to drink it down faster. It tasted awful, so I poured it out. This would not be the last time I would try to put an end to my misery. I often overmedicated myself on prescribed or over the counter medicines, thinking and hoping that if I took more, I would get better faster. I was hoping that the pain would ease and give me some relief from my problems. Once I started driving, I would drive recklessly when upset. During my last years of high school, I realized that I needed to make changes about how I handled medicine due to my stress and anger and pain. It wasn't until I was in college that I began to understand the destructiveness of my driving and misuse of medication was a response to my need for a strategy to cope with my problems.

No one noticed these issues in my life. I believe because I hid them well. I was the smart Black girl. I went to school, church, and attended social functions while hiding behind a mask. This mask was that I was smart, and it appeared that this couldn't happen to me! I wanted to be the perfect granddaughter for my grandparents who were raising me. I didn't want them to have any reason to be ashamed of me or be upset with me. There was only one crack in the mask that I portrayed. I had anger issues that seemed to pour out at the wrong time, and with the wrong people. I would hold everything in, and as soon as one small thing would happen I would explode at my friends. I remember two vivid incidents in junior high and high school where I hit one of my friends very hard because of my anger issues and almost lost those friendships.

The reader may want to know what happened in between those years. What interventions did you experience? Who "noticed" these things and offered help? How did you cope in college? There is a big jump from middle/high school to 40 years old.

Now as I finish my 40th year on this earth, I am so glad that each suicidal attempt is just a tattoo on my soul that says I survived. As I survived each moment I felt different. I survived each moment, I felt I was unlovable, ugly, and unneeded. I survived each arrow that was designed to kill my future. Those arrows hurt, left scars, and modified my trajectory, but I survived. I look back and wonder what would I tell myself if I could go back in time. What would I say to heal myself? What would I tell myself to cope in more constructive ways?

One: *Tell somebody who is trustworthy.* I held everything in. I felt I needed to protect others. I was raised by my grandparents and I didn't want to hurt them. I took the job of protector, but I was a child. I understood that my truth would strain relationships and change the lives of our small community. In my mind, if I kept quiet, no one would get hurt. I didn't understand I was hurting myself and maybe allowing others to be hurt like I was. At the time, I believed it was me. It was my fault. I believed I attracted these abusers in my life. I was unlovable—my mother and father did not want me, so I must be damaged in some way.

Being gifted or smart was not enough to buffer such rejection and abandonment. It would take until I was in my twenties, when I became a mother, to see that this thinking, this rationalizing, for the fallacy that it was. As I was raising my own daughter, I wanted her to be outspoken and direct, and to be effective at coping with challenges in her life. As I began to self-reflect, I realized one reason for this was that I still blamed myself because I was shy and quiet. I wanted her to be more self-assertive, so such things would not happen to her.

Two: *This is only temporary, even though it feels permanent.* I was making permanent decisions based on temporary circumstances. I wanted to die based on the current situation—not realizing that my future was so much brighter. I finally began to see the light at the end of the tunnel when I started college on an academic scholarship. This was when I began to heal and bloom. My second year in college, I finally trusted someone with my secrets and began to let go of some of my destructive behaviors. However, healing can't be rushed and it takes time. You have to be open to the process and know sometimes there will be setbacks. Life and growing is a process of ebb and flow... of moving forward and backward.

As I write this I cry, not a full blown cry, but I can feel the tears in my eyes. I want to go back and be the protector and champion for the little girl I was. But I can't. I hope this encourages some little girl, who like me blames herself, hides herself, and wonders... why should I go on? You should go on because tomorrow will come and another tomorrow after that. I am here to let you know, you are a survivor and you will be successful. I have been happily married for almost 18 years and have five daughters. I have one bachelor's degree, two master's degrees, and a doctoral degree. I have traveled abroad. Almost everything that I dreamed about having or doing when I was middle school and high school, I have been able to accomplish, and you will too—if you keep putting one foot in front of the other and knowing you are not alone. Someone else has been where you have been and felt what you have felt. You are not hopeless; you are a survivor because you are still here.

Quinita Ogletree, PhD, is a Lecturer at Texas A&M University. Her research interests are achievement disparities, literacy, gifted education, early childhood and urban education. She received her bachelor's degree in Psychology and her Master of Divinity from Virginia Union University. Dr. Ogletree has a master's degree in Educational Psychology from the University of Houston and her doctorate in Curriculum and Instruction from Texas A&M University.

CHAPTER 45

ADVERSITY IS KNOCKING...
LET SUCCESS ANSWER IT

Charissa M. Owens

> **Key Challenges:** underachievement, low/negative academic self-concept, single parent, loss of parent

I graduated high school in the top 10% and entered college with the sophomoric expectation of easily earning high marks in all my college courses. However, in the fall of my freshman year, I was failing two thirds of my classes. I called my mom before fall break in a panic. I ranted, "How can these professors expect me to read so much in so little time and still get the content of the text? What makes them think that I can remember all the information in multiple chapters? I can't keep up with all the papers, projects, and due dates for each class. I am well in over my head."

In my mind, I didn't feel smart enough for college and I felt my professors did not want me to succeed. For about 10 minutes, she just listened. I expected her to commend me for trying and help me figure out how to withdraw from classes. To my surprise, she started explaining that my poor performance was not because of my professors but rather my limited

Gumbo for the Soul, pages 253–256

experience in facing adversity. She went on to say, "You are from an intelligent, college-educated family, and you'll graduate from college. Go, take a walk, Chari. Then come back to your room with a plan to improve your grades." I did just as she asked. As I walked down the dorm hallway, I pushed a heavy door ajar to a small courtyard and I reflected on what she said. The moment I opened the door, memories and stories about my family's history flooded my mind.

LEARN FROM THE PAST

I recalled my mother sitting to my left and my sister to my right. We sat in the first row. After attending many Sunday services at a Baptist church, I knew this was an honor. But an honor for what? I didn't understand why we were being honored. But I enjoyed the honor of sitting in the front row. After a while, we were escorted to a limousine and back to my Grandma Ivey's home for lunch. This is what I remember from what I was told was my father's funeral. He died at 32 years old. I was five, my sister was two, and my brother was days from being born.

Having two small children and pregnant with her third child was a heavy burden for my mother to carry at a very tragic time. It definitely was not a part of the dreams my mother had for herself and our family. With much support from my extended family, she took on her new life as a single working mother. A few years passed and she realized that the help of my West Indian family wasn't enough to support the vision she had for herself and children. So, in church one Sunday, she told God that she would do everything in her power to be a good mother but she would need HIM to be the father. With that prayer, she was reminded of what our elders achieved and chose to embrace her power to do all things through hard work and faith.

That was over 30 years ago. Since then, my mother made difficult decisions in order to keep our family fed, clothed, sheltered, and happy. She made the choice to work longer hours at her current job. She also took on seasonal jobs. My mother leaned on her strengths and faith, believing that one day she would be able to see the dream she had for her family manifest. She focused her energy on balancing work, raising her children, and going to school; something that she saw my own grandmother accomplish. Today, she holds a master's degree, which has enabled her to earn higher paying leadership positions in her organization and improve the quality of life we had as a family.

"You come from an intelligent, college-educated family" was a phrase she repeated to us through the years. College wasn't an option, it was a requirement for my siblings and me. She wanted to be sure that we knew our family's story. It was the platform she used to remind us that we can do and achieve anything. She would describe a time in society when most Blacks residing in the south were discouraged from going to school. Using historical facts, family pictures, and other government documents that were in our possession, the stories of my elders' accomplishments unfolded. My great-grandfather earned his medical degree and became one of the first Black doctors in Florida. My great-aunts and grandmother all graduated from college and became teachers and nurses. With a stern, yet nurturing voice my mom would end the stories by saying, "This is the stock you come from." I did not understand the significance of my family's story and my mother's experience until the moment I pushed opened my college dorm's door.

When I opened the door, the memory of these stories showed me that I was capable of succeeding. In that moment, it became clear to me that my mother and elders did not cower in fear when they were challenged. They didn't run away or, in my case withdraw, from adversity. Instead, they faced it and overcame the problem by working harder, making sacrifices, and seizing opportunities.

I understood the significance of my elders' educational accomplishments. Their lives and what they were able to do was a testimony to what could be gained when faced with adversity. They confronted hate, economic inequalities, and sub-human status. Yet, they did not give up. They choose to work harder with less resources. When the opportunity became available, they attended and graduated from a Black college in order to achieve more than society expected.

My mother's experience after the death of my father showed me that I would need to make hard decisions and choose to accomplish my dreams—no matter what. My mother believed that she could achieve what she wanted because she saw my grandmother and other elders accomplish their dreams in the face of adversity. It took my mother many years of sacrifice to balance three demanding roles—single mother, employee, and student. Her accomplishments led not only to her dream of earning a graduate degree, but also seeing her three children complete college with graduate degrees. Today, my sister and I hold doctorate degrees in counseling and special education, respectively. My brother, the child my mother was carrying when my father passed away, has graduated with a bachelor's degree in business and is working toward completing his master's degree in business administration.

After reflecting on what my family achieved during times of adversity, it was clear that I needed to put into practice the same principles. When I returned to my dorm room, I stayed up late getting organized for my classes. Over the next week, I sought opportunities to work in study groups. I also set up meetings with my professors to ask for clarification for each assignment. The library became my second dorm room. Within weeks, I began to see an improvement in my grades. More importantly, I learned that adversity is not a roadblock, but rather a platform for an opportunity for another level of success.

CHOOSE TO EMBRACE ADVERSITY

I believe, at its core, adversity is an opportunity to learn what one is capable of doing in order to be successful. You can choose to succumb to the problem and become its victim or work hard to surmount it and become a victor. Even now, as I face uncertainty, I consciously make the choice to believe that I have what it takes to take on adversity so that I can experience a greater level of success.

What makes me believe that what I am doing will help me be more successful at the end of this moment of adversity? Well, I have a record of overcoming hardships starting with that moment in college. You will never be free of experiencing hardships. Each challenge will be more difficult than the last. But, you can embrace moments of adversity by believing in your ability to succeed. You will need to work hard, make some sacrifices, and seize opportunities as they come. In the end, I can assure you that you will be propelled to the next level of success. So, accept life's adversity and allow it to open doors to opportunities that will lead you to achieving your dreams.

Charissa M. Owens, PhD, is a Visiting Assistant Professor at the College of Charleston and state certified public school special education teacher. Her work focuses on educating culturally and linguistically diverse students who are twice-exceptional. She is currently working on expanding access to academically rigorous schools that embrace diversity.

CHAPTER 46

A FAMILY AND A DREAM

A Journey from South Central to Life Beyond

Alexis Riley

Key Challenges: identity, school challenges, self-esteem, first generation college student

---

South Central—a place where home ownership determined the presence of depth of poverty, violence and drugs. Growing up in this part of town, required knowledge of location and familiarity. My father would often warn me against wandering past the streetlight and watched me like a hawk while I played outside. Unprotected by the confines of my parents' car I understood that by leaving my block I opened doors to the dangers of homelessness and gang members on the streets that paralleled my own. Of course, simply remaining on my block did not shield me from everything, but I remained steadfast in focusing on our family's dream of making it to college.

Growing up I felt like I was living in a place filled with love yet with two parents who occupied separate habits of cultivating my childhood.

Gumbo for the Soul, pages 257–260
Copyright © 2017 by Information Age Publishing
All rights of reproduction in any form reserved.

My mother tended to the practice of instilling focus and structure within me and my father lived in the land of music and exploration. Seemingly my parents only had one clear vision in their marriage and that was the development of their children—my sister and I. Continuing their familial lineage from separate towns in Louisiana, they both viewed college as the key to success for their daughters, and a feat that they themselves never witnessed or achieved.

My home growing up was also my mother's childhood home in the 1970s. When Black, female ownership was rare and treasured, my maternal grandmother, Nana, handed over the property to my mother when she was at the tender age of 18. At the time, my mother was in school and working a full time job. Eventually, she realized that college wasn't really 'her thing' so she dropped out before finishing her associate degree at California State University, Los Angeles. Similarly, my father grew up moving from home to home in around Compton and dropped out of high school at the age of 17, eventually earning a GED at 19. He then decided to focus on searching for purpose in the church. This led to my parents meeting in 1987, and married when my mother was pregnant with me two years later.

Two years after my birth, my parents decided to have one more child. Struggling to pay bills and finance two children, my father worked a full time job as a banker, while my mother stayed at home on food stamps, taking care of two children and getting paid to babysit some of the toddlers in the neighborhood until I was five. I can still envision my father holding heavy grocery bags from bus to bus from Downtown Los Angeles to home, and my mom daily providing all she could spiritually and emotionally. My parents made the decision to sacrifice financially, with my mother staying home because they felt no one else would raise their child. They had a keen sense of the importance of early years of development. After a certain point, my parents seemed to only be teammates when raising their babies. Even when their inevitable divorce occurred in 2005, and emotions were at a high, they still kept my sister and me as their central priority.

Although none of my parents, aunts and uncles went to college, getting a Bachelor's degree was a constant and natural part of the conversation that they had with me when I was a child. College was talked about as if it were a huge planet outside of our solar system that I had to figure out how to travel to, and I found myself fully committed and determined to take on the challenge.

Inspired by the lack of an effective father figure he saw in his own life, my dad strived to 'learn while teaching' when parenting me. He would instill within me to work twice as hard as everyone else. By the time I was in first grade, my father started working the graveyard-shift at Bank of America in order to become part-time staff at my elementary school, known by all the staff and students (which wasn't a problem until my more impressionable fifth grade hormones kicked in). Looking back, I'm not sure when either of my parents slept, both with full-time employment and two children. With my father randomly popping into classrooms from K–fifth grade, I excelled academically and landed comfortably in the role of 'teacher's pet'. Where some students seemed as if they naturally understood skills like fifth grade math or technical skills like handwriting, I repeatedly found myself having to go home and repetitively study and write down vocabulary and math rules to really understand. In order to keep up with the exponential pacing in the classroom, I tackled emotions of failure and sacrificed recess and after-school activities for studying. Rewards and verbal affirmations from family made me think I could reach my goals of A's, and although sometimes I received B's, becoming Student of the Year in fifth grade and honored with writing a speech at graduation made me start to really believe I was great in this academic world.

Even with all the affirmations and goals, none of this could combat the failings of the Los Angeles Unified School District. Walking into fifth grade at a second grade reading level, I met a woman with these strange and magical letters after her name, "PhD" for the first time. She was my fifth grade teacher and I named her, *Black Classroom Superhero*. I did all that I could at home and school to impress her and meet her goal for me to be over grade-level by the end of the year. I hit my reading goal and her accomplishments are still idolized by me today as I map out my next steps in life.

In high school, my drive and strong desire to impress helped me understand what my teachers really expected of me. After earning life crushing B's in ninth/tenth grade, I finally got my footing by eleventh grade, with AP classes and joining a number of student groups. My parents' co-workers and friends kept repeating one thing about eleventh grade, and it was that it was the most important year that colleges looked at. With that information I could start to smell the air of the college solar system getting closer and closer. I lived and breathed college FAQs sheets, making sure my UC 4.2 and high school 3.8 GPA was good enough to get into my top three colleges, Barnard, Smith, and University of Pennsylvania, respectively.

After being rejected from Barnard, heartbreak led my decision to extend my time in California, delay my dreams of moving to New York and attend the top UC (University of California) College I was accepted to, University of California, Santa Barbara. With a 2.7% Black and 50% White population, the pro-Black upbringing that I received at home combined with my lack of foundational writing skills resulted in a 2.5 GPA my first quarter in college, while having two jobs. Both crushed and confused as to how to recover from such a failure in this strange land, I realized I was no longer within the safety confines of 81st street with my father watching over. I had to overcome my academic gaps, work three times as hard as my White peers and study late nights and while at work. Memories of my family were always there to wipe my glasses clean when I lost sight of that degree at the far end of the galaxy. I had to constantly reaffirm all of the lessons and quotes that were spoken over my life while in South Central, with occasional visits home just to be held by both of my parents' warm embrace. Academically, I started to find my way, and by my third year, I found myself with three jobs, including undergraduate research assistant and A's in all five of my classes. By my fourth year at UCSB, I stepped out of the spaceship and achieved my childhood goal in earning my Bachelor's degree with a 3.3 GPA in 2011 with both parents by my side. But somehow my thirst for the galaxy beyond the sky was unquenched and I kept yearning for the next step!

I continue to stand on the shoulders of my ancestors before me, I hold their vision of my success near and am continuously reminded of where I come from, the paths I have surpassed and the future steps that God has ordered. Now ending my fifth year as a teacher with a Master's in Science of Teaching from Fordham University's Graduate School of Education, I have extended branches of the tree of success that my families planted in the soil of Louisiana many decades ago. Despite all my accomplishments, in all honesty, that PhD, at the end of my name is still what I daydream about when imagining the next stop on the galaxy of my parents' dreams. My life is a story of a family's aspirations coming full circle, where sacrifices turned into triumph for myself and the future generations. Currently as a teacher, I strive to set an example like the one I saw from my Black classroom superhero, being a presence that is uplifting, demanding and honest about the realities of the world that students of color experience. As a child and now as an adult I continue to bridge the gaps where schools have failed and somehow still inspire me. Bridging these gaps by learning the lessons of failure and overcoming expected adversity as a Black woman by remaining faithful to the dreams of that fifth grade girl who dreamt of colleges and making her family proud.

Alexis Riley is currently a High School Physics teacher in Brooklyn, New York. Her research interests include the success of second-generation Black/Brown college students, the development of racial identity amongst Black/Brown students in a predominantly White teaching environment and culturally responsive pedagogy, tentatively. While teaching, she has continued to found and facilitate student activist groups and performs as a Teacher-Leader.

CHAPTER 47

BEYOND OVERCOMING

Living Out God's Plan

Cynthia Rivers

> **Key Challenges:** single parent family, school challenges, poverty

*Overcomer: I have been young, and now am old. Yet I have not seen
the righteous forsaken, nor his seed begging for bread.*
—Psalms 37:25

Growing up in the projects, I was the youngest of 10 children. My mother was married but in many ways, still single. Married at a very young age, my father did not know how to be a dad or committed husband. So, he was absent most of my life. He was what the old folks called a rolling stone . . . *wherever he laid his hat was his home.* I don't even remember my father living with me. However, I do remember longing to fill a void that was missing in my life. But, since I was only three years old, I didn't quite know what that void was.

I remember fluttering butterflies during the summer days and the rhythmic flashing of lighting bugs when night hit the sky. The twirls of box fans in

---

Gumbo for the Soul, pages 261–265

the windows made a low humming sound, and neighbors sat on their porches trying to catch a cool breeze. Our houses were so close, you could walk out the front door and touch the door of your neighbors; and the walls were so thin, you could hear every conversation of the family. People hung out in the middle of the day on the street corners. The sight of public transportation and the smell of chemicals from the Proctor & Gamble plant down the street and trash from the city dump located literally in my backyard were prevalent. Many of the kids in the neighborhood would 'shop' at the dump. If we were lucky, we would be able to find dolls and cars to play with.

Life comforts were rare . . . almost non-existent. I recall vividly how we ate syrup and condiment sandwiches and used a string of soda bottles in the window sills as our burglar system. The question in the back of my mind was, "Are we poor?" as I happily sat on a potato chip can that also served as a makeshift chair because there were not enough chairs at the kitchen table in my house. I remember playing outside until the street lights came on and creating games that allowed our imagination to run wild, as my mother watched from the front living room window. We could only afford one pair of skates, so my friend and I would share the pair . . . I would wear one skate and she would wear the other. We made tents out of bed sheets and swings from old clotheslines and used and a piece of a card board box as a seat. We had so much fun.

When it was time to sleep, it was like the lottery. I would go from room to room to determine who would have the 'privilege' to 'triple up' with me in the twin bed that slept two (in my house) but would accommodate three if necessary. I remember my brother or sister calling out, "I will take little Cindy Sue tonight." I would then crawl up in the middle of my siblings and enjoy the bond. Yet, in the back of my mind, the same question would creep up, "Are we poor?"

I remember standing in the neighborhood line for free cheese, rice, powdered milk and honey. I remember my mother reaching into her purse and pulling out pretty colored coins and paper food stamps so that my brother could run to the store and buy a dollars' worth of red skinned bologna, a twenty-five cent loaf of bread, and a bag of chips to feed the family.

Growing up we made do with what we had. Baking soda was a wonderful product to have on hand—it was cheap and did wonders. We used it to as deodorant and a household cleaning agent. We also used it to wash clothes and brush our teeth. We always ate as a family, but I never understood why mama didn't eat. When I would inquire, she would say "I'll get something later." I watched as the food quickly disappeared. There was barely enough to feed us, and her 'later' never came. Again, I would ask myself, "Are we poor?" But when I saw the love in her eyes and smile on her face, I sensed that we were not poor as defined by traditional standards or criteria.

I frequently watched mama in the kitchen. She would always whip something up and I never understood how she could make a feast out of three small items. I thought that she had to be the thirteenth disciple because she was an amazing cook and she could make items stretch to feed the multitudes. Everyone in the neighborhood loved to come to our house and, on many occasions, Mama could feed her 10 children along with another two or three children in the neighborhood. She feed us all with the items purchased with a few colored coins and a book of paper stamps. "Mama, how do you do this?" I asked. She replied, "Child, it is the Lord that is doing this." At that point, I began to seek the Lord that my mother spoke so highly of. I began to do what she did. When I would get into trouble, she would say "Bring me the Bible. Let's see what the Bible says about this." She would then go on to read, "Honor thy father and thy mother that thy days be long upon the earth." Shortly thereafter, she gave my brother and me a small bible of our own. And so it was, that I began to read at an early age. I was an advanced student.

I also prayed and asked the Lord to give me understanding. Little did I know, at that time, I was actually praying and seeking the Lord for myself... and that void that I longed to be filled as a three year old was suddenly filled.

I would always go to church with my mother and she would teach me the ways of the Lord through her love, generosity and kindness. She taught me how to give out of my lack. She also taught me that if you trust God, He is a God of multiplication. It was from our conversations, my reading, and my answered prayers for understanding, that I learned that having a closed fist meant that you were not able to receive anything, or give anything. I learned that I needed to be willing to give my time and my talents, that if I give, it would be given back to me, in good measure, pressed down, shaken together and running over.

Many of my friends were allowed to run the streets. They embraced their surroundings and accepted what was before them. But my mother would always say, "*Living in the projects does not mean the projects live in you. Take pride in where you live.*" Mama made us clean up the neighborhood. We picked up paper and made sure that no one defaced the property. She also taught the other children in the neighborhood to have purpose and a sense of pride and she actually paid them if their yard was clean and free of debris.

Mama would always recite Phillippians 4:3 to me. "You can do all things through Christ who strengthens you." She would go on to say, "You can do anything and be whatever you want to be. You have a good head on my shoulders." I was always encouraged and did well in school.

As I grew, I knew that I wanted to be a businesswoman. So, I would constantly remind myself, as well as others, that we could do all things through Christ who strengthens us. As a young lady in middle and high school, I would dress the part. I went to school in business casual attire and enrolled in classes that emphasized the goals I wanted to reach. I was noticed by a teacher who recommended me for a job to work in the school office. In the summer, I worked in the rental office of the apartments where we lived. And this prepared me to be the owner of a photography business that my husband of 19 years and I now own. My gifts and talents as a businesswoman are being fulfilled.

As I grew up, I always asked myself, "Are We Poor?" As an adult, I can now answer firmly and boldly, "No, we were not." Although we did not have the resources or money to eat choice foods or, at times, not enough to buy some of the necessities like clothes, we were very rich. Because of our faith and perseverance, we were not forsaken or begging for anything. God provided. We were wealthy in love, family, community, giving, sharing, knowledge, wisdom and God. We were taught to not allow our circumstances to define us. We were taught that what we had could not be purchased with money. It was a gift freely given to all of those whom desired.

I could have been a statistic of a young gifted African American woman who came from a broken home in poverty. I could have been 'stuck'. Instead, I remembered what I was taught; if you can dream it, you can have it. I sought knowledge and wisdom. I knew who I was and what I was created to be. I also knew that I had to go back to God, the one who created me. I looked to the word of God, the Bible and in Jeremiah 32:27 it reads, "I am the LORD, the God of all mankind. Is anything too hard for me?" My answer is "certainly not!" God is the one who can take a young Black girl from the projects of Cincinnati, Ohio and make her into an overcomer! One who overcame the obstacles before me. One who overcame the words spoken over her; that she would not amount to anything. One who overcame not having my father in the home. One who overcame inadequate education because of where she lived and the lack of books and resources. One who overcame not being considered because of the color of her skin. One who overcame not having the proper necessities. One who overcame obstacle after obstacle . . . obstacles too numerous to count. By dealing with and gaining control of a difficult situation, I am able to affect the lives of others through my faith. I am an *overcomer* and this is my desire for other gifted Black females. Have faith, work hard, and you, too, can overcome.

Cynthia Rivers, is a business owner, Prayer Leader, Certified marriage coach, devoted wife and loving mother of two. Cynthia's life speaks to God's great love for others through her leadership, friendships, family, and counseling. Cynthia has worked as a reading coordinator to improve children's literacy and develop the reading skills of students in low-income elementary schools through shared reading experiences. As a certified marriage coach, Cynthia and her husband have a passion for helping couples grow their relationships and solidify their marriages on strong biblical principles. Only God can turn a mess into a message. *"Do small things with great love"*—Mother Teresa

CHAPTER 48

THE OTHER "BIG C"

Kelly A. Rodgers

Key Challenges: divorce, homelessness, parental drug abuse and addiction, school challenges

We had the nicest house on the block. Our neighborhood in north St. Louis in the 1980s was a mixture of two-parent and traditional, mostly working class Black families. When I was four, my parents bought their first home and moved our family from the projects. My parents were young, not quite 25, newly married and itching to grow their family. When my first brother was born, my father surprised my mother by buying the home down the street that she had been cooing over for at least three years, and there we set up shop.

Our family would eventually grow to include five children; I was seven years older than my next sibling, but the four of them came in fairly rapid succession, each year, with the final year ending with the twins. As my mother usually described it while chuckling, "I had one in '84, another in '85, I skipped '86 but then I doubled up in '87." As a stay-at-home mother, she cooked, cleaned, attended PTA meetings, and baked cupcakes for my class. On weekends, my father took over and would rise early with my siblings and me to make breakfast. We took family trips down south in our

Gumbo for the Soul, pages 267–271

station wagon, and weekend outings to the zoo or amusement parks. By all accounts, we were living that little slice of the American dream that was reserved for working to middle class Black folks in the inner city.

But, as an adolescent in a house full of young kids who demanded my parents' attention, I often felt lost in the shuffle. I was quiet and sensitive and kept to myself, save for a few close neighborhood and school friends. I had always been that way. I lived somewhat on the outskirts of everything. My sixth grade year, on the suggestion of elementary school teachers, I had begun at Classical Junior Academy (CJA), which at the time was the only full-time gifted middle school program in St. Louis. At CJA, I found something that I never knew to desire: a building full of beautiful, brilliant witty Black kids. As a part of the school desegregation program, CJA also drew a significant number of White kids from the suburbs. We were a motley crew by anyone's standards, and in all of our individual weirdness, we found a home in the spirit of CJA, a home in which we still live and remain a very close-knit group even as we prepare to enter our 40s.

Things at school were good, but things at home were unraveling. There were hushed conversations between my parents late at night, and I'd creep to my bedroom door and strained to hear. "Laid-off." What did that mean? It sounded for sure like Daddy wouldn't be going to work. But for how long? Laid-off. That sounded temporary. You got laid off for a period of time and then you go back, right? That was different than being fired. I watched as week after week passed, with my father never going to work. When the phone rang, I again strained to hear that joyous moment when he would be told when he was no longer "laid off." But, that call never came.

What did come was foreclosure. We were going to lose our gorgeous house; the house I loved with the bedroom done in pink Holly Hobby just for me. The house I'd lived in since I was four-years-old. One afternoon, when I came home from school, my father was sitting on the couch, as he was so many days since being laid off. He was sullen, and he said he wanted to talk to me. I was starving and asked him to let me make a sandwich first, but he wanted to talk to me right then. Incredulous, I dropped my backpack at the door and sat next to him on the couch. He was sadder than I've ever seen him, even to this day. His eyes were red and he wouldn't focus them directly on me.

Cocaine. The singular word that would shape my life from that day forward, and which would always seem to be omnipresent. My father was addicted to crack cocaine. It was the early 90s and crack was something that teachers and after school programs urged you to "just say no" to. It wasn't real to me, but then it was. That's why he lost his job. That's why he couldn't get another job. That's why we were losing our house. That's why we would be moving in with his mother, on a street two blocks over.

What followed the two years I spent sleeping on my grandmother's couch was a flurry of moves that shifted so quickly that I could barely catch my breath. First, my father got a job in Florida, just outside of Jacksonville. He moved first, and we followed soon after. It wasn't long, though, before the increasingly obvious telltale signs of drug use emerged. The paychecks disappeared, the appliances were pawned and then lost. We returned back to St. Louis, but my spot at CJA had been given to another child on the waiting list. I was crestfallen but, as she would do so many times in the intervening years, my mother came to the rescue, calling my school, speaking with the principal and somehow got her to agree to allow me to return. I needed that. School was my sanctuary. I watched everything I'd known tumble down around me, but I kept my head down and pressed on.

The pattern would repeat itself several times, beginning a year later, when my mother's cousin turned her two-bedroom apartment over to us when she enlisted in the Army. I was in high school then and was forced, as the result of the school desegregation order, to abandon Metro College Prep, the gifted high school I attended with most of my classmates from CJA, and to enroll in the predominantly White high school in the suburban district in which we lived. Missing paychecks and appliances. Rinse and repeat. Head down, persevere on. Next came a three-month stint in a shelter for women and children, meaning that my father would not be living with us for the first time in our lives. We'd long since gone on welfare to provide food; my father worked, but smoked his pay just as fast as he earned it. With the support of the shelter, my mother was able to save some money and we were able to move into a temporary home in south St. Louis. My mother started working again and a year later, we were in our own place, a spacious new townhome in south St. Louis. A sense of normalcy settled over our house and I prepared to enter my senior year.

My father had moved to Chicago, still trying to outrun his addiction. He had a good job and was renting a house from a guy with whom he worked. He was clean and ready to have his family with him again. But the question was, would we come? I was growing increasingly disgusted by my father and the crap that he put us through. I didn't want to go. Through all of our changes since I had to leave Metro, my mother had worked hard to make sure that I didn't have to change schools again and I'd settled in my suburban high school for more than two years. My teachers and administrators were amazing and they spoke with my mother to try to keep me involved with things, including the annual leadership camp when I was the first Black kid bussed in from the city who had been chosen to participate. Despite this, I still had no strong ties to that high school, but was concerned about what this meant for my college applications. Would everything transfer? Would I lose out on some things I needed to know to do well on the

ACT? This would be my third high school. Would that be too many for colleges to consider me? Would they view me as being as unsettled as I felt?

As with Jacksonville, Chicago was short-lived, the Big C (cocaine) commanding attention yet again. By January, my mother, seven-year-old sister and I were headed back to St. Louis for the last time and I returned to my high school for my final semester. I was behind a bit on the college application process because of the senior year move, but I scrambled to get everything together.

My parents would never be together again and divorced a year later. My father kept my three brothers, as they both thought it was best that they have the presence of a man in their lives. He was, after all, what my mother called a "functioning crack addict." After his initial lay-off so many years ago, he always managed to keep a job, usually a well-paying one, too; yet his addiction just wouldn't allow him to prosper in the job. So my brothers would be safe, at the very least. I began my first year of college, aided by a generous full-tuition scholarship and a heap-load of loans and grants to provide room and board. I chose to stay close to home, attending a small predominantly White private college two hours from St. Louis. My mother, sister and I shared a one-bedroom apartment, and my newly divorced parents were time-sharing my siblings over holidays between St. Louis and Chicago, albeit oftentimes contentiously. With my home life stabilized at last, I was ready to leave the nest, but I did not want to wander too far. My mother and I had gone through the fire together, again and again. She was shelling out chunks of money to support my brothers in Chicago as my father continued to use crack cocaine, so money was usually tight, but she was spectacular at sending care packages and ordering birthday cakes for me to share with my friends during finals week. I made it through college on a wing and a prayer, perseverance and with the love and support of my family.

Today, my father is clean and has been so for so long that I have had the luxury of having lost track of how long. My parents are still divorced, yet both of them are living happily and successfully apart, having rebuilt their lives and in doing so, they helped the five of us rebuild ours. However, many of the scars and lessons remain. I don't get wrapped up in "things." I've seen my family have "things" and I've seen us lose it all, over and over again. I can and will stand through the fire and the flames, but I also know when to escape out the back door. I love loyally and honestly. I believe in struggle and in triumph. Through the process, my mother and school have remained my constants. Wherever we were living, whatever madness we were going through, I buried myself in education so that when I got to graduate school and I taught my first course as a teaching assistant in the math department, I had no doubts about what I wanted to do with the rest of my life. I earned a Master's degree and then a PhD, and in the stands, cheering embarrassingly just as I had instructed them not to do, as I made my way across the stage, were my four siblings, my mother and my father.

Kelly A. Rodgers, PhD is an Assistant Professor of Psychology at the Borough of Manhattan Community College at the City University of New York. She received her dual BA in mathematics and Spanish from Westminster College, and her MA and PhD in Educational Psychology from the University of Missouri. Dr. Rodgers' research centers around the socioemotional aspects of the college experience, such as issues of identity, self-understanding and motivation for students of color in general and in STEM in particular, and how these contribute to student persistence and institutional retention.

CHAPTER 49

MY JOURNEY FROM THE SOUTH BRONX TO THE ACADEMY

Yolanda Sealey-Ruiz

Key Challenges: poverty, immigrant family, college academic under-preparation

I came of age during the 1980s in the South Bronx. Other than its fame as the birthplace of rap music, my neighborhood was similar to many 'hoods' in America. It was a poor community that was rich in potential and possibility because of its youth. I was privileged to grow up at a time when rap music and the Hip Hop movement were guiding principles in defining and redefining what it meant to be young and Black in Urban America. The 'godfather of rap, Grandmaster Flash, lived a few blocks away, and a member of the Cold Crush Brothers, one of the first widely recognized rap groups, was a family friend who lived five floors above my family's apartment.

Our neighborhood of housing projects and tenement buildings enveloped the youth of my community in security. We were young, we were

Black, and we had dreams. Our parents 'made a way out of no way,' and it wasn't until we grew up and moved out of the neighborhood that many of us realized we were quite poor.

My father occasionally owned a business. Sometimes he was proprietor of a liquor store or dry cleaners, and when those businesses failed, he worked for a man named Maxi, whom I later came to know as Uncle Maxi. Uncle Maxi was a full-bellied, gray-haired Greek man who was a loan shark to many and a numbers runner to most. He became very close to my family, and I'm certain that, for many years, he was my father's only friend because whenever dad needed anything, Maxi was his go-to person.

My mother was a stay-at-home mom. This was out of necessity, since she was taking care of my two siblings, my diabetic grandmother, and me. My father rarely kept a steady job, despite his skills and education (he was trained as a pharmacist on the island of Barbados), but he was adamant that mom stay home to watch us (his sketchy employment record didn't seem to matter when it came to this topic). He did not want us to become latchkey kids who roamed the streets and got into trouble while both parents were at work. The subject was not open to debate. According to him, and those who subscribed to the 'cult of true womanhood' philosophy, a mother's place was in the home; her job was to take care of her husband and children. I think during those years that my mother was so overburdened with raising the three of us, dealing with the drama my father put her through, and caring for her sick mother, that even if she had the inclination to protest 'her place,' she probably didn't have the energy to sustain her objection.

Time has a way of making things apparent, and I believe I have thought deeply about the many issues I experienced as a child because of my intellectual maturity. At a young age, I was able to understand the complex situations going on in my home, school, and community. In a very real way, these situations encouraged me to work even harder in school in order to put myself in situations where educational opportunities would be offered to me. As a result, I qualified and was placed in a gifted and talented program in middle school, and attended a renowned gifted and talented educational program every weekend at the Fieldston School in New York City. Education was often my solace to the issues that were taking place at home.

Mom and dad were often at odds about money, especially during those high-pressured 'back to school' moments; however, my maternal grandmother and uncles managed to rally their funds together to guarantee that my siblings and I return to school each year in the 'flyest' gear. But, it wasn't just about the clothes, although this was very important to most kids in my community, particularly those who went to the schools in the neighborhood. The start of a new school year was also the one chance that we had to rock 'fresh gear' for a least one-week straight, and give the impression that your family was better off than the other families in the community. It was also a chance to show off, get noticed, and gain/get respect.

Although my father flaked on our 'back to school clothes' money several years in a row, we never believed that our education was not important to him. Both of our parents made one thing clear to me and my siblings—there were things they could not afford to provide; however, a solid education would grant access to those things and offer us a passport to the vast world that existed beyond the boundary of our South Bronx neighborhood.

As I grew older, I began to realize and fully appreciate what my parents did for us—they did their best. I witnessed many sour moments between my parents due to the lack of money and my father's infidelity, but my siblings and I managed to create a somewhat pleasant childhood (most of the time) and create a decent life for ourselves. We emerged as professionals; I earned my doctoral degree, my brother David is a CPA, and my sister Donna is a Registered Nurse.

My father, a Bajan, migrated to the United States during the late 1950s. He was a licensed pharmacist on the island of Barbados, and received a full scholarship to continue his studies at Columbia University in New York City. My mother left Auburn, Alabama at the age of 16 and moved to New York City in hopes for a better life. In the years before she met and married my father, she worked as a housekeeper and home health aide. One year after her arrival to New York, mom met and fell in love with my dad. A few months later, mother was pregnant with my sister, and my father's college plans were postponed. He decided to look for work and become a family man. With every passing year, the hope of going to Columbia faded, and by the time I came along, he was faced with the task of caring for a family of three children, a wife, and a sick mother-in-law.

On the surface, dad and mom seemed to be mismatched. My mom, a southern girl from Alabama, left her home and a life of poverty for a new start in New York City. My dad, who came to New York in his early twenties, was forced to leave Barbados after a tragedy that resulted from a medication he prescribed. Although a licensed pharmacist, he prescribed an unauthorized drug akin to the "morning after pill." The young lady who took the pill hoping to terminate her pregnancy died of internal bleeding. Since my dad's family was middle-class and well connected, they were able to get him off of the island before he could face a penalty. Though their lives seemed worlds apart, together, mom and dad were the exact parents my siblings and I needed to get us through the toughness of the South Bronx as we were developing into productive citizens.

The truth is, my father threatened us if we didn't get good grades and he did not hesitate when it came to following through on his threats. My mother was motivated by a determination that we each would go further in school than her (she left school at 16 to come to New York). I'm not quite sure what influenced me most back then: the threat of being beat with a stalk of sugar cane by my father, or the disappointment that surely would fill my mother's eyes if I brought home failing grades. In any case, I bought home grades of 90 through 99; my mom was ecstatic, but my dad asked where the 100s were.

Mom continued to encourage us with a remarkable dedication to our success. Each morning, she would rise early, make us toast with peanut butter, serve us a glass of juice and send us on our way. Mother didn't depend on the schools to feed us. She saw that as her job. From her impoverished childhood days, she learned that a child cannot concentrate in school if she is not fed. My mother knew nothing of Maslow's Hierarchy of Needs (1943), but she understood that her children needed to be fed and receive proper care if they were going to reach our full potential in school. Although her devotion was not enough to prevent my brother from dropping out of high school (as do many young Black males for various reasons), it was what was needed to encourage my sister to complete her A.A.S. in nursing and convince me to buy into the notion of lifelong learning.

My sister received fairly good grades and passed through school in an uneventful, middle-child-syndrome sort of way. But school had to be different for me. I had to excel. It was the only way to show my mother what her dedication meant to us, and to help heal the wound that my brother inflicted on her heart when he dropped out of high school. Although I was the youngest child, I felt this immense pressure to make up for my brother's failure and uphold the family's definition of educational success. I began to bring home report cards with 100s in many subjects, entered and won local and national storytelling contests, and secured a place in a weekend gifted and talented program at the elite Fieldston School in Riverdale. I wrote poetry, short stories, joined the debate team and the weather club; my participation in the weather club even won me 15 seconds of fame on a local television news program. By the time I was in my final year of junior high school, I realized that my mom's encouragement sparked what already lived in me—a love of school and a passion for learning.

I was considered an exceptional student in junior high (I was bestowed the honor of valedictorian of my eighth grade class) and I did very well in high school (I graduated with a 98 average); however, it was not until my first year in college that I began to experience the effects of my inadequate public school education. All was fine when I academically competed against other poor Black and Latino kids from communities like mine, but when I entered the collegiate arena and had classes with White and Black kids from middle- and upper-class backgrounds, excelling became a challenge for me. I realized that my classmates knew much more than me; they'd read books I'd never heard of and visited places that I had only seen on television. There was a significant gap in the quality of our education, and my education was clearly on the lowest end of that gap. I played catch up during my four years in college and managed to graduate (after taking remedial math and writing classes my first year) and finish with a 3.3 grade point average. In spite of my GRE scores, my GPA, along with my personal statement, got me into Teacher's College, Columbia University. I was no longer new to the game, and though I was deficient in many areas that my classmates were not, I found a way to excel at Columbia, while holding down a full-time job as a marketing manager. I worked hard, embraced the challenges before me, and made a vow to earn my PhD even before I fully understood or could imagine what it meant to complete the terminal degree.

Although I continued to love learning, I cannot say that my first four years of college were easy for me. I had just started at Columbia, married and moved to Manhattan's Greenwich Village. I was an evening student and worked for *The New York Times* as a marketing manager during the day. I made a decent salary, but without my PhD—the degree I vowed I would earn a decade before—I was not completely satisfied. After spending seven years at *The New York Times*, I went to work for another media company, and then a large college. I was earning a nearly six-figure income when I decided to walk away from the money and the career I had carved out for myself and become a graduate student at New York University's School of Education. I was about to become a doctoral student and I was determined to not let anything—a successful job or lack of money—stand in my way.

I earned the PhD in 2005, and began to move forward with my new career. In retrospect, I realize that I have been fortunate enough to become a career changer who has made a successful switch to my life's work—teaching (and learning). Shortly after earning my doctorate from New York University, I began teaching at Kingsborough Community College in Brooklyn, New York. Within two years, I had my daughter Olivia and decided that it was not wise for me to work 90 minutes away from my newborn baby. I applied for, and was granted, a postdoctoral fellowship at my alma mater, NYU and went on to become a Research Associate with its Metropolitan Center for Urban Education.

After two years at the Center, I received a phone call that would change my professional life forever. After meeting my former practicum professor in Ossining, New York during research fieldwork, I received a call and was invited to teach a course at Teachers College in the very program from which I graduated over 15 years ago. I accepted the offer and after 18 months as a research associate, I applied for and received one of two-tenure track positions in the program. From that moment, I decided to spend each day engaged in hard work and prayer; my focus was tenure even though no one had received tenure in the program for almost two decades.

Much has changed since my days in the South Bronx. Recently, I received tenure at my alma mater, Teachers College, Columbia University. It was not an easy road to travel. My story is one of hard work, prayer, perseverance and serendipity. I vowed long ago to make a difference for students—particularly for those who may need to be reminded of their gifts and greatness. This approach makes me somewhat popular with students, which keeps me very busy, but I find my work to be very rewarding.

I worked hard, believed, and gave it my all. There are still days that I am in awe of where God's blessings and my hard work have taken me. It's been a long road from the streets of my South Bronx neighborhood to a tenured position at Columbia University. There is still more work for me to do, but, for now, I take some comfort in where I am on this journey, and in the fascinating possibility of just how far this little Black girl from the South Bronx can go.

REFERENCE

Maslow, A. H. (1943). A theory of human motivation. *Psychological Review, 50*(4), 370–396.

Yolanda Sealey-Ruiz, PhD, is an Associate Professor of English Education at Teachers College, Columbia University. Her research interests include racial literacy, culturally responsive pedagogy, literacy and urban school environments. She is founder and faculty sponsor of the *Racial Literacy Roundtables Series* at Teachers College.

*Your story could be the key that unlocks
someone else's prison. Don't be afraid
to share it.*

—Anonymous

CHAPTER 50

WHY NOT YOU?

My Story of Inspiration and Determination

Chinequa Shelander

> **Key Challenges:** divorce, extended family, anger, over-achieving

The smell of bacon loomed in the air as my father stood in the kitchen fixing breakfast; I woke up and began dressing for church. It felt like a typical Sunday morning, except that it was not a typical day. My mom entered my room to say good-bye. You see, my mom was moving out and back to Georgia to start another life without my father. What made this so unusual was that she was leaving my brothers and me behind. Though it was hard to understand at the time, I knew it was in our best interest. I was in my first semester of ninth grade when she left, I can remember thinking, "What am I going to do now?" We left for church and hugged my mother one last time, because I knew when we returned from church, she would be gone.

High school was supposed to be a time for dances, fun, and maybe a little freedom, but that was not the case for me. When my mom left, it put a strain

Gumbo for the Soul, pages 281–283
Copyright © 2017 by Information Age Publishing
All rights of reproduction in any form reserved.

on my father. Being a firefighter, he worked 24-hour shifts and the need for childcare grew. Luckily for us, we had a strong supportive extended family. We stayed with relatives on the nights that dad worked, up until I turned 16. Every other day, we would stay the night with cousins and although it was fun, it was also taxing.

March 27, 1997 was a Thursday. It was also, my sixteenth birthday. I recall being at school and counting down the hours until the final release bell rang. I had a lot of built up excitement because I was going to get my driver's license. As soon as the bell rang, I ran down the hall, said good-bye to my friends and practically ran through the school building door and jumped into the car. Not only was I going to get my driver's license, I was also going to get a car! Some called me lucky but that luck came with a price. I became responsible for being "mommy" to my two younger brothers. As a high school sophomore, I would pick my siblings up from school, go home, make sure my homework and their homework was completed and then prepared dinner. I had to ensure they had clothes picked out for school and that they went to bed at a reasonable hour, all as I tried to excel in school and be an athlete.

Enduring much responsibility at such a young age was really tough. All my friends were able to enjoy high school, while I was thrown into pseudo-motherhood. "Why me?" I would ask. "Why can't I just have a normal life?" Although the responsibility was great, as a gifted young woman, I did not let my situation become a crutch. I wanted to be the very best at any and everything that I did. School became my outlet. I threw myself into school and succeeded tremendously. The same school year my mother left, I decided that I would not allow this situation to define my academic career in a negative manner? I chose to remain positive and excelled in my classes. I was also inducted to my high school's 4.0 club, a prestigious "club" that required one to maintain an average of 4.0 or higher for the entire school year. I averaged a 4.1 GPA during my tenth grade year!

As I matriculated through high school, I had my troubles. Maturing into a young woman without a mother's guidance made me angry. Angry with mostly my mother, and as a result, our relationship suffered. It took a great deal of effort, mostly from me, to mend the relationship with my mother. Although I only saw her a few times a year, my attitude and feelings toward her were cold. I blamed her for everything, because I felt as though she ruined my life.

After years of harvested feelings and counseling, my mother and I are very close. She is now my best friend and one of my biggest supporters. Holding a grudge against her did not hurt her, but it weighed on me. In order for me to succeed in life, I had to forgive and let go.

As an adult, I am now able to reflect on my high school years. I wish that things transpired differently, but I realize that my experiences are my story. A story is defined as an account of past events in someone's life or in the evolution of something. You are that something, you are evolving as a gifted student, as a woman, you are becoming older and wiser and your story is being created. Though the road may not be easy, keep going. When you find yourself asking "Why me?" Immediately ask yourself, "Why not me?" Allow whatever you are going through to be your motivator. Being fatherless, motherless, and friendless or just adjusting to being gifted can be tough but use these trials and dissension to excel. Your story can and will help someone one day, like mine has!

Chinequa Shelander, EdD is a science educator in Atlanta, GA. She has a BS in Biological Sciences from Clark Atlanta University, a MS in Biochemistry and Molecular Biology and a MAT in secondary science from Wayne State University, and an EdD from Argosy University in Educational leadership. She is currently working on becoming a professional certified educational therapist through the National Institutes for Learning development and Southeastern University. Her research interests include increasing the presence of minority women in STEM, and the use of culturally responsive teaching for twice-exceptional students.

CHAPTER 51

A JOURNEY INTO RACIAL IDENTITY

A Black Woman and White Socialisation

Victoria Showunmi

> **Key Challenges:** foster family, identity, self-esteem, perseverance

I start my story with the recurring question 'Who am I?' as it forms the basis of my frames of reference. If I were with you, you would observe, visibly, a Black and confident female. However, what you are unable to see is that I was raised by upper-middle class, German Jewish parents. I have since coined the phrase "socialised White" as I am Black and was raised in a middle class White environment.

I started my journey into whiteness when I was given away at six months old by my biological mother in the middle of a busy London station in the United Kingdom. From there, I took up my place in a house in North East Devon, which is located in the South West of England. As I grew up, there were times that I would ask my mother[1] "why did God make me this colour?" I was surrounded with unfamiliar faces that did not look like me.

Gumbo for the Soul, pages 285–288

Such unfamiliar faces included my mother's immediate family (her husband and children), an elderly friend of her mother's, and my mother's acquaintance who became a long-term lodger.

At the age of three, my parents sold their large house and bought a significantly smaller one that was located in a small village in the South West of England. The village consisted of a population of just under 1,000. I taught myself to read, and at three and a half I started school. The school consisted of three to four classrooms. The days at the school were hard as I was not just the only Black child in the school, but in the entire village. This made me ask myself many questions about who I was; and where I belonged. I would continue to ask these questions for years to come. In my mother's innocence or perhaps her naiveté, she made up a poem for me to quote at school, which read something on the lines of:

> ...when I was a baby I was dropped in gravy that was why I was a little brown girl, when Flo was a baby she was dropped in snow and that was why she was a little white girl.

I knew at a young age that being Black would be problematic because of who surrounded me. Playtime was traumatic as that was when most of the racism in school took place. There was a particular game called British Bull Dog 123. The object of the game was for the players to run from side to side, and in the middle was the bulldog. The bulldog was tasked to catch the other players as they ran. Because I was different, the kids insisted that I be the bulldog. This experience was very unkind and deeply hurt me. Whenever I experienced difficult times like these, my mom told me that I should recite the poem she taught me, and if the poem did not work to console me, she would tell me to say: *"sticks and bones can break my bones but names will never hurt me."* Can you imagine? Here I am a five year old with the knowledge to combat the racism I was experiencing was through a poem and song.

I also remember a time when some of the children I lived with in the village wanted me to come out to play. I went out to play with them, not knowing what I was getting myself into. We walked along to the local playing field to play football. Before long, one of the boys in the group asked if I was 'that colour all over'. I did not understand what he meant. He and the others who were more streetwise than demanded that I take all my clothes off so that they could see if I was brown all over. It was raining, but I did as they asked. Imagine, a little girl standing in a playing field naked with the rain falling and not knowing what to do. I was left to get dressed and walk home on my own. In the midst of all of this, my mother lacked the understanding of culture or anything remotely African. I think she was even confused about the way she should view me. My first and most memorable introduction to racism within my home was when my mother would refer to me as her little 'piccaninny.' She somehow thought this was an expression of love.

I was surrounded by very upper-middle class people who viewed my staying with my mother in terms of that of my being a guest. My mother saw me as her *own child*—but at the same time as a child who needed to be grateful for what was being offered; for being adopted and accepted as part of her family. So I grew up with very mixed messages of belonging.

School was another matter. Instead of doing my A levels, I was channeled into a path that mimicked the approach that the English upper class had for daughters that prepared them for domestic work. Moving swiftly on, I did not attend college after graduation. I married a Black man at 19, bought my first house, and had two daughters by the time I was 21. I signed up to do my first college degree when my oldest daughter was just one week old. I passed my degree with ease, as I found learning very easy, even in formal school settings.

By the time my daughters were three and four, their father announced that he was gay. This news rocked my family and me. I knew I had to make a new future for my girls and me. I decided to focus on myself, and earn a Master's degree. I began my Master's in Women Studies since I was very interested in women's development. I worked as a teacher and then a lecturer before stepping into a career in higher education. My career has been as interesting as my personal life as I have been a business owner, strategic consultant, researcher, Senior Lecturer and head of section. My professional life has included working in the corporate world and at universities across different parts of the United Kingdom.

So what can be learned from my experiences as a Black gifted female raised by a White family? Firstly, what I have shared is just a vignette of my life in these short and limited pages. The important part of sharing this story is that it offers insight into those things that enabled me to survive. I have the ability to put a positive spin on every critical incident that occurs. So if something happens, I look for ways to turn it around into something that can be built upon and used at a later time. I have learned that life is a journey with twists and turns, yet if you keep your eye on the prize, you can achieve your goals and dreams. Furthermore, I have the ability (quite rightly or wrongly) to minimalize painful experiences which form part of my life's journey. With all of my experience, and the trauma I experienced in childhood, I have been able to develop a deep level of resilience that has assisted me throughout my life, and helped me to understand the value of knowing who you are and always separating that from the single stories people have of who you are or who you should.

NOTE

1. Mother refers to German Jewish Mother unless otherwise stated.

Victoria Showunmi, EdD, is a lecturer at UCL IOE London, England. Dr. Showunmi received her doctorate from University of Sheffield, Masters from Institute of Education London and BA hons from University of Greenwich. She is an international scholar whose research interests explore (a) gender and leadership; and (b) Black girls/young women and their well-being. She uses a feminist approach, along with narrative, as lens to analyze her work.

CHAPTER 52

NO SAFE SPACE

Aisha K. Staggers

Key Challenges: health issues, physical abuse/sexual assault, police brutality, racism, single parenting

One day late in June of 2012, I wanted to get away and think, but didn't want to go too far from home. So, I checked into a local hotel on the Northeast side of Columbia, South Carolina. I hadn't been feeling well throughout the day and wanted to rest. There was also some relationship drama going on in my life and I just wanted a break and change of scenery while my daughter was visiting her father.

As the day progressed, I began vomiting. This wasn't uncommon for someone coping with ulcers that had recently began bleeding. After about an hour, I was vomiting blood, profusely. I called my father who lived less than a mile away to take me to the ER. I don't know why I chose to go to the Lexington Medical Center, all the way across town in the very county where the Charleston shooter was from. I don't know why I told my father I would be fine and he could go home because I was certain I would be admitted. I guess it was because it had happened so many times before, I knew what to expect. Or so I thought.

They took a blood sample. I kept throwing up. They took a urine sample. I kept throwing up. They did a chest x-ray. I kept throwing up. A few hours had passed, I continued throwing up and each time it was blood, in massive amounts, to the point I felt light-headed. Then there was the pain, I was in excruciating pain just below the breastbone, like having the wind kicked out of me with a steel-toed boot. At last, the nurse returned with pain meds and I drifted off to sleep. I remember being shaken awake by the doctor who, earlier, barely wanted to touch me to examine me with his face close to mine asking, "How long have you had a crack problem?" I was stunned.

First, I have never touched crack or any other illicit drug in my life. I was always a "good kid." I always got good grades, an over-achiever who strived to be the best, went to college and straight to graduate school. For the first time in my adult life, no one was looking at my college transcripts; no one cared that my graduate school GPA was nearly a 3.9. Second, I was quite disoriented from the pain, the pain meds, and coming out of my sleep in this manner. Third, as I opened my mouth to protest, blood dripped from my mouth, kind of like when you see someone in a movie get punched in the mouth and a long trail of blood is dripping down to the floor.

Gurgling through my own blood, I told the doctor to "get out of my face" and that I didn't know what he was talking about. The only thing I had been taking was Maalox. And I had been drinking that like water for months. Still, the doctor insisted that high levels of crack were in my bloodstream and he was discharging me to go home. I knew he was wrong.

I also knew I was violently ill. So, I asked for a second opinion and more tests. The doctor dismissed my request and sent a nurse in to talk with me. She began going over discharge instructions and telling my about outpatient services to help with my "addiction." I told her that I didn't have an addiction and bleeding as I was and with the pain I was in, I didn't feel safe going home. I explicitly told her that I feared I was "going to bleed out" and I wanted a second opinion. She said, "Fine." I thought she was going to get another doctor, but she brought back a police officer instead.

The police officer entered the room as I was throwing up, again. I figured he would see this wasn't a safe situation and that I was in dire need of treatment. I was wrong. He ordered me to get dressed and leave or he would arrest me for trespassing. I didn't object or resist. I just figured I would go to another hospital and called my father to come get me.

The police officer had parked himself in front of the door while I was on the phone, on the inside facing me. I asked for privacy because I was nude under my robe from the chest x-ray. He refused to leave and I refused to dress. He ordered me to dress or risk being arrested. Again, I asked for privacy and, again, he refused. I realized at that moment, everything I had known as a student and instructor of social science was true, there are no safe spaces for African American women. We are considered a threat. Even in our most vulnerable states; like being in a hospital, naked under a gown and vomiting blood, we are viewed as subhuman, a cultural anomaly. As such, our modesty, our womanhood often goes unprotected. I knew that if I had been a White woman, this would not fly; he would have bowed out and given me my privacy when asked the first time. Instead, he called for backup. Three other officers joined him and all four, White men, stood in the room shouting at me to dress.

I sat there stunned and alone. Then one pulled out this thing that looked like some kind of tie or tether and affixed it around my wrists while another told me I was being arrested and they called the nurse who brought the first cop in, telling her to dress me. As she removed the gown, I closed my eyes. I was completely naked. They could see me, but I didn't want to see them looking at me.

The first one dragged me out and the others went to go get their car and said they would meet at the car of the officer with his hand gripping my arm. As unsafe as I felt in that moment, my heart fell to my knees when those other cops left. I knew I didn't want to be alone with that officer and I knew why. I was right.

He forced me into the back of the cruiser on my back. His car was in an isolated part of the parking lot and it was so dark, no streetlights, and no witnesses. I could feel myself screaming, "No, stop, please don't do this," as he unbuttoned my jeans and slid them, along with my underwear, below my hips, exposing me. He leaned over me and I could hear him unbuckling his belt. All I could do was cry. Then I saw headlights from afar shining in the window just above my head. He saw them, too, then buckled his pants and slid my clothes back up to my waist, leaving my pants unbuttoned.

The other cruiser pulled beside him and one of the officers climbed into the front seat alongside the first. They drove me to Lexington Detention Center where I was booked, denied a phone call, and broke out in hives due to an allergic reaction to the industrial detergent used to wash the orange jumpsuit that I was issued and forced into by three female officers. I told them of my severe allergies beforehand. They ignored me and refused me medical attention. I finally got to make a call the next afternoon and I called my mother in Connecticut.

She told me that when my father got to the hospital to pick me up, they told him I left and drove myself home; all of which he knew to be untrue having driven me himself. For nearly 24 hours, my family had no idea where I was or what happened to me. I mentioned to my mother what happened in the cruiser and she reminded me that our conversation was being recorded. I said that I didn't care because at that time, I felt that after being sexually assaulted, and having my head slammed onto concrete while the female officers dressed me, I had suffered the worst.

I went before a judge later that day. I was released without bail or bond and the case remanded to traffic court. Yes, traffic court! I was still throwing up blood the whole time. When my father picked me up, I had him take me to another hospital where I was admitted after 20 minutes because my blood count was so low and I required five units of blood. They also did an endoscopy and found that my ulcer was larger than I thought and was bleeding. I was there for 13 days. Upon being discharged, a good friend and her husband came to get me. She's a nurse and so she looked at my labs, she is also a woman of color, Native American, and understood my mistrust of the doctor discharging me, especially after my ordeal.

That's when we found it, the reason the whole thing started. In the records they requested from my primary care doctor were test results and medical background information for me and for another patient of his who happened to be in the ER the same time I was. Her records were mixed with mine. She had a drug problem. She was also White and 59. I am Black and was 37 at the time. But they couldn't wrap their minds around the fact that an older White woman could possibly be the drug addict, it had to be me; the Black woman, their stereotype.

As Black women, we have the unique complexity of being both Black and female; a complexity that lends itself to our being constantly disregarded in the struggle for Black justice and women's rights. That is why the deaths of Black women at the hands of law enforcement or White people, who frighten too easily by our very existence, often go unmentioned. It is also why we must not forget them and continue to speak their names because they could be you, your sister, your best friend, or even me. In fact, it was me.

When Sandra Bland's death while in police custody made national news, everything in me was shaken. All the security I had built around me, all my emotional walls, everything gone. Then I saw her mug shot and I knew. I knew, even before seeing the video, the relative possibility that she was assaulted, whether sexual, physical or both, just like me. I knew that if it was suicide, and I believe that to be a big if, that her being assaulted and/or violated in some way had to be the reason why. I knew because in the days after my assault while in custody, I felt as though I didn't want to live any longer because this was a kind of injustice I couldn't bear. I asked for a psychologist while in the other hospital those 13 days and they sent me a White male who mentally victimized me all over again. When I finally got home, I just felt a sense of hopelessness. I filed a report and when they dismissed it, I felt even worse. Then when I was dropped by my PCP, after he realized his office's mistake and that a suit may ensue, I was done with it all. The only thing that kept me going was my daughter and knowing I had to survive this and move past it for her.

Coping with racial and sexual trauma is never an easy feat. As Black women, we are to believe we have unfathomable strength and resiliency and that our suffering does not exist or isn't worthy of exposure. We believe it and everyone around us believes it too, so they mistreat, denigrate, and abuse us. How do we survive this kind of soul murder? Do we survive it at all? The truth is, the pain of it doesn't go away, it lingers; we just find ways of living through the pain only to find we aren't really living at all. When we find the strength to say, "I'm not okay," and find the things that heal us, do we begin living again? For me the healing is in writing. When I hurt, I write. It is liberating and it brings life into my soul. Acknowledging my fragility by writing has allowed me to see myself wholly and not just as a victim. Even more, when I write with purpose, I feel a sense of solidarity with my sisters who have suffered the same. Like Ida B. Wells, Phyllis Wheatley, and Ntozake Shange, and I write to uplift and empower. I am a writer-activist, I soldier through my sorrows using words and images; and I cope with my own trauma by telling the stories of others.

Like Sandra Bland, I am an educated, professional black woman, but I know, firsthand, none of that will protect me from the systemic racism and sexism we face daily. For this reason, those of us who survive must continue to advocate for ourselves, and our sisters who die in this manner. We must continue to speak their names and share their stories, as well as our own. I failed Sandra Bland and so many others by not talking about my experience in depth until now. I became brutally aware of that when a month after Sandra Bland's death, Charnesia Corley was sexually assaulted by White police officers, not far from where Bland died. I refuse to fail another young Black woman, so I speak their names . . . and I vow, also, to speak my own.

Aisha K. Staggers, MA, is a writer and lecturer of Psychology and Sociology. She was a regular contributor to Atlanta Blackstar and has also written for "For Harriet," Huffington Post Blog and a host of other online media outlets and traditional news organizations. She is the former editor-in-chief of *On The Rise,* an e-zine that showcases the works of independent music artists and former co-host of a weekly radio talk show. In addition to her experience as a professor of social sciences, Aisha previously served as the African American Affairs Coordinator for the South Carolina Commission for Minority Affairs and Assistant Director for the Center for Social Policy and Research at Central Connecticut State University. She currently resides in Connecticut with her daughter.

CHAPTER 53

BEING ABOVE AVERAGE

Hearing, Accepting, and Believing

Michelle Trotman Scott

> **Key Challenges:** parental loss, single parent family, resilience, underachievement

He sat at the piano and hit the key, "This is the middle C. Can you sing that note?" "Hmmmm" I hummed. "That's good, baby! What about this note?" I hummed that note, too. "That was great!" He played a combination of rhythms and notes and asked me to mimic the notes, rhythms and tunes. This went on and on and he chuckled and played as I hummed along. "Daddy, this is fun!" I replied. He agreed, "Yes, it is."

I was only two years old and I am able to retell this information because my father documented the account via a recording. I was the first born of four children (2 boys and 2 girls) and I was a Daddy's girl! He loved to capture meaningful moments (pictures and tapes) and his love allowed me to recall this first memory of engaging in the learning process.

Gumbo for the Soul, pages 295–299
Copyright © 2017 by Information Age Publishing
All rights of reproduction in any form reserved.

My father was a child prodigy. He started playing music in church when he was five years old. He was an excellent vocalist, arranger and composer. He was gifted with the ability to "play by ear" and was a prolific sight reader. My father, in short, was above average so, to him, it was only natural and expected that his children would be above average, too. "You're above average" was a phrase that I heard quite often.

I've always been on the move. In utero, when my mother moved, so did I. I was supposed to be born in March; but I was born three weeks early. I was supposed to be less than five pounds; but I was almost seven pounds. I had a desire to move and be physically and mentally engaged at all times. But, my parents taught me that there was a time and place for everything. As I grew older, I was taught how to exhibit self-control, how to focus, and how to have discipline. I learned to sit quietly through rehearsals as my father directed orchestras and requiems. I learned to be patient as he worked with concert choirs and gospel choirs. I learned to watch intently as my father appeared as a guest and/or hosted television shows. I learned to listen as I sat through operas, speeches, and sermons. I learned when to speak, when to be quiet, when to move, and when to be still. I learned to listen and to be aware of my surroundings. I learned to use every opportunity as an opportunity to learn. I also learned to be honest and tell the truth. I did all of this . . . because I was above average.

My father's intention was to make sure that I met my potential . . . to be all that I could be. He insisted that I do my best and did everything in his power to make sure that he was there for me. He protected me and taught me how to protect myself. Daddy would say "You are a Frazier, so that means you are important. You are above average" and I believed him.

Academic excellence was a priority for daddy and mom. For example, in the kindergarten, I was placed in the 'highest' reading and math groups and I was expected to excel academically, socially, and musically. As I grew older, I would sit through group and individual music sessions with my parents so much that I would begin to sing along. I could hear the rhythms in the rain and the windshield wipers. I would mimic the rhythms and create dances and songs. I joined the children's choir at church and attended Sunday school every week. I also demonstrated the ability to move to the rhythmic beats of music, so my parents enrolled me in a church dance class. I flourished, competed on the national level, and even became a national dance champion. "You need to stretch, you need to practice," Daddy would say. Even when I didn't want to comply, I would do it because I knew my Daddy knew what was best for me. I was above average.

When Daddy got a job as a music professor at the State University of New York at Buffalo, we moved from Ohio to New York. At that time I was eight years old. As my parents enrolled us in school, my father emphasized to the school personnel that I was gifted and capable of doing above average work.

I was pulled out of class for more challenging academic work and later I took violin classes to nurture my musical abilities.

The following year my music teacher continuously wanted me to inquire if Daddy would come in and perform at an assembly for the school. Daddy loved the community, so he obliged. When my female friends saw that I had a father who was engaged and actively involved in my life, they began to taunt me. "You think you're better than us because your father comes to the school! You think you are so smart! You talk so White." I kept it to myself, but one day, I let the cat out of the bag while at home. "Daddy, please don't come to my school anymore. The girls in my class are mean to me because you performed at the assembly. They say that I think that I am smart, and that I think that I am White."

My Daddy responded, "Shelli, are you White?"

"No, Sir."

He asked, "Are you smart?"

"Yes, Sir."

He affirmed, "Not only are you smart; you are above average, aren't you?"

"Yes, Sir."

"Good. Then, tomorrow, you tell the teacher what the students are saying and doing to you. Once you do that, if they put their hands on you, you have my permission to fight; to defend yourself." There were a few more incidents. But, during this time, I realized that I had to choose my friends wisely to stay on track.

That year, on the last day of school, when I was ten years old, my Daddy died of a heart attack in his sleep at the age of 35. I was devastated. One of my biggest fans was gone. I was lost, angry, and confused. He was no longer there for me. I went from being in a two-parent home to a single parent home—my life dramatically changed.

We moved back to Ohio and moved into our former home. Mom had to find a job, which was somewhat difficult because she had not been in the workforce for over five years because she was a stay at home mother. Also, at the time, there were no gifted services offered in my school district. Since her children were gifted, mom looked for schools that would nurture us and she found a school that specialized in "the arts."

Being in the new school was a joke! I received good grades without even trying. By the time I entered sixth grade, my study habits were lacking and it showed. I earned two "F's" and one "D" during my first quarter of school. Mom was furious! I was punished and all extracurricular activity ceased. I eventually got back on track, but it was challenging. I missed my Daddy and I no longer believed that I had the skills to show that I was smart and above average.

My Mom reminded me of my heritage. She reminded me that I was a descendant of kings and queens. She reminded me that I could do all things through Christ who strengthened me (Philippians 4:3). My attitude began to change. I began to remember the sermons I heard and the Sunday school lessons that were taught. I began to remember the family conversations around the dinner table when Daddy was alive. I began to really listen to my mother and take heed to the advice she offered. I began to believe that I was "above average" again.

I also began to excel in the classroom again. In high school, I started to think about college. Mom told me that she could not afford to send me to college so I needed to earn a scholarship. She also suggested that I try out for the track team so I did as she requested. I made the team and excelled, and in the end, I earned academic and athletic scholarships to The Ohio State University. I realized that it was actually true . . . I was above average, just as my daddy told me.

In college, I slipped a little but then I got back on the academic plow and worked hard on the track. I made the Dean's List, broke school records in track and field, and won athletic honors. At times, I would feel as if I were living a life of someone else, but all along, my Mom (like my Dad) would tell me that I was "above average."

The day before graduating from college, I sat down and wrote my deceased father a letter. I thanked him for instilling values in me. But I also chastised him for making me spend so many fathers' days without him, for not being there when I needed his encouragement . . . for leaving me. The day before graduation, I was in tears. But Mom was there and told me how proud she was and how proud Daddy was too. Again, she reminded me that I was "above average."

I have since embraced this truth. This is the truth that has guided throughout my entire adult life. I went on to obtain a Master's Degree and a PhD. I got married and had a beautiful daughter. I have been a middle school teacher, a coach of multiple sports, a principal, a superintendent, and am now a college professor. Every day, I think about my Daddy and remember his advice and encouragement. I also talk to my mom multiple times a day and she always encourages me. Every day, I think and believe that I am above average and I tell my daughter the same thing! I am leaving a legacy. And you can, too! We all face tragedies. Mine was losing my father. But in the short time he lived . . . my daddy inspired me. Treasure whatever time you have with your father or mother. Remember these priceless messages one or both parents and loved ones teach you. Remember, that you are smart, beautiful, and above average. Remember that it takes hard work, patience, and effort to propel you forward into a successful future, but you must believe in yourself first!

Michelle Frazier Trotman Scott, PhD, is an Associate Professor in the College of Education at the University of West Georgia. All degrees are from

The Ohio State University. She teaches graduate and undergraduate courses in special education and undergraduate courses in diversity. Dr. Trotman Scott's research foci are the over-representation minorities in special education, under-representation of minorities in gifted education, the achievement gap, and parenting. She has published and consulted in all areas. Prior to her appointment at UWG, Dr. Trotman Scott was a middle school teacher, a middle and high school coach, a principal of an elementary school and a superintendent of a charter school in Ohio, and then an adjunct professor at The Ohio State University.

CHAPTER 54

SCHOOL CHANGED MY LIFE

Desireé Vega

Key Challenges: divorce, violence (fights, excessive spankings)

I often reflect on my childhood and think to myself, "I shouldn't be here. How did I make it?" Growing up in my household was not always easy. My parents married and had children at a young age and in my opinion, they were not prepared to be "grown-ups." I describe my home life as chaotic but that is putting it gently; screaming, yelling, and 'whoopins' were commonplace for little to no reason.

This experience is difficult to write about for many reasons. I love my family and believe they did the best they could, so I do not want to portray them in a negative light. Additionally, it is difficult; opening up old wounds because the pain still runs deep. I take pride in being a strong and independent woman, so this level of vulnerability and openness is hard to share. But if I am going to keep it real, I will say that growing up in my household was awful at times. I still vividly remember screaming to my father around age 10, "I wish I was dead!" This happened in the midst of my parents' first divorce from each other. I am thankful to be alive today and feel like I have had so many amazing opportunities and blessings in my life, but I *did* wish

Gumbo for the Soul, pages 301–304
Copyright © 2017 by Information Age Publishing
All rights of reproduction in any form reserved.

I was dead many times as a child and adolescent. No one knew that at the time, but now everyone does.

School saved me. I was in gifted programs in elementary school and took dual-credit classes in high school. I am a first-generation college student and when I am asked about my experiences, I share that I loved school, I did well in school, and I had people who believed in me. That is a small part of a deeper story. School literally saved me from my home life. School was a safe space for me; to some degree, I felt free from "getting in trouble" for something I didn't do, which was often the case at home.

We are all products of our environment, therefore, we learn from what we see. I am certain that my parents had their own traumas growing up that carried over into their relationship and how they raised my two brothers and myself. I frequently witnessed my parents hitting each other and then take their frustrations out on us. I recall them fighting in the bathroom one day and I begged my older brother to knock on the bathroom door to stop them from hitting each other. It was too much to handle, but it happened so often.

When I was in school, I felt smart and loved. I felt that way at home, but not consistently. One minute, I could be getting hugs and kisses and then if I spilled milk, I was getting beat. So I walked on eggshells and lived in fear at home. One day, my older brother and I were getting ready for school; it was cold and snowy outside. We were in elementary school at the time. I could not for the life of me find my snow boots. Well, once my mother found out, it was over for me. I will spare the specifics, but I got a beating for being unable to find my boots. A few days later, I found my snow boots under my parents' bed. They were simply misplaced. Like most kids, I'd lose things.

In some unconscious way, it is possible that I did well in school to make my parents happy and avoid "getting in trouble" at home. But I did love school; like I said, it was my safe haven. However, the fear I carried from home was so paralyzing that I did not speak unless spoken to, my teachers would always comment on how quiet and shy I was. This carried over throughout most of my educational career. My advisor from graduate school still reminds me of how quiet I was when I was her student several years ago. I carried this terrible anxiety with me for too long because I never felt I had a voice. I did not think my voice was worthy of being heard because it was not while growing up.

I eventually figured out that school was my ticket out of my parents' home. College would get me out of the toxic environment in which I was living. I sure wish someone had told me that earlier, but no one knew what was going on at home. I was always happy at school, I basically checked my baggage from home at the school door. So no one would ever suspect World War III was occurring at home. In high school, I ran track and worked part-time to limit my time at home. I successfully managed to balance these responsibilities and maintain my high grades. When I was home, I stayed in my room with the door shut and read for hours as an escape. My track coach in high school, who was also my math teacher, played a big role in me leaving home to go away for college. He saw potential in me and never gave up on me. He became like a second father to me; I still have contact with him to this day! He encouraged me to look at colleges and guided me through much of the exploration process as he knew that I did not have anyone at home to help me apply for college in the way that college-educated parents help their children.

I often think that without having had a love for school and people in school, such as my coach/math teacher that fostered my love of learning and provided me support and guidance that I would not be where I am today, working as a school psychologist. My life experiences, while painful, do not define me, but they have certainly shaped my worldview. I recognize the important role a person can play in another one's life. When you meet someone, you do not know what battles they are fighting. I went to school and all my troubles disappeared for a short amount of time. No one knew what I experienced outside of school. I also learned that I needed to leave home to be myself. Going away for college and subsequently for graduate school and work allowed me to find my voice. I love my family, but I needed the distance from the unhealthy environment to grow and heal.

My experiences have taught me the importance of putting one's own needs first, developing healthy boundaries, and ending toxic relationships. As a child and adolescent, I did not have this freedom and instead sought to please my parents to avoid punishment. I was helpless and I do wish I had spoken up to someone that I trusted to free myself of the pain I was experiencing. However, I do not know if the alternative of being removed from my home would have been better. I cannot change the past, only the future. So I focus on my successes and the wonderful blessings that I have had occur in my life. I have many supportive people in my life and a career that I love. Because of my experiences, I find it important to mentor my graduate students, particularly, those of color, who may experience isolation because of their skin color and gender and also feel like they are not enough because of their background experiences. While I have had my share of challenges and continue to live with them today, I have used these experiences as life lessons and, in my heart, want others to feel supported and encouraged to achieve dreams that they may not think they are capable of reaching. School allowed me to achieve my dreams and shaped me into the person I am today. School literally saved my life.

Desireé Vega, PhD, is an Assistant Professor in the School Psychology Program at the University of Arizona. She earned her BA in Psychology from Binghamton University and both her MA and PhD in School Psychology from

The Ohio State University. Dr. Vega worked as a school psychologist for three years with the Omaha Public Schools district. Her research and teaching interests focus on best practices in the assessment of culturally and linguistically diverse students and the preparation of bilingual and culturally competent school psychologists. Her research also explores the significant factors that contribute to the academic success of African American and Latino youth in the K–12 pipeline and access to higher education among urban youth, including the role of school psychologists in the transition from high school to college. Dr. Vega served as a co-principal investigator on a grant funded by The Office of Special Education Programs to prepare bilingual (Spanish–English) school psychologists to address the critical and growing need for bilingual school psychology services.

CHAPTER 55

I AM BECAUSE OF HER

Nicole McZeal Walters

> **Key Challenges:** parent alcohol addiction and abuse, parental loss, poverty, overcoming

"Nicole McZeal, please report to the front office." All eyes in my AP English Literature class turned to me as I slid out of my seat. As I passed by the door, TJ snickered, "What it is THIS time?" Ignoring her, I made my way down the long hallway to the front office. The walk this particular day seemed to last forever.

My heart beat so loudly (I swear it could be heard outside my uniform shirt) as I saw my grandmother waiting for me inside. "What is it, Granny?" Mrs. Cate, my principal, asked me quietly, "Where is your backpack? Your grandmother is here to pick you up early. I'll go and get it from your classroom so you can speak with her." With that, she disappeared.

I whipped around to face my grandmother, "What's wrong, Granny? What's going on? Why are you here to pick me up early?" I demanded. "Nikki, we need to go home. It's Judy Kristi...." her voice trailed off. She didn't need to go any further.

Gumbo for the Soul, pages 305–309
Copyright © 2017 by Information Age Publishing
All rights of reproduction in any form reserved.

Walking to my grandmother's beat up brown station wagon, I opened the heavy door and got inside. "What happened now, Granny?" My grandmother tried to start the car, but the engine wouldn't turn. I could see her frustration as she tried again and again. Third time was a charm. Finally, we drove home in silence. I finally spoke up softly, "What did she do *this* time, Granny?"

Judy Kristi, my mother, who also struggled with drug and alcohol abuse for the greater part of my teen years, all the way through my adulthood. When she was clean, she was a joy. She was loving, caring, intelligent, beautiful, could dance a mean two-step, and was hilarious. But, when she went in "one of her periods" it would be a dark time; she was mean, combative, and self-destructive. When I was 13 and my sister was three, my grandmother took us in so we would no longer be victims to her and my stepfather's lifestyle. My biological father and mother had divorced when I was younger, and during the latter part of my teenage years, I had little contact with him. My grandmother, school, and membership in various organizations kept me sane—and served as my refuge.

You see, I attended one of the most prestigious all girl's Catholic schools in my city. When I went to school, even though I wore uniforms, I was always "together." My hair was done, uniforms were neatly pressed, nails clean, loafers shiny, and all of my materials were in place. I excelled in Spanish, English, History, Reading, and Theater. I struggled in Math and Science, and really had to work hard in order to maintain a high grade point average to remain a member of The National Honor Society.

I loved my friends and had plenty of them! Out of a class of 64, I was one of five Black girls, so everyone knew who I was. What they didn't know is my deep dark secret about my mother. All they knew was that she was "sick" and I lived with my grandmother. No one probed and thankfully, I didn't have to make up a story about her "sickness." Looking back, I'm sure they felt it was odd that my mother only showed up to attend my high school graduation.

My grandmother worked as a domestic for a wealthy White family who allowed her to drop off and pick me up from school which was located about 20 miles from my family home. She wore a simple skirt and shirt, which she later told me she gladly washed and pressed the same three skirts in order for me to have what I needed and not feel out of place with the White kids. She was also a dynamic speaker, writer, mother, grandmother, wife, friend, community activist, and champion of women's rights. She was my hero.

Each morning, my grandmother would drop me off and say, "Now Nikki, this school better not call me for anything ridiculous. You know we don't have money like these White folks, and I have to stay at my job." With that, she would drive away in her beat up brown station wagon, leaving a cloud of smoke behind.

I used my comedic timing, quick wit, and intelligence to gain popularity and the following of a large group of friends, many of whom I had known from my middle school years. From time to time, I envied some of my buddies who appeared, from the outside looking in, to have more of the finer accouterments in life.

What I didn't know then, but learned later, was that many of them had parents with an abundance of money, yet they didn't spend the quality time with their parents as Granny did with me. Granny's quality time ensured that my development and progress were on track. There was quantity but not quality, so to speak, in their lives. I was in every group known to a teenager at that time—remnants felt even today, as I am active in many, many organizations, boards, and community endeavors. I've always been BUSY.

My grandmother instilled the importance of education and the importance of using my brain—my intelligence—to further myself. She would often tell me, "One thing they can't take away from you is your brain, education, and thinking. You have a lot of strong qualities from your mother. Just don't make the same mistakes she did by letting a man run your life."

My mother had succumbed to drugs and alcohol during her third marriage. Unfortunately her last divorce left her depressed, and she spiraled even further. She would fight the urge, go to rehab, come out, and repeat the cycle again and again.

It was the example of my mother's tenacity as she tried to fight through her addiction that once I put my mind toward something, I could not be stopped. My principal, headmistress of our school, and guidance counselors became my family away from home. It was there that I took solace in knowing that I would one day overcome all that I experienced. I just had to work really hard and keep looking at the light at the end of the tunnel.

If education was my ticket out, I had to exercise my brain to ensure I gained all the knowledge, skills, connections, and opportunities to overcome the obstacles of having to deal with my mother's illness. Reflecting on this time, it is here where I developed empathy for those who suffered from depression, addiction, or battled other social ills.

There were days that would go by when my sister and I wouldn't see my mother. I would hear my grandmother frantically calling around asking if anyone had seen her, "Where was she last? Who was she with? How did she look?" This ritual would go on for days on end until my mother would reappear apologetically saying, "She had stayed with friends." Anger that I had would dissipate because I was just glad that she made it back home.

I was very angry during this time as a teenager, and resented her not being "normal" like the other mothers in my class. My sister was too young to understand what was going on, but knew that something was not right with our mother and I did all I could do to protect and shelter her. Each day, if I didn't have an afterschool activity, I would rush home to spend time with her. She was bratty for sure, but she was still my sister and I adored her and today, I am blessed to consider her my best friend.

As I sailed through high school, it became a place that I used to continue to shelter me from the storm of a home life that was often marked by turbulence. I would make up excuses as to why friends couldn't stay over. My best friend during this time, one of the few who knew my secret, asked if she could spend the night. I remember the first time as I was so nervous because I didn't know what she might see. She asked, "Hey Nick, my parents are going out of town overnight. Is it ok if I crash at your place tonight?" Panicked, I flew into a million excuses why that would not be a good idea.

She reassured me, "Nick. It's cool. I don't care. You're my friend, and it's gonna be fine." Upon arriving home, my grandmother welcomed her to what we had. Dinner that particular night consisted of pinto beans, rice, cornbread, and cabbage with ham. I skeptically looked at her and wondered if she would judge me for not eating "fancy food."

While she was also Black, she lived a more affluent life and I had never seen my kind of food at her home. She devoured dinner and asked, "Granny, may I have seconds, please?" My grandmother was tickled pink and heaped her plate with more food. "Of course you can my child, and there's plenty more where that came from." Where we lacked in other material goods, we always had plenty of food. My grandmother would always say, "You can always give someone shelter and a warm meal if you have it."

My mother stayed away that night and I attributed it to my serious prayer and 10 Hail Marys. I chanted in my head on the car ride home. When we were dropped off at school the next morning, Granny didn't give me my usual speech. Instead she said, "Stacy, I am so glad that you stayed over. You are welcome anytime." I bounded out of the brown station wagon feeling more confident. I had a sleepover and mom didn't mess it up! Later on she told me she saw us get out of the car and decided to stay away to save me from the embarrassment. I had pep in my step for the remainder of the week.

Throughout my final years in high school, I learned to respect humanity, understand the fragility of life and human suffering, and decided that my career path would be something to help others. I also learned important character traits like grit, resilience, and unwavering confidence in my abilities. I continued to love my mother through her addiction and continued to beseech her to get help. My daily mantra I would repeat in the mirror was "You are young, gifted, and Black. You got *this!*"

I eventually graduated from college and as an educator; I kept the same character traits I learned in high school close. My career has focused on working with people, namely children, who were considered the "have nots" and it has served my life purpose in helping others. I also continue to volunteer heavily with girls' education and was asked to serve on my alma mater's board of trustees, making me the only Black person—male or female—in this position. Every time I walk on campus, I feel a sense of pride and reflect on the beat up brown station wagon that dropped me off in a cloud of smoke.

Adversity has certainly stared me in the face many times … But, I would look it directly in the face, square my shoulders, and repeat, "You are young, gifted, and Black. You got *this!*" Be encouraged during times of challenge, seek mentors and role models to support you, and never give up on your dreams. *You* are the one we have been waiting for.

When people first look at me, they only see the outside, the vibrant smile, and the gleaming dark skin of a woman, with her hair and clothing in place. What they don't know is, I am I because of her.

Nicole McZeal Walters, EdD, is a former P–12 teacher and administrator who now serves as the Associate Dean for Graduate Programs and Assistant Professor in Educational Leadership at the University of St. Thomas in Houston, Texas. Her research foci include minority females, special education, equity and accountability as it relates to culturally relevant leadership. She has been in the field of education for over 20 years and is most interested in research related to marginalized populations and the impact of leadership in today's schools.

CHAPTER 56

MOVE OVER WORLD...
HERE I AM

Tuwana Wingfield

> **Key Challenges:** peer pressure, isolation, academic challenges, poor mentoring

At the tender age of seven, I had this yellow t-shirt embossed with the words, *Move Over World . . . Here I Am!* sprawled across my chest. I can still remember posing for the camera as momma prepared to take the picture. My hands rested on my undeveloped hips as I positioned my chest forward and held my head high. Let my momma tell the story, she would say that I was a little *character* with always something to say—inquisitive with a smile that would light up a room. At the age of seven, I had no idea what the words "move over world," meant.

Now over 30 years later, I still want to be seen and heard. My journey of pushing my way through the world and making my way has not been without its fair share of challenges. I have experienced setbacks that made me question my worth and overall purpose in life. *Where did this little girl go who had so much confidence? What was behind the smile now that used to light up a room? How did she/I break through and become the woman that I am today at 40 years of age?* I hope by telling my story of pushing through the world to be seen and heard will help other young Black and Brown girls and women overcome obstacles in their path toward becoming their more authentic selves.

Growing up in a predominately Black community and attending predominately Black schools from primary through secondary, I was protected and shielded from the realities of growing up Black in White America. I never questioned my ability to perform academically because my teachers, who were mostly Black, affirmed and confirmed that I was a bright child. I made high grades in school and was placed in the higher tracked classes with other bright students. My teachers would always tell my mom at parent-teacher conferences, "She's so smart . . . she's a little leader and always wants to help others." These were all qualities that confirmed I was smart. In my family, I was called a "book worm" because I always had a book in my hand or was begging my mother to take me to the library. "Doing school" was easy for me. Then came junior high and high school but "doing school" didn't seem as easy to me, but I still knew that I had what it took to be successful. I just had to work a little harder.

Working harder meant reading more, writing more, calculating more, and studying more, because I was in advanced classes. I took biology, chemistry, physics, geometry, trigonometry, and advanced placement (AP) calculus. Every step of the way it got a little more difficult, but I didn't let that keep me from moving forward; pushing through. I had a core group of friends that I studied with to stay on top of things in school. We were a tight knit group. We pushed and challenged each other to be better; smarter. There was competition, but it was a good form of competition. None of us wanted to see the other fail.

After successfully getting through junior high and high school, I was on my way to college. In the early 90s, the television show, *A Different World* was so important in affirming for me that college was possible for me and many others who looked like me, even still, I had no idea what I was getting myself into. I was a long way from all that I was familiar with and from what gave me comfort. Now in an unfamiliar world, I felt like I was in a strange, White, and unwelcoming place. While attending a predominately White institution (PWI), far from home and all that was familiar to me, I felt isolated because I was Black. All throughout my elementary, junior high, and high school, I had the comfort of being surrounded by people who looked like me and who supported me. Now in college, at this PWI I had no idea who I could trust and depend on for support. This was the first time in my young adult life that I felt different from everyone around me. I no longer had the protection of my family, my community, and school. I felt alone and yet I knew that I had to figure out how to survive in this strange new world . . . college.

The transition from high school to college was none like I had ever experienced. I was living on my own, away from family and all that was familiar to me. In my classes, I was sometimes the *only* Black person in the sea of Whiteness. I had to learn how to make new friends, get around campus, get a job, and negotiate living in a predominately White community. Doing all of this required a smartness that was different from book smarts; I needed to tap into my street smarts. Being street smart meant that I had to be strategic about navigating through my college experience so that I could survive and thrive in a place that didn't seem to want me there—A place where my smile didn't light up the room when I walked in. More often than not, I was overlooked or even ignored in class, which made me feel uncomfortable and unwanted. For example, I can remember sitting at the front of the lecture and the professor, a White man, overlooked my raised hand when I was trying to respond to a question posed to the class. Other times, which felt like all of the time, I was the representative of the entire African American race when issues of race came up in class. Imagine sitting in class, and where everyone looks to you to be the spokesperson for everything about Black culture. This was my experience.

Learning how to survive and thrive in college was not easy for me and as a result my grades suffered at the end of the first semester of my sophomore year. I found myself on academic probation and I desperately needed to figure out how I was going to get off of probation. I had to learn how to ask for help with something that used to come so easy for me—how to do school at the college level. It was a humbling experience to ask for help in an environment that was unwelcoming. I eventually met someone who advised, mentored, and connected me to key faculty and staff that were willing to help.

I met my mentor in a chance encounter; while I was studying at the Black Cultural Center (BCC) and one of my friends from high school was giving a newly hired staff member a tour of the campus. Mr. Wayne was an African American man, hired to be one of the admissions counselors at the college. When I was introduced to him, he asked me what my major was and wanted to know about my experience at this PWI. Of course, I told him briefly about myself and what I experienced up to this point in my academic career. A few weeks after our meeting, there was a message left for me at the BCC to meet Mr. Wayne at his office.

When we finally met again at his office, he asked me, *"How can I help you young lady?"*

I didn't know how to respond to his question, so I said that I didn't need his help because I am already a student at the university. His response is what allowed me to let my guard down and accept his help. Mr. Wayne said, "I am well aware that you are a student, however it is my responsibility to ensure that you remain one . . . I've looked at your grades and know that you need help." In that moment I was so embarrassed and ashamed that my grade point average was a 1.0 and that I had no idea what I needed to do to turn things around. Sensing my embarrassment, Mr. Wayne said that he was willing to help me get off of academic probation. He introduced me to a new academic advisor and encouraged me to sign up for a non-credit hour course designed to assist students struggling academically to develop time management and improve study skills.

Through my relationship with my mentor, I learned to share my fears about success and failure. I learned that it was OK to allow someone to help me because I couldn't do it all by myself. I also learned that it wasn't enough to be smart and do school; you also have to learn how to leverage the relationships and connections made—to build a community of support around you. In time, I figured out how to create that community amongst my peers, faculty, and staff. It truly took a community to help me push through surviving and thriving in a predominately White institution so that I could be successful and pursue my dream of attending graduate school. The lessons that I learned—identifying others who genuinely care about your well-being, humbling yourself to ask for help from your teachers, peers, faculty, and staff were invaluable. The most important lesson learned was the missteps I made, made me much stronger and determined to do things differently.

I opened this piece with the words *move over world . . . here I am* to capture the essence of what it means to believe in yourself. To believe that you can accomplish anything that you put your mind to. The inquisitive little girl child is still a part of who I am today. I know that I have a place in this world and will continue to use my voice; pushing through to be seen, heard, and listened to. My place in this world is to share the lessons that I learned and quite frankly continue to learn. I want to be in a position to help other young Black and Brown women navigate these white spaces, learn their worth, and empower them to tell their story; reaching back to pull others up along the way. I will end with the words from one of my favorite poems by Countee Cullen:

> *Hey, Black Child*
> *Do you know who you are?*
> *Who you really are*
> *Do you know you can be*
> *What you want to be*
> *If you try to be*
> *What you can be?*

In my journey, I learned who I once was, who I am currently, and who I want to be; my authentic self—to live in the fullness of who I am as Black woman. May my words give you courage as you continue pushing through so the world can move over and make room for you and see you as the dynamic gifted Black or Brown woman that you are!

Tuwana T. Wingfield is a fifth-year doctoral student in the Educational Administration and Foundations higher education program in the College of Education at Illinois State University. She received her graduate degree in social work at the University of Chicago, School of Social Service Administration and is a licensed clinical social worker in the State of Illinois. Her areas of interest are feminism, critical theories, culturally responsive education, social justice, identity development, mentoring, and research methods in education.

CHAPTER 57

FROM SPECIAL ED TO HIGHER ED

A Black Girl's Journey in Discovering Her Giftedness

Jemimah L. Young

Key Challenges: biracial, English as a Second Language, special education misdiagnosis, behavioral challenges, juvenile delinquency, underachievement

Growing up, I grew to loathe the question "Where are you from?" As a military family, we've had the opportunity to explore the world, enriching both my lived and educational experiences. My journey is unique because I have experienced a multitude of educational environments, and from each I draw strength and wisdom to complete my current work as a Multicultural scholar. In the following narrative, I share part of my journey from "Special Ed to Higher Ed."

Gumbo for the Soul, pages 317–322
Copyright © 2017 by Information Age Publishing
All rights of reproduction in any form reserved.

TURNING POINT 1: THE MISEDUCATION OF ME

My mother is Korean and my father is African American, but in the eyes of the world, I was a Black girl. I quickly discovered that schools were not designed, nor prepared to capitalize on the strengths of my cultural background and its influence on my learning.

My formal schooling began internationally, with a curriculum, structures, and customs that were uniquely different from American schooling. Of what I can remember, the focus and purpose of school was to learn academics, almost exclusively reading, writing, math, and science. Several years later, we moved to the United States and I began elementary school, as a little Black girl who was not English proficient. I was inappropriately placed in special education. I was perceived to be verbally behind and my accent and circumstance were not taken into account. As most educators are aware, once funneled into special education, it is often difficult to transition out of these services. From second to fourth grade, I continued to receive special education services, despite tremendous progress in English proficiency and above average grades. It was at this point where I experienced one of three educational turning points.

At the end of my fourth grade year, I received a perfect score on my mathematics state assessment, which less than 1% of students in the entire state accomplished that year on any content assessment, let alone mathematics. There was an award ceremony established in my honor and several school leaders began to speculate how notable this was given that I was identified as a student with special needs. Although high-stakes testing can be seen as a point of contention, in this situation it worked in my favor, and I was appropriately removed from special education and placed in an English as a Second Language (ESL) program, which I graduated from within a year.

Middle school also marked an important transition in the journey. Like most adolescents, I attempted to find my proper place in a world that was both unfamiliar and unaccommodating to me. One common theme throughout my journey was high academic achievement, but unfortunately my behavior did not align with traditional classroom expectations. Like many high-achieving students, my view of the world and of learning did not adhere to the pedagogical traditions of American schooling. This disconnect lead to an escalation of behavioral infractions that landed me in alternative school. As I reflect on this time, I can draw many parallels between the school's discipline policy and the legal system. Once I was identified as a behavioral problem, I was placed on a "strikes" system and needless to say, after I returned back to the traditional middle school campus, I was sent again to alternative school for "stealing" a $.30 carton of milk.

I remember this day vividly, as I forgot to get the milk (included with the purchase of my lunch) and asked a teacher, who was responsible for monitoring the lunch line, if I could avoid the line to retrieve my milk. I thought nothing of this, until the next day, when I was called into the principal's office and accused of stealing. There were many witnesses, in addition to the monitoring teacher, who vouched for me. However, due to a strict zero-tolerance policy that was in place for any discipline related incidents that occurred within 90-days of returning to the middle school, I found myself back in alternative school. Armed with a new distain for the system and a mistrust for authority, I began to acquiesce to the culture of misbehavior and underachievement fostered by this alternative education setting. Needless to say, I continued along this path until I was sentenced to 60 days in a juvenile education center.

At this point, I would be remiss not to mention that I came from a stable, two-parent household and my mother was a non-native English speaker. Many of the disciplinary issues were not clearly articulated to her, and since the school district lacked a Korean translator, by default I was charged with the task of translating during these meetings with my mom. You can imagine how much of the truth was actually conveyed with a child (who is in trouble) serving as the translator. My father, from whom I get my tenacious nature, was a long distance truck driver and solider that was very passionate about my success; however, he traveled much of the time. My grades were always good, so in many respects both my parents felt little need to be concerned. However, once I was sentenced to the juvenile school, both my parents made the concerted effort to remove me from the public school system.

TURNING POINT 2: FROM THE BOTTOM TO THE TOP

Private school was marked by the redefining and remediation of my academic identity. Private school exposed me to museums and cultural experiences I never received from traditional middle or alternative school instruction. Moreover, because the curriculum was self-paced, I was able to remain on task all day because I was free to work ahead. Unbeknownst to me, I was even able to cover many of the credits lost during my sentence and earn enough credits to start high school as a sophomore. Given my accelerated learning trajectory and the absence of any and all discipline infractions, my parents, either by want or financial necessity, decided to send me back to public school to attend high school. Unfortunately, our local school district had other plans.

Given my newly discovered academic identity, I was on a quest to finish high school, as soon as possible. I earned sufficient credits to enter as a sophomore, but the high school refused to honor the earned credits because they were accredited nationally, but not by the state accrediting agency. Our persistence in pursuing these credits initiated an investigation, because in the process of looking into my transcripts, the school discovered that I did not complete my 60-day sentence at the Juvenile center. Once this was brought to their attention, they insisted that I return to the juvenile campus and complete my time before starting traditional high school.

By this time, my parents were more informed, better prepared, and like myself, ready to fight. They notified the school officials that they retained an attorney and soon after, the issue was put to rest. The remainder of my freshman year was rather uneventful. I was tested and placed into a Gifted and Talented program, took honors (Pre-AP and AP) courses, played several sports, started a lucrative snow cone business, and managed a 4.0 G.P.A. However, it was not until my sophomore year that I finally recognized my giftedness and capabilities, despite my past experiences.

TURNING POINT 3: THE MANTRA

The third and final turning point for me was not an event, rather a person. This person was a teacher that I met my sophomore year, and she mentored me throughout high school. She invested her time, energy, and passion to ensure my success and encouraged me to be active academically, beyond the walls of our classroom. Before meeting her, I knew I would go to college; however, I had little direction and drive beyond going thru the perpetual motions of taking classes. I graduated high school within the top 5% of my class with honors and was accepted to 27 universities, with over half a million dollars in scholarships between these institutions. I remember nervously asking my teacher for advice before I left for college. I braced myself for a wealth of information, but her advice was short and simple—"You can be anything and everything, just *never* take no for an answer."

This advice became a mantra during my college career and beyond. When I was told I couldn't complete my bachelors in two years—I didn't take no for an answer. When I was told I could not work and complete my masters in one year—I didn't take no for an answer. When I was told I could not take a full-time faculty position and complete my doctorate—I didn't take no for an answer. And now, as I'm told I can't have a successful family and career balance—I will not accept no as an answer.

CONCLUSION

Having experienced a host of educational settings—from international, special education, ESL, alternative school, Juvenile, private, Advanced Placement, Gifted and Talented, college, and now the academy, I often reflect on what would have happened if each of these transitions did not occur. If I had missed one question on the state assessment, would I have remained in special education? With the financial sacrifice my parents made to remove me from the public school system, I cannot help but ponder whether that choice is the reason why I am a researcher of the school-to-prison pipeline, rather than a participant within it. Finally, if my teacher did not mentor me and cultivate my resilience, would I be writing this narrative today? Hence, I would like to provide the following words as suggestions for success to other Brown and Black girls:

1. Embrace the struggle. Everyone's education comes with hurdles. Knowing how to navigate the system is essential to current and future success. First, sometimes it is important to go over the hurdles and other times it is important to circumvent or avoid the hurdle altogether. This is where your awareness and the support of mentors and family are essential. I struggled through my time in special education and ESL, but when it came to spending valuable middle grades learning time in a juvenile education center on a technicality, it was time to "cheat," rather than "beat" the system, given the importance of this crucial learning time.

2. Recognize the turning points. Turning points in life are crucial moments in time that can dictate your success and failure with enduring ramifications. In my educational journey, I can identify three specific moments that kept me on a positive trajectory toward success. One misstep at any of these junctions could have prevented me from achieving even a modicum of success. Therefore, I charge you to think critically about every decision you make and never allow the educational system or institution to have autonomy in your academic journey.

3. "Never take No for an answer." One thing that I have learned by adopting this mantra is that it is harder than you think for some people to say "no," especially when you are staring them in the face. Thus, I suggest that you not only, *never take no for an answer*, but become a bold and active participate in your journey toward success. To this end, you should be uncompromisingly unapologetic when advocating on your own behalf. Remain present and attentive at all times, and seek the most appropriate resources to support you along the way. Finally, when someone tells you no (and they inevitably will), you must know how to regroup, recharge, and press on toward your goal.

Jemimah L. Young, PhD is an Assistant professor of Multicultural and Urban Education at the University of North Texas. Her research interests include the academic achievement of Black Girls, achievement gap research, in addition culturally responsive pedagogy—particularly in STEM. She implores critical lens and mixed methods research to investigate the impact of learning for marginalized groups.

Made in the USA
Middletown, DE
22 March 2018